IN THE SHADOW OF EBENEZER

In the Shadow of Ebenezer

A Black Catholic Parish in the Age of Civil Rights and Vatican II

Leah Mickens

NEW YORK UNIVERSITY PRESS
New York

NEW YORK UNIVERSITY PRESS
New York
www.nyupress.org

© 2022 by New York University
All rights reserved

References to Internet websites (URLs) were accurate at the time of writing. Neither the author nor New York University Press is responsible for URLs that may have expired or changed since the manuscript was prepared.

Please contact the Library of Congress for Cataloging-in-Publication data.
ISBN: 9781479816491 (hardback)
ISBN: 9781479816507 (paperback)
ISBN: 9781479816521 (library ebook)
ISBN: 9781479816514 (consumer ebook)

New York University Press books are printed on acid-free paper, and their binding materials are chosen for strength and durability. We strive to use environmentally responsible suppliers and materials to the greatest extent possible in publishing our books.

Manufactured in the United States of America

10 9 8 7 6 5 4 3 2 1

Also available as an ebook

CONTENTS

Introduction — 1

1. Race and the Catholic Church, in Theory and Practice — 19

2. Atlanta's Religious and Political Ecology and the Establishment of Our Lady of Lourdes — 35

3. Our Lady of Lourdes, the Civil Rights Movement, and School Desegregation — 60

4. Liturgical Renewal and the Second Vatican Council in Atlanta — 88

5. The Withdrawal of the Sisters of the Blessed Sacrament from Our Lady of Lourdes — 112

6. Reviving Our Lady of Lourdes through Liturgical Renewal and Liturgical Justice — 134

Conclusion — 161

Acknowledgments — 169

Notes — 171

Index — 193

About the Author — 205

Introduction

On May 24, 1963, the Archdiocese of Atlanta ordained its first Black priest, Fr. William Calhoun, at the Cathedral of Christ the King. Calhoun had been a member of Our Lady of Lourdes Catholic Church, a nonterritorial parish located on Auburn Avenue that the archdiocese had designated for the "Negro apostolate." After graduating from Our Lady of Lourdes School, Calhoun embarked upon a vocation as a priest, graduating from St. Mary's Seminary in Baltimore before returning to Atlanta to prepare for his ordination. The ceremony itself was conducted entirely in Latin, and Roscoe Thomas, an Our Lady of Lourdes parishioner, explained the content and meaning of the proceedings to Calhoun's parents, who were Baptists. Once Holy Orders were conferred on Calhoun and Matthew Kemp, a white seminarian who was being ordained that same day, they spent the next hour blessing those in the audience, a mix of Blacks and whites as well as Catholics and non-Catholics.

The elevation of William Calhoun to the priesthood was a particular source of pride for the Sisters of the Blessed Sacrament (SBS), the religious order that founded Our Lady of Lourdes in 1911 and whose members also taught at the parish's school. The SBS was founded by Philadelphia heiress, religious sister, and canonized saint Katharine Drexel in 1891 as a missionary women's teaching order that established schools for Native Americans and Blacks. They were an unusually progressive voice within American Catholicism in the Jim Crow era, ministering to marginalized peoples whom the wider Church often ignored in favor of the European immigrants transforming the Church in the North. In many dioceses, including in Atlanta, the SBS was regarded as the religious order to consult with about "the Negro Question," as its members were often the only religious leaders in the locality who had any substantial contact with the local Black communities.[1]

Since their arrival in Atlanta, the SBS had been advocating for Black priests as a means to better evangelize and increase the visibility of the

Church among Blacks, and they perceived the ordination of William Calhoun to be the culmination of their decades of work. As the sisters' annals recorded, they felt the ceremony represented

> the Church in action, in her greatest action, the Liturgy, acting out what she teaches before hundreds of our Separated Brethren [i.e., Protestants] to whom it was so new. Here was the Ecumenical Movement reaching out to souls. Then, too, for us it had the added intensity that comes when someone you know and admire, one of our own, receives the great power of the priesthood. But this was in Georgia with all of its anti-Catholic, anti-Negro mileau [sic] crumbling before this demonstration of Christ acting in His Church for all men and through allmen [sic]. It has truly been a privledge [sic] for us to be here this day.

The ordination of Fr. Calhoun was not only a vindication of the universality of Catholicism and the truth of the Church's social teachings but also a glimpse into how liturgical action could bring about social change. Disparate individuals came together to pray in unison, which in turn gave them the strength to put Catholic social teachings into practice. There was even a link to the ongoing Civil Rights Movement, as Fr. Calhoun's parents were members of West Hunter Baptist Church, the congregation pastored by Rev. Ralph David Abernathy, Rev. Martin Luther King Jr.'s second in command. Indeed, the SBS wrote of their disappointment when Abernathy was unable to attend the reception Our Lady of Lourdes gave in honor of Calhoun on the Sunday after the ordination, although his wife, Juanita, was present.[2]

The circumstances surrounding the ordination of Fr. Calhoun challenge many assumptions about how pre–Vatican II Catholicism operated in the United States. First, the ceremony took place in the South, a region that was extremely antagonistic to Catholicism. Second, present was a large contingent of Protestants, who followed the ceremony to the best of their ability. Last, and most important, there was a significant Black presence at the event, although it is unknown whether the audience was segregated. The Black invitees, like Fr. Calhoun himself, were all connected to Our Lady of Lourdes in some way, whether as current parishioners, former students and parents of Our Lady of Lourdes School, or Protestants with familial and/or social ties to Our Lady of Lourdes members.

That so many Blacks in Atlanta had a relationship of some kind to Our Lady of Lourdes stems from its status as the "Mother Church" for Black Catholics in the Archdiocese and the fact that it was adjacent to what was once considered "the richest Negro street in the world," Auburn Avenue. While its Protestant neighbors—Big Bethel African Methodist Episcopal Church, Wheat Street Baptist Church, and especially Ebenezer Baptist Church—are better known to historians and the public, Our Lady of Lourdes has an equally storied history that can inform the fields of Black history, Catholic history, and the history of Southern race relations. The experiences of white ethnic Catholics in the industrial North have often been treated as the default when discussing the history and sociology of the Catholic Church in the United States. However, such a Eurocentric focus fails to explain the history of a historically Black Southern parish like Our Lady of Lourdes. The Black Catholic experience in Atlanta, Georgia, is fundamentally different from that in the Northern, European immigrant Catholic parishes that sociologists and historians usually study, and those differences have much to teach us.

Although Southern Catholics constituted a minority of the region's population, they were not walled in a "Catholic ghetto" like their coreligionists in the North. For example, a letter Francis E. Hyland, auxiliary bishop of Savannah-Atlanta, circulated to the diocese's Catholics in 1950 revealed that of Georgia's 159 counties, "there are regularly established parishes in only 24 Counties; There is a Catholic Church or chapel in only 42 Counties; There is a Catholic School in only 15 Counties."[3] The city of Atlanta was unusual in that it contained five parishes, including Our Lady of Lourdes and what was then the Co-cathedral of Christ the King, but this was a small number compared to the scores of Protestant churches that surrounded them. For example, Immaculate Conception Church (now the Shrine of the Immaculate Conception), the first Catholic parish in Atlanta, is surrounded by Central Presbyterian Church and Trinity United Methodist Church. Our Lady of Lourdes shares the Auburn Avenue neighborhood with a variety of Protestant churches affiliated with historically Black denominations, most notably Ebenezer Baptist Church, the church formerly pastored by Rev. Dr. Martin Luther King Jr. If the Northern Catholic ghetto enabled white ethnic Catholics to exist in environments where they could believe that Catholicism was the default religion, Catholics in Atlanta were acutely, spatially aware of their minority status.

The centrality of the Black-white racial binary to the Southern political and social order shaped the Southern Catholic experience as well. It meant that Atlanta's Catholics prioritized their identification with the culture and interest of their racial community, rather than religious solidarity with Catholics of the opposite race. The paranoia about the perceived ethnic and theological "otherness" of Catholicism among white Protestants in the South made white Catholics eager to demonstrate their devotion to the "Southern way of life" (i.e., white supremacy) and the Lost Cause, even though the Catholic Church was officially opposed to racism and segregation. The advent of the Civil Rights Movement exposed the inherent contradiction of white Catholics who considered themselves to be loyal to the teachings of their religion yet ignored their Church's teachings on the evils of racism and segregation.[4]

Although persistent anti-Catholicism throughout the twentieth century was an irritant for Atlanta's white Catholics, their European heritage meant that they enjoyed full access to Southern society, including political participation, the use of public facilities, and all of the archdiocese's Catholic institutions. The same was not true of Atlanta's Black Catholics, who were geographically concentrated in the Auburn Avenue area and Southwest Atlanta, and until the construction of the city's second Black parish, St. Paul of the Cross in 1954, were confined to a single parish.

The insular nature of the city's Black community, combined with the small size of Our Lady of Lourdes's congregation also affected relations between Catholics and Protestants. Atlanta's Black Catholics did not regard Protestants as "heretics" existing outside of the community, as was often the case for white ethnic Catholics in the North. More often, they were family members who just happened to attend other churches. Some writers, such as E. Franklin Frazier and Fr. Lawrence Lucas, accused Black Catholics of being "whitewashed" or self-hating social climbers, but members of Our Lady of Lourdes during the Jim Crow era were so segregated that "becoming white" simply was not an option. Atlanta's Blacks generally had few interactions with whites of any religious persuasion, other than the SBS and the Society of African Missions (SAM) priests assigned to the parish.[5]

The SBS occupied an unusual position in Atlanta's racial and religious ecology, in that they could move back and forth between the world of white Catholics and that of Black Catholics without attracting undue attention. This most likely occurred because as a mission group, the SBS still retained a paternalistic relationship to the Black community that was deemed unthreatening to the racial status quo. However, the SBS espoused an interracialist position that was at odds with the Southern way of life. For example, Sr. Mary Thomas Aquinas, the first principal of the Our Lady of Lourdes School, described the shocked reaction she received from the bishop of Savannah when she inquired about the feasibility of Black priests. In an undated letter to Katharine Drexel from around the early 1920s, she said,

> I asked [Bishop Michael Joseph Keyes] what he thought of the Colored priest in the South. He looked at me for a few minutes, trying to read my meaning, then he said, "What do you mean?" I said, "Well, Bishop, I mean what do you think about Colored priests in the South, how the Colored people would receive them, whether they could come into the Church any quicker." "No, they should start in the North with Colored priests and gradually bring them down South. The white people would never stand a Colored priest. Imagine Fr. Horton having to invite a Colored priest to Sacred Heart Church sit at the table with him." Says Fr. Horton, "I'd ask him for another job." "No, the South is not ready for the Colored priests yet," said the Bishop.[6]

Though the SBS was considered to be the religious order to consult with about "the Negro Question" in the United States, they always had to walk a fine line between supporting Black communities in their efforts for political and social liberation and the Church's desire to appear respectable to white America.

The changes wrought in the 1960s by the Second Vatican Council (i.e., Vatican II) and the Civil Rights Movement upset the uneasy dynamic between white Catholics, Black Catholics, and the SBS in Atlanta. Of the two events, the Civil Rights Movement had the most immediate and disruptive effects because it struck at the heart of the Southern way of life that white Southerners, Catholic and Protestant, took for granted.

Many members of Our Lady of Lourdes and St. Paul of the Cross participated in protests and boycotts along with Black Protestants to end the segregation of public facilities in the city.[7]

The most immediate and obvious way Vatican II impacted Atlanta's Catholics was the changes to the liturgy that came shortly after Fr. Calhoun's ordination. The form of the Mass that Frs. Calhoun and Kemp would have learned in seminary was the Tridentine Latin Mass (TLM), which was developed in the aftermath of the Council of Trent in 1570. The form of the TLM differed greatly from the low church Protestantism that was normative in the South; it was performed in Latin, required no participation from laypeople, and had the officiant spend the bulk of the ceremony with his back to the congregation. The changes enacted by Vatican II led to fundamental transformations to Catholic theology—a renewed emphasis on Scripture, the empowerment of "the People of God," an openness to other religions, and a more expansive ecclesiology—that were subsequently embodied by the reformed liturgy.[8]

Paul Hallinan, the archbishop of Atlanta at the time of Fr. Calhoun's ordination, was a vocal advocate of liturgical reform. He believed that the renewed liturgy in the United States would be consistent across racial and ethnic lines, but some Black Catholics quickly saw the new vistas for cultural self-expression that the council opened to them. By the end of the 1960s, inspired by Vatican II, Black Catholics in Northern cities such as Chicago staged highly political Masses with pan-African and Black Power themes. But the full implications of inculturation and liturgical renewal would not come for the parishioners of Our Lady of Lourdes until the 1990s.[9]

Race is intertwined with all aspects of everyday life in the United States, so it should be no surprise that Black Catholics experienced liturgical change differently from whites. How people worship, where they live, what legal rights they have, and who their neighbors are have affected the history of Black Catholics in the South, shaping a course of events that is distinct from the history that assumes the white experience as normative. Black Catholics in general are an understudied demographic among sociologists and historians. Increasing our knowledge of this group holds promise for expanding our understanding of the intersection of race, religious tradition, and religious activism in the United States. By examining how the Civil Rights Movement and Vatican II affected African American Catholics in Atlanta, this book illustrates how religious change and social change intersected. The story unfolds through a particular focus on the parish of Our Lady of Lourdes in the Old Fourth Ward / Sweet Auburn District. Through archival and oral history sources, the people of this particular local Black Catholic context help to expand the received history.

Our Lady of Lourdes is the focus of this volume for several reasons. First, it is the "Mother Church" for African American Catholics in Atlanta, being the oldest historically Black parish in the city. Second, Our Lady of Lourdes is one block away from Ebenezer Baptist Church, the congregation in which the Rev. Dr. Martin Luther King Jr. was raised and later copastored. A major question that this work aims to answer is the extent to which the congregants of Our Lady of Lourdes were aware of and/or supportive of the political activities of their neighbors at Ebenezer. Third, the city of Atlanta is well-known for being a "Black mecca" with a large, politically active African American middle class. In addition to Ebenezer, Our Lady of Lourdes is also close to several other influential historically Black congregations, including Big Bethel African Methodist Episcopal Church and Wheat Street Baptist Church. Examining these congregations in relation to Our Lady of Lourdes allows for an assessment of how the latter was similar to and different from these Protestant congregations and whether and how they all were mutually shaped by their literal place at the center of the civil rights struggle. This parish, sitting at the intersection of Black church activism and Black Catholicism, provides a window into how race and local context transform and are transformed by religious tradition at a pivotal moment in history.

Race in Histories of American Catholics

General histories of American Catholicism have treated white ethnic Catholics as the default, while Black Catholics are relegated to a few scant pages (if any). The term "white ethnic" was first coined in the 1960s, but the general concept appears to have been in existence since the end of World War II as a way to describe non-Protestant, non-Anglo-Saxon whites from Europe. A "white ethnic revival" occurred in the late 1960s and early 1970s, as second- and third-generation Americans from European immigrant backgrounds began to embrace their particular ethnic backgrounds as a source of cultural and political power. In many but not all cases this newfound ethnic consciousness was used to mobilize white ethnic communities against political and civil rights gains made by Blacks in Northern cities. The development of white ethnic identity fit not only into the story of the United States as a nation of immigrants but also into the Catholic Church's own "Immigrant Church" narrative. Overemphasizing the immigrant roots of the American Church also enabled white Catholics to sidestep the issue of the role of Catholicism in slavery and racism since Catholic immigrants who had arrived after the Civil War and settled in Northern cities could hardly be responsible for the behavior of white Protestants in the Antebellum South.[10]

This tendency to see white ethnic Catholics as the default in American Catholicism is most obvious in older, pre–civil rights / pre–Vatican II works. In *Protestant, Catholic, Jew: An Essay in American Religious Sociology* by Will Herberg, for example, the Catholic Church is defined as "a foreign church, or rather, a conglomerate of foreign churches, recruited from the waves of foreign immigration." His chapter on Catholics invariably revolves around white ethnics, especially the Irish, and their fraught relationship to the white Protestant majority. Although Herberg admits the existence of "a small group of Negro Catholics," he considers Black Catholics, along with Hispanic Catholics, to be unassimilable in the Irish-dominated American Church.[11] Similarly, post–civil rights works such as Jay P. Dolan's *The American Catholic Experience: A History from Colonial Times to the Present* and more recent studies such as *The Spirit of Vatican II: A History of Catholic Reform in America* by Colleen McDannell also take for granted that the story of American Catholicism is essentially that of the European immigrant, with Black Catholics relegated to a handful of pages about segregation.[12]

John T. McGreevy's *Parish Boundaries: The Catholic Encounter with Race in the Twentieth-Century Urban North* is generally considered to be the foundational text on how white Catholics in the North interpreted issues pertaining to race. His thesis is that white ethnic Catholics classified themselves and others by their respective neighborhood parish, which due to de facto segregation meant that these congregations were almost always monoethnic. Race, ethnicity, and religious devotion were all embodied in the parish and the particulars of the neighborhood in question, giving the community and its people a holy quality. Thus, white Catholics perceived that their neighborhoods were "despoiled" when racially and religiously alien Blacks began moving to those areas in large numbers in the 1960s and disrupted the organic unity of ethnicity, religion, and place.[13]

As the title indicates, *Parish Boundaries* is specifically about race and ethnicity among Catholics in the North. What McGreevy describes points to key differences that set Catholics in the South apart. White Catholics in the North most often identified with their ethnic group (e.g., Irish, Polish, Italian), whereas their Southern coreligionists existed in a strict racial binary of Black versus white with no qualifiers. The relationship between white Catholics and Blacks (whether Protestant or Catholic) was shaped by the perverse logic of Jim Crow rather than the Northern de facto segregation that created the "parish boundaries" model posited by McGreevy. Under Jim Crow, Southern racial boundaries were far more overt. Bursts of white paternalism were deployed as the carrot to the stick of institutional and extrajudicial violence to ensure Black submission. In the case of Our Lady of Lourdes, this paternalism ranged from donations by white Catholics desirous to support a "colored mission" to the white priests and sisters attempting to convert the wider community, interspersed with disenfranchisement and racist violence, such as the Atlanta Race Riot of 1906.

Catholics in the Northern parishes McGreevy described were also far more isolated from Protestants than were Catholics in the overwhelmingly Protestant South. Black Protestants were even more of a presence at Our Lady of Lourdes, since the majority of the parents at the parish school were Protestant, and all of the members had friends and relatives who were non-Catholic. Unlike the white ethnic parishes described by McGreevy, which were walled off from other religious and ethnic groups, people of other races and religions were always part of the Our Lady of Lourdes story, in spite of the strict separation of the races demanded by Jim Crow.

Gerald Gamm's 1999 work *Urban Exodus: Why the Jews Left Boston and the Catholics Stayed* builds on McGreevy's thesis about how the organizational structure of Catholicism (i.e., the neighborhood parish) compelled white Catholics to remain in the Roxbury and Dorchester communities longer than Jewish residents of the same neighborhoods. He agrees with McGreevy that the tight identification of the parish with the neighborhood made white Catholics loath to leave for the suburbs. However, he also notes that this territorialism made white Catholics more hostile to Blacks who moved into the area, whereas those Jews who remained in their original communities tended to be tolerant of their Black neighbors. Black Catholics are mentioned only briefly to illustrate how their shared religion was insufficient to build affinity with their white coreligionists.[14]

Cyprian Davis's 1990 monograph *The History of Black Catholics in the United States* was the first comprehensive effort to put the Black Catholic experience at the center of the American Catholic story. The book begins with the Ethiopian eunuch mentioned in the New Testament book of Acts and ends with the 1980s controversy over whether a separate African American Rite should be established. Davis illustrates how Black Catholic history is related to the story of the overall history of Catholicism in the United States, while emphasizing how slavery and institutionalized racism meant that they had a fundamentally different interpretation of what it meant to be Catholic and American than their white ethnic coreligionists.

Still, the history that Davis recounts is more about bishops, priests, and sisters than about ordinary Black Catholics (although educated laypeople also play a role in the story he tells). Much of this is out of necessity, as most Black Catholics would have been illiterate until the twentieth century and thus unable to commit their thoughts to writing. However, it means that Davis omits details of what the nuts and bolts of lived religion must have been like among the masses of the Black laity. *The History of Black Catholics in the United States* is, then, a necessary beginning, a general overview of the subject, and a springboard for future research, leaving much still to be explored.[15]

Since Davis was a Benedictine monk, his criticism of the hierarchy for their failures tends to be more muted than that of a secular scholar, a trait that is not shared by Fr. Lawrence E. Lucas. His 1970 *cri de coeur* against institutional racism in the Catholic Church, *Black Priest/White Church: Catholics and Racism* is partially an autobiographical account of being a Black Catholic in a white-dominated religious institution, while also attempting to field ideas about how the Catholic Church could improve its record on racial issues. Lucas's primary complaint about the Catholic Church is that it is a white supremacist organization that socializes Black Catholics to "whitewash" themselves in thought and behavior. He is especially critical of the psychologically damaging effects of having white priests and sisters acting as authority figures in Black parishes and parochial schools. The book ends with Lucas stating that white Catholics need to take the ethical and moral teachings of the Church seriously, rather than obsessing about an individualistic and devotional piety. Similarly, the hierarchy needed to use its moral power to force white Catholics and American society in general to not only condemn racist attitudes and institutions but also inspire them to be proactive about becoming actively antiracist.

Like many works about American Catholicism, *Black Priest / White Church* is also very much focused on Catholics, regardless of race, in Northern cities. Lucas's account reinforces Herberg's observation that Blacks, regardless of religious affiliation, exist outside of mainstream American religious life. Lucas argues that the Church always referred to "us" with regard to white ethnics, whereas for Blacks it was a case of "us" and "them." However, as we will see, Our Lady of Lourdes members did not consider this "us" versus "them" dichotomy to be a problem, perhaps because they were so segregated that white Catholics were seldom a point of comparison.[16]

Black Catholics in the North are also the focus of Matthew Cressler's 2017 book, *Authentically Black and Truly Catholic: The Rise of Black Catholicism in the Great Migration*. As the title makes clear, he is less concerned with "whitewashing" and more interested in how Black Catholics made a religious world for themselves. Cressler explains that he chose Chicago as the site for his work because it contains one of the nation's largest Black Catholic communities, one that primarily comprises the descendants of Black migrants who converted during the Great Migration. Because of this migration, there are intimate ties between Chicago and Southern Black Catholic communities, including Our Lady of Lourdes. Chicago was also a hotbed of Black Power activism in the years following Vatican II, activism that crept into the discourses and liturgies created among the city's Black Catholics. The book tracks the varying ways that Chicago's Black Catholics understood what it meant to be Black and Catholic in the pre- and post–Vatican II periods and how political trends in the Black community as a whole affected how they conceived of these dual identities.¹⁷ His work suggests that Black Catholic life must be understood both in relation to the Civil Rights Movement and in relation to Vatican II. Building off that work, this book takes that intertwined history into the South.

There were, of course, already ties between Black communities in the North and the South. Cressler does not mention that some of the Southern migrants who settled in Chicago were already Catholic, either because they hailed from culturally Catholic areas such as Louisiana or because they had converted to Catholicism prior to traveling north. This issue directly affected Our Lady of Lourdes in the early twentieth century because many of the parish's initial converts left Atlanta to "go to Detroit," thus negatively impacting the struggling mission's already tenuous financial state.¹⁸ The parishioners of Our Lady of Lourdes had very different religious concerns from those of the Black Catholics from Chicago whom Cressler profiles in his book.

Works examining Southern Catholicism—Black or white—have been sparse, especially when compared to the body of work about Catholicism in Northern urban centers. Those that exist have been published relatively recently, which suggests that this gap in the research is finally being addressed. For example, Mark Newman's 2018 monograph, *Desegregating Dixie: The Catholic Church in the South and Desegregation, 1945–1992*, examines how Southern Catholics, both Black and white, responded to the Civil Rights Movement. It focuses on the South as a region, pointing to the different ways that segregationist white Catholics, progressive white Catholics, Black Catholics, and the Catholic Church as an institution responded to the call for civil rights. Many of those patterns are evident in the life of Our Lady of Lourdes and its sister churches in the Archdiocese of Atlanta. The history of Our Lady of Lourdes both illustrates and complicates the larger regional picture.¹⁹

The situation of Catholics as a minority in the South is the subject of Andrew S. Moore's *The South's Tolerable Aliens*, a 2007 history of Catholics in postwar Georgia and Alabama. As the title suggests, the book focuses on how white Catholics constituted a religious "other" in a region where racial and denominational identity was rigidly defined within a caste-like structure. To compensate for this "otherness," white Catholics demonstrated their willingness to defend the Southern way of life (i.e., segregation), even though this was antithetical to the universal nature of Catholicism. Once the Civil Rights Movement commenced and American bishops began to take a more active stance against racism in U.S. society, white Catholics in the South were forced to choose between their religious loyalty and racial solidarity. Moore juxtaposed the experiences of Paul Hallinan, the archbishop of Atlanta, and those of Thomas Joseph Toollen, bishop of Mobile, Alabama, to illustrate liberal versus conservative approaches to civil rights issues among the Southern hierarchy. However, Black Catholics are mostly in the background of Moore's narrative.[20]

Black Catholics—and specifically Our Lady of Lourdes—come to the fore in Moore's contribution to the 2018 edited volume, *Catholics in the Vatican II Era: Local Histories of a Global Event*.[21] His is a concise history of the parish within the context of the shifting racial and religious dynamics caused by the Civil Rights Movement and Vatican II. His primary focus is Archbishop Paul Hallinan's implementation of liturgical and racial reforms during and after Vatican II. Moore illustrates that although Hallinan was widely regarded as "liberal," on both liturgical and racial issues, his color-blind vision for the post–Vatican II Church failed to take into account the needs and desires of Black Catholics. The experiences of Our Lady of Lourdes members, both pre- and post–Vatican II, demonstrate the messy reality of how Black Catholics in Atlanta experienced reforms in their church and attempts at desegregation and urban renewal in the city at large. This book expands on that messy history, especially to include the parish's pre–Vatican II history and the factors that led to its revitalization in the late 1980s.

A recent work that uses the lens of region, race, and transnational ties to examine the history and development of American Catholicism is *The Making of American Catholicism: Regional Culture and the Catholic Experience* by Michael J. Pfeifer. The book's five chapters examine how regionally distinct iterations of Catholicism arose in different parts of the United States. Each chapter is framed around a particular parish that exemplifies the regional culture, both secular and religious, in question. Of particular interest for the purposes of my own work is chapter 1, which focuses on Our Lady of Lourdes Catholic Church in New Orleans, Louisiana. Founded in 1905 as an all-white parish until desegregation began in the 1950s, Our Lady of Lourdes was an amalgamation of various African Diasporic cultures—the Black Creoles native to New Orleans, Black Protestant converts, West African priests and sisters—all of which led to a uniquely African / African American worship experience. Our Lady of Lourdes was shuttered in 2006 after suffering catastrophic damage from Hurricane Katrina, forcing its remaining parishioners to migrate to other parishes.[22]

Although the Atlanta and New Orleans Our Lady of Lourdes parishes have much in common by way of being majority-Black parishes located in major Southern cities, there are substantial regional and cultural differences. With New Orleans's beginning as French territory, Catholicism was the default religion for much of its history, whereas it is a minority religion in Atlanta. New Orleans's Francophone culture also led to the development of a racial dynamic that was very different from what arose in Atlanta. While Atlanta traditionally operated under a strict racial binary of Black-white, New Orleans contained a more complex system consisting of white Creoles, Creoles of Color, Blacks, and European immigrants from a variety of ethnic backgrounds. Jim Crow segregation would eventually be superimposed onto New Orleans society, but it always uneasily coexisted with the preexisting French-derived racial hierarchy. It is for this reason that Pfeifer states in his introduction that Randall Miller's notion of Catholic "cultural captivity" (i.e., the idea that white Catholics in the South shaped their religious culture to fit into white Protestant political and social norms, rather than one guided by Catholic social teachings) does not apply in Southern Louisiana, where Catholics were traditionally in the majority. Consequently, the insights gained from the experiences of the parishioners of the New Orleans Our Lady of Lourdes are not necessarily applicable to those of the Atlanta Our Lady of Lourdes.[23]

Structure and Methods

This book builds upon preexisting literature but also uses primary sources and oral histories collected over a period of months. The Archives of the Sisters of the Blessed Sacrament, located at the Catholic Historical Research Center of the Archdiocese of Philadelphia, was an invaluable aid. The annals and letters produced by the SBS assigned to Our Lady of Lourdes from 1912 to 1974 provided a timeline for every major event that occurred during their tenure at the parish. While the members of the SBS were observing the occurrences of Our Lady of Lourdes from the perspective of white outsiders, they were accepted by the residents, Catholic or not, as part of the Black community.

Most of the documents pertaining to the internal workings of the Catholic Church in Atlanta were obtained at the Office of Archives and Records of the Archdiocese of Atlanta. These items include correspondence between diocesan officials, Sunday bulletins, and publications produced by Our Lady of Lourdes itself. Materials related to the Drexel Catholic High School controversy of the late 1960s came from the collection of the same name at the Auburn Avenue Research Library, an institution devoted to the study and preservation of Atlanta's Black history. The correspondence between Bishop Benjamin Keiley and Cardinal James Gibbons that is cited in chapter 1 originated from summaries and quotes provided by the Roman Catholic Diocese of Savannah from their unprocessed bishops' collections. The bulk of the primary sources pertaining to Archbishop Paul Hallinan and the implementation of the Second Vatican Council in Atlanta originated from the archives of the Catholic University of America in Washington, D.C. The materials focusing on Archbishops Eugene Marino and James P. Lyke originated from copies of the *Georgia Bulletin* housed at the Xavier University of Louisiana Archives and Special Collections.

Oral histories from twelve individuals who were members of Our Lady of Lourdes during the Civil Rights Movement and Vatican II were obtained to allow Black Catholics to describe this time period in their own voices. An additional oral history was secured from a religious sister of the Sisters of the Immaculate Heart of Mary who was the principal of the Our Lady of Lourdes School in the late 1970s. Twelve oral histories were collected from Blacks who attended the three major Protestant churches on Auburn Avenue—Wheat Street Baptist Church, Big Bethel African Methodist Episcopal Church, and Ebenezer Baptist Church—to ascertain the relationships between Black Protestants and Black Catholics during the pre–Vatican II / Jim Crow era. Seven of these interviewees were members of Big Bethel, two were from Wheat Street, and three were from Ebenezer. One interview was obtained from a member of St. Paul of the Cross. The interviewees ranged in age from fifty-nine to ninety-three. Eleven interviewees were members and/or alumni of Our Lady of Lourdes Catholic Church and the Our Lady of Lourdes School. At least four of the Our Lady of Lourdes interviewees remain active members of the parish. They are involved in a wide range of ministries, and one was a secretary of the parish. Other Our Lady of Lourdes interviewees are no longer active at the parish because of moves to other states or changes in church memberships. At least seven of the interviewees from the Protestant churches have been lifelong members of their congregations. Two of these interviewees were members of more than one of these congregations at one time or another. Most have been active in a range of ministries (e.g., as deacons, Sunday school teachers, choir members, ushers, and musicians). Only one interviewee from the Protestant locations is no longer a member of her Auburn Avenue church location.

Chapter Outline

Chapter 1 provides a general overview of how the Catholic Church struggled with issues pertaining to race in the nineteenth and twentieth centuries. It juxtaposes the pre–Vatican II ecclesiastical and soteriological mandate to incorporate as many people as possible into the "True Church" with the reality that the American Church tended to be ambivalent about actively engaging with the Black community. This ambivalence occurred because the American hierarchy did not want to be too closely associated with a group (i.e., Blacks) that was even less popular than already suspect white ethnic Catholics. In addition, the reactionary ideology of pre–Vatican II Catholicism lacked the conceptual language to criticize slavery and structural racism, even when these societal forces interfered with its missionary impulses.

Chapter 2 describes the establishment and development of the parish of Our Lady of Lourdes from its founding in 1911 until 1962, when the Civil Rights Movement was in earnest and Vatican II had just been convened. Details from oral histories flesh out the exact nature of the devotional and community life of Our Lady of Lourdes during the Jim Crow era. Brief histories of the major Protestant churches that are neighbors of Our Lady of Lourdes (Ebenezer Baptist Church, Wheat Street Baptist Church, and Big Bethel AME Church) show how this Catholic congregation fit into the overall religious ecology of the Old Fourth

Ward / Sweet Auburn neighborhoods at the dawn of this significant era of social and religious change. There are revelations as to why Our Lady of Lourdes parishioners chose to be Catholic at a time when and in a place where Protestantism was the norm.

Chapter 3 focuses on how the Our Lady of Lourdes community was affected by the Civil Rights Movement and the desegregation of Atlanta's public and parochial schools. We will see the ways in which Black Catholics and the SBS assigned to Our Lady of Lourdes were involved in the Civil Rights Movement and the desegregation of Catholic institutions within the Archdiocese of Atlanta. The chapter also examines how Bishop Francis Hyland and Archbishop Paul Hallinan handled desegregation, with a focus on the controversy surrounding the closing of Atlanta's only Black parochial high school, Drexel Catholic High School.

Chapter 4 traces how Vatican II and liturgical reform impacted Our Lady of Lourdes during the 1960s and 1970s. It touches on the context behind liturgical reform, especially the tension between popular devotions and "active participation" among the laity during the Mass, to explain why the Council Fathers felt a need to change the supposedly unchangeable Mass. The chapter indicates that while the reformed liturgy was accepted with minimal conflict at Our Lady of Lourdes, it was reflective of neither pre–Vatican II Catholicism nor the ethnic makeup of the parish.

Chapter 5 discusses the events and context leading to the SBS's withdrawal from Our Lady of Lourdes School in 1974. It reveals how the renewal of religious life demanded by Vatican II led to extensive changes in SBS practices and how the order understood its charism. Part of this reevaluation process involved hard decisions about how the SBS should use its increasingly limited personnel, which included withdrawing from institutions that were perceived to no longer be in need of the order's services. The chapter also details how Our Lady of Lourdes managed to keep the school operational until 2001, when the Archdiocese of Atlanta finally withdrew funding.

Chapter 6 relates how Our Lady of Lourdes entered a period of contraction during the 1970s and 1980s and how it reversed this downward trend by embracing an inculturated liturgy that reflected its unique history. The chapter begins with a brief description of how Auburn Avenue and its surroundings fell into a state of decline because of changing

Black residential patterns, rising crime, and the encroachment of the interstate highway system into the neighborhood. Compounding Our Lady of Lourdes's woes was the sense of abandonment it and the other majority-Black urban parishes felt, as the archdiocese turned its attention and resources toward the increasingly suburban white Catholic population. The chapter ends with a discussion of the theory behind Black inculturated liturgies and how implementing liturgical change revitalized Our Lady of Lourdes in the 1990s.

This book sheds light on how Black Catholics were affected by the convergence of the Civil Rights Movement and Vatican II by examining the history of a specific parish in Atlanta. In particular, it challenges the notion that the post–Vatican II period in American Catholicism was uniformly characterized by institutional and devotional shrinkage, as decline at Our Lady of Lourdes was a product of factors far more tied to its history in a segregated South and a segregated Church. Significant growth came some thirty years after the council when inculturated liturgical change took hold, casting doubt on the common assertion that the renewed liturgy invariably led to declines in participation and piety levels. Rather, the struggles and renewal of Our Lady of Lourdes provide insight into the dynamics of race relations in the Catholic Church in the South, especially how Jim Crow social relations created a Black Catholicism that was often separate from that practiced by their white coreligionists, yet intimately related to the forms of religious expression created by their Black Protestant neighbors.

1

Race and the Catholic Church, in Theory and Practice

To grasp the unusual place that Our Lady of Lourdes occupied in Atlanta's early twentieth-century religious ecology requires an understanding of the historical and ideological contexts in which this parish was established. While the idea of a single segregated parish for all Black Catholics residing in a major Southern city may seem unremarkable according to the social conventions of Jim Crow, it was actually a grudging concession granted by the Vatican, a sign of how white Catholics in the United States acquiesced to the wider culture rather than attempting to change it. From the viewpoint of the Vatican, the ability to visit any Catholic church and be accepted as a fellow believer was a privilege held by every baptized Catholic; condemning Catholics of a particular race to a certain parish because their coreligionists of another race refused to tolerate their presence was not only a failure of charity but antithetical to the idea of a truly universal church. Despite the institutional conservatism of the Catholic Church, the Vatican was frustrated with the inability or unwillingness of Catholic prelates in the United States to make significant inroads among Blacks, especially when compared to the fruitful gains experienced by Catholic missionary efforts in sub-Saharan Africa.[1]

However, the Vatican itself had historically given American Catholics mixed messages on slavery, and its theological and social teachings gave no guidance about how Catholics were supposed to reconcile the dehumanizing nature of chattel slavery and anti-Black racism with the imperative for universal evangelization. Until the post–Vatican II period, Catholic social teachings (CST) were formulated by European intellectuals responding to problems that were unique to Continental European political concerns. Even those who were sympathetic to the plight of nonwhites as a matter of charity still held paternalistic views about how Western influence, whether religious or secular, would be helpful for "backward peoples." Consequently, the Vatican lacked the conceptual framework necessary to challenge the anti-Black attitudes that made evangelizing Blacks in the United States so difficult.

Nonetheless, there was nothing in the theological or philosophical underpinning of pre–Vatican II Catholicism that would support the anti-Black policies enacted by the American Church. The official position of the nineteenth- and early twentieth-century Catholic Church was that it was the "True Church" ordained by God and that every human, regardless of race or ethnicity, was obliged to join. Because the Catholic Church was the organization established by God to fulfill his will on Earth, it was impossible for any human to be saved if they were outside of the Church. Individuals who willfully refused to join the church that Christ founded thus had no hope of salvation. It was possible, but extremely difficult, for non-Catholics to enter heaven under the pre–Vatican II view of soteriology; knowingly rejecting the Catholic Church meant rejecting not only an institution but also the Mass, the Eucharist, and the other sources of grace that only Catholicism could provide. Even if non-Catholics did have a chance for salvation, it was contingent on the extent to which their beliefs and behavior conformed to the natural law as interpreted by the Catholic Church's Magisterium. Thus, the Church was obliged, by both God and the duties of charity, to bring non-Catholics, including baptized Protestants, into its fold.[2]

Although Catholic theology, ecclesiology, and soteriology demanded a robust proselytization program to bring the unchurched to the True Church, the antebellum Church showed little interest in evangelizing among the enslaved in the United States. Contrary to the popular image of slave masters using Christianity and "white Jesus" as a means of social control, most slave masters, whether Catholic or Protestant, were ambivalent about the desirability of mission work among slaves. One of the main justifications for enslaving Africans in the seventeenth century was that it was permissible to enslave "heathens" but not Christians. There was a fear that should slaves become baptized, they might seek emancipation, as was their right under British law. State legislatures of slave states eventually passed laws that decreed that baptism made no difference in individuals' enslaved status, but many planters still refused to allow missionaries among their slaves for a variety of reasons: baptism made slaves "saucy," allowing time for religious instruction and practice cut into work hours, and Africans were too "brutish" for evangelization to have any merit. Even when missionaries touted evangelization as a way to create slaves who were more accepting of the slave-master hierarchy, many planters remained fearful of the egalitarian implications of Christian doctrine.[3]

Another stumbling block to evangelizing slaves was a shortage of clergy to serve the far-flung farms and plantations where most of the Southern populace lived. An acute priest shortage, especially in rural areas, made it difficult to organize the kind of congregational religious and social activities that would maintain Catholic identity and practices. The priests who were available tended to be Continental European immigrants who spoke poor English and struggled to communicate effectively to their congregations. Their inept preaching not only repelled Anglo-American Catholics but also made the Catholic Church seem even more foreign to Protestants. The primary function of Catholic priests was to act as an "alter Christus" who could dispense the sacraments to the faithful, especially the Eucharist during the celebration of the Mass. Preaching was a useful but not a necessary skill for the priest to have, a sentiment that put the Catholic Church at a disadvantage in a region where the oratory skill of a preacher was a major attraction for would-be churchgoers.

Randall Miller's examination of sacramental records throughout the Deep South (Louisiana, Mississippi, Alabama, and Maryland) indicates that many slaves received a Catholic baptism, but there is no evidence that they identified as Catholic, received the other sacraments, or had an identifiably Catholic devotional life. Priests blamed this lack of Catholic convictions on slave masters who neglected their obligation to provide slaves with religious instruction, while the planters claimed that they could not evangelize their slaves because there were not enough priests, the unspoken assumption being that converting the souls of the enslaved was not as pressing a matter as converting their white coreligionists.[4] Both of these claims were cited in a letter William Henry Elder, bishop of Natchez, wrote to the Society for the Propagation of the Faith concerning his lack of progress in evangelization among Blacks:

> These poor negroes form in some respects my chief anxiety. I believe they are generally well cared for, so far as health and the necessaries of life are concerned. But for learning and practicing religion, they have at present

very little opportunity indeed. Commonly the Masters are well disposed to allow them religious instruction, and sometimes they pay Ministers to come and preach on the plantation. They do not like to let the negroes go to a public church, because there is danger of their misbehaving when they are away from home, and out of sight of the Overseer. . . . Catholic masters of course are taught that it is their duty to furnish their slaves with opportunities for being well instructed, and for practicing their religion. And here is my anxiety, that I cannot enable those masters to do their duty because there are not Priests enough.[5]

Elder went on to say that the priests who were at his disposal were already serving in organized congregations and could not be recalled to become missionary priests to far-flung plantations. However, he rejected the idea of building a church that might serve multiple plantations, as Elder worried that the number of slaves in the congregation would be so great that they would crowd out the white population, suggesting that it was more important not to make white Catholics uncomfortable than to bring Blacks into the Church.

As Elder's letter illustrates, the American bishops did not see any point in spending their limited resources on a group of people even less popular than white Catholics, when there was a seemingly endless number of already Catholic immigrants from Europe arriving in the North on a daily basis. The Catholic Church's strategy of focusing its resources on retaining white Catholics to the exclusion of attracting converts among Blacks would intensify, as anti-Catholicism strengthened after the Civil War.[6]

Anti-Catholicism in Late Nineteenth- and Early Twentieth-Century Atlanta

The post–Civil War political environment created new challenges for the Catholic Church in the South, as organized anti-Catholicism became a major part of the region's political discourse. Anti-Catholicism in the South, as least as a political issue, had been considerably less prominent during the antebellum period than it was after the war. Until the surge in Catholic immigration in the 1840s, the ethnic composition of the Catholic Church in America had been overwhelmingly Anglo. Thus, while

Southern Protestants might take issue with Catholicism for theological reasons, the ethnic background of white Catholics was unobjectionable. In early nineteenth-century America, Catholic officials in the United States were also keenly aware of being minorities in a heavily Protestant nation. They focused their energy and resources on strengthening the Church's institutional base, rather than extending its political or social influence. Perhaps most importantly, white Catholics in the Old South accepted slavery as a given and eagerly supported the Confederacy during the Civil War. This helped the Catholic Church weather the nativist controversy in the 1850s, since its acceptance of the "peculiar institution" proved that it was not a threat to the status quo.[7]

The guarded tolerance afforded to white Catholics in the Old South should not be misinterpreted to mean that the Catholic Church was not seriously unproblematic for white Protestants. The highly ritualized nature of the Tridentine Mass smacked of "idolatry" and offended the supposedly egalitarian religious tastes of American Protestants, especially in the South where low church Baptists and Methodists predominated. Even during the Civil War, when white solidarity was needed to sustain the faltering Confederacy, it was not uncommon for white Protestants to look down on Catholic contributions to the war effort. However, this distaste for Catholicism did not manifest itself in de jure segregation or government action against Catholic institutions. White Catholics were more of a curiosity compared to the constant existential threat posed to the antebellum social order by emancipated Black slaves.[8]

This grudging acceptance turned into fear and paranoia after the Civil War as a direct result of the political and social unrest caused by the end of slavery. Although foreign immigration to the South virtually dried up after the Civil War and did not recover until the mid-1960s, Southern white Protestants were obsessed with the possibility of a foreign invasion that would further destabilize the region's delicate racial ecology through the undermining of white supremacy, a fear that was no doubt influenced by what was then the very recent experience of federal troops occupying the South. Because the vast majority of Catholic immigrants settled in urban areas in the North, they embodied all of the aspects of the post–Civil War United States that white Southerners detested: the hated industrial North, foreigners who degraded native-born American "racial stock," the coy suggestion of racial intermixing (whether between Blacks and whites or between WASPS and Catholics), and the vices and degeneracy that rural Southerners associated with city life. White Protestants in the South feared that the Catholic Church was luring Blacks into its fold with subversive promises of integrated worship, Catholic education, and "gaudy, elaborate rituals" that appealed to their "superstitious and childlike" nature.[9] Discriminating against Catholic immigrants as a racialized and religiously different other was not unique to the South, but the way in which post–Civil War white Southern Protestants feared Catholicism for its potential to undermine white supremacy was.

No figure personified white Southern anti-Catholicism more than Thomas Edward Watson, an influential populist politician from Thomson, Georgia. Watson began his political career in the U.S. House of Representatives critical of the oppressive structures of Gilded Age industrial capitalism, and he was sympathetic toward Blacks and poor whites who had been sacrificed in the name of "progress." By the end of the nineteenth century, Watson had not only soured on the possibility and desirability of an integrated populist movement but also become convinced that Catholics and Jews posed an imminent threat to the republican virtue of the United States in general and the South in particular. Watson believed that the only virtuous nation in the world was the United States because it was founded upon republican ideals as embodied by the white Anglo-Saxon yeoman farmer. Anything that threatened to erode this ideal, be it industrialization, foreign trade, Blacks, or non-WASP immigration, would lead to a diminishment of American civic virtue.

Watson's obsession with the Catholic Church appears to have begun shortly before World War I, an era that was characterized by a historic period of international trade and global migration. For Watson, Catholic immigration contaminated American republican virtues because of the inferior values he associated with the Catholic Church: autocracy, technological backwardness, and pagan rituals and superstition. Catholic priests represented a particular threat to the American social fabric because Watson believed their ostensible celibacy was a mask for their uncontrollable sexual appetites. If disreputable Italian and Irish priests were already raping respectable white Protestant women, Watson concluded, it was only a matter of time before Black priests followed suit. From Watson's perspective, Catholicism represented everything he disliked about the modern world, including his fear that Blacks were easily duped political pawns who could be utilized by any outside group to undermine the ideal white Anglo-Saxon Protestant Southern community.[10]

The ways in which anti-Catholicism and anti-Blackness converged in early twentieth-century Atlanta are evident in the 1916 persecution of Julia Riordan, a white Catholic teacher at the Davis Street School, by the Klan-dominated Atlanta Board of Education. Riordan first came to the attention of the board when she was accused of teaching Catholic triumphalism in the classroom. Since referring to the Catholic Church at all, even in a historical context, in Atlanta's public schools was considered subversive at this time, it is possible that Riordan may merely have mentioned the Church's contributions to European history. Five years later, in 1921, the board rejected Riordan as a candidate for principalship, not just for being Catholic but also for organizing with a teachers union against a proposed pay cut and because she allegedly prayed at a "Negro church" on a regular basis. Although the identity of the "Negro church" is not known, it is likely to have been Our Lady of Lourdes, as it is improbable that a white Catholic in the pre–Vatican II era would have visited a Black Protestant church. By 1922, anti-Catholicism had become a pressing issue in Atlanta politics, and the board had become stacked with persons who were either Klan members themselves or sympathetic to the Klan's views. The Riordan affair illustrated how white Georgians feared the potential of Catholicism to undermine Protestant normativity, white supremacy, and the economic order.[11]

Anti-Catholicism of the sort exhibited by the likes of Tom Watson or the Atlanta School Board of the 1910s and 1920s does not appear to have been present among Atlanta's Blacks. The white supremacist concerns that motivated such sentiments were inapplicable to Black communities. The lurid stories of licentious priests and the supposed threat of parochial schools to the common school movement that outraged and panicked white Protestants held little interest for Blacks. They were more concerned with their own survival than the supposed machinations of a religious organization they cared little about.

Black communities in the North did sour on Catholic immigrants, however, especially when the Irish adopted the same anti-Black attitudes as native-born whites. Catholic immigrants were also perceived to be an economic threat to the already precarious state of free Black laborers in the North, and there was considerable resentment among Blacks concerning the free ability for recent arrivals to immediately exercise the political rights that had been denied to them for generations. Unlike nativist sentiment found among white Protestants, however, Black indignation toward white ethnic Catholics never gained institutional power, not only because Blacks were shut out of Northern political machines but also because it was Catholics' perceived whiteness, rather than their religion, that made them a threat to Black self-preservation.[12]

Nevertheless, it is unclear if Southern Blacks had enough contact or knowledge of Catholicism or Catholic immigrants to form an opinion, negative or otherwise. In the case of Black Atlantans, there appears to have been a general antipathy toward what was perceived to be a "white church," but it is not clear how widely that was shared. For example, Janis Griffin, a current congregant of Our Lady of Lourdes, recalls in an interview with Andrew Moore that her family was a member of Ebenezer Baptist Church when she and her siblings attended Our Lady of Lourdes School in the 1950s. Martin Luther King Sr. ("Daddy King"), the head pastor of Ebenezer at the time, disapproved of the elder Griffin sending his children to the school at "that white church" (i.e., Our Lady of Lourdes).[13] Nevertheless, this utterance was most likely a frustrated jab against a perceived religious rival in the already crowded religious marketplace of Auburn Avenue rather than the expression of an ingrained belief that the Catholic Church was an active threat to the Black community. A 1921 article from the *Bulletin of the Catholic Laymen's Association of Georgia* on the work of the Society of African Missions (SAM) in Georgia asserted,

> When the Rt. Rev. Benjamin Keiley, Bishop of Savannah, entrusted the work of evangelization of the negroes of his diocese to these missionaries, he realized that the field was an extensive one, and that every inch of ground had to be cleared of various prejudices before any encouraging results could be expected.... As years went by, it became evident that the colored man showed little or no hostility against the Church, and that his prejudices against it were not of the bitter kind which not only refuses a fair investigation, but a priori places the ban on everything that comes within the narrow boundaries of its intolerance.[14]

Pre–Vatican II white Catholic accounts of racial issues are inclined to be self-congratulatory and paternalistic, but the *Bulletin*'s assessment that Black Protestants did not express the same kind of kneejerk hatred at Catholicism as their white coreligionists appears to have been accurate.

Although Southern Blacks remained largely indifferent to pre–Vatican II forms of Catholic liturgy and spirituality, they were very interested in parochial schools because of the poor quality of segregated public schools. Like parochial schools in the North, Catholic schools in the South reflected the ethnic makeup of their neighborhood. However, in the South this meant that the majority of students who attended Black parochial schools were Protestants with little to no preexisting knowledge of Catholicism. In the specific case of Our Lady of Lourdes, Catholic schools proved to be fruitful in encouraging conversions among Blacks, although most of the families that patronized them remained Protestant. Yet the presence and availability of Catholic schools as an alternative to public schools improved the image of the Catholic Church among Southern Blacks.[15]

Since Blacks and Native Americans were designated as "heathens" in need of conversion, missionary religious orders, rather than diocesan clergy, were tasked with serving them. One of these orders was the Sisters of the Blessed Sacrament for Indians and Colored People (SBS), which would staff the Our Lady of Lourdes School from 1912 to 1973. The SBS was founded by Philadelphia heiress Katharine Drexel, who used her substantial inheritance to establish a women's teaching order that would evangelize Blacks and Native Americans through education. Teaching sisters were trained at the SBS Motherhouse in Cornwall, Pennsylvania, and sent to schools that were often founded by the order itself. Drexel also provided funding to build churches for Blacks and Native Americans, including Our Lady of Lourdes. Most SBS schools and parishes were established in the first two decades of the twentieth century, and the ones aimed at the Black community were usually located in the South. The most impressive SBS institution was Xavier University of Louisiana, the only historically Black Catholic university in the United States, which was founded in 1925.

The SBS would always suffer from the inherent contradiction of having to tacitly accept Jim Crow norms to reach the Black community.

For example, Drexel's activities as a private citizen—she was a lifelong member of the NAACP and contributed to the Scottsboro Boys defense fund—demonstrate that she was personally committed to advancing the civil rights of Blacks. However, the institutions she founded would inadvertently contribute to the continuance of segregation. During Vatican II, the SBS and other religious orders that ministered to Black people would begin to reevaluate their respective charisms in light of the concerns raised by the Civil Rights Movement.[16]

Despite the indifference of the American hierarchy, evangelization and population movements led to a steady increase in the number of Black conversions during the period between Reconstruction and Vatican II. Rural Black migrants encountered Catholicism when they arrived in cities in the North and South via the Great Migration, and other religious orders took up working with Blacks.[17] In addition to the SBS, the Society of St. Joseph of the Sacred Heart (i.e., Josephites), the Society of the Divine Word (or Divine Word Missionaries), and the Society of African Missions (SAM) were also involved in the "Negro apostolate." All of these orders had a sincere desire to provide spiritual and material succor to Blacks, but these priests and sisters often harbored the same paternalistic and racist views as other whites of the time. Keeping Black ministry restricted to a handful of religious orders, however, relieved bishops of the need to divert money and resources away from white Catholics and kept clergy and sisters outside of those orders ignorant of Black Catholic concerns. The onus to advocate for Blacks within the Church fell on white Catholics with an unusual interest in the issue, such as Katharine Drexel, rather than the hierarchy, which theoretically bore this responsibility.[18]

Catholic Social Teachings, the Community, and the "Negro Question"

The disinterest of the hierarchy in the United States toward evangelizing Blacks was not only contrary to Catholic teachings on missiology and soteriology but also a violation of Catholic social teachings (CST). Catholic evangelization entailed both enlarging the membership of a particular religious organization and spreading a worldview that was supposed to affect the fabric of the sociopolitical order. Unlike the extreme individualism that typifies many American Protestant groups, Catholicism is presumed to be a total way of life that is practiced within a community structure. Being Catholic meant accepting the authority of an ecclesiastical hierarchy, both local and international, that had something to say about everything from labor relations to contraception. These episcopal pronouncements about political and social issues compose CST, and they are considered normative for all people, Catholic or not. Papal encyclicals occupy a place of primacy in terms of establishing an unofficial canon of CST, especially Leo XIII's *Rerum Novarum* and the encyclicals written in honor of it on various anniversaries (e.g., *Quadragesima Anno, Mater et Magistra, Centensimus Annus*).[19]

The intellectual foundation of CST is rooted in the nineteenth-century Catholic Thomistic revival. Much like its medieval iteration, the neo-Thomism that emerged during the nineteenth century was intended to be a comprehensive worldview that explained all aspects of the human existence, from the metaphysical underpinnings of reality to how the individual should make ethical choices. The neo-Thomists posited that the ideal social order should be characterized by communitarianism ethics embodied by organically developed communities that are run by a clearly defined hierarchy. Individuals were prized by the Thomists insofar as they played their predetermined role in contributing to the welfare of the entire society as defined by traditional community leaders. The neo-Thomist emphasis on the acceptance and embrace of hierarchical relationships proposed that seemingly antagonistic political actors, such as labor/capital or ruler/ruled, could peacefully coexist if each party fulfilled its respective duty to the other and the common good. In the case of labor relations, this meant that workers had the duty to work hard, obey their employers, and not engage in socially disruptive behavior, such as strikes or protests, whereas bosses had to offer a living wage, provide safe workplaces, and respect the religious and familial duties of laborers.[20]

While community was defined in different ways for white American Catholics in the North and South, both iterations required Blacks to be marginal participants. As the works of John McGreevy have indicated, white ethnics in the North treated their neighborhoods as sacred spaces because they were consecrated by the presence of the Catholic parish associated with the neighborhood and ethnic group in question. In this scheme, each white ethnic group made up its own "natural" community with the parish and the priest at the center, thereby approximating the organic community of neo-Thomist thought. However, this also meant that Black migration became an existential threat to the organic, mono-ethnic nature of the sacred area. Once the Black population reached a critical mass, the neighborhood became "despoiled" by their foreign religious and ethnic traditions, thus forcing the original inhabitants to abandon it. In the "parish boundaries" model, the community is defined by a common ethnic identity that is expressed by living in a particular area, which automatically excludes individuals from other ethnic and/or religious groups from membership.

In comparison, white Catholics in the South sacralized the racial hierarchy and a particular understanding of white Southern history more than specific physical spaces. This was illustrated not just by their tacit assent to Jim Crow but also in the way they eagerly participated in the post–Civil War cult of the Lost Cause. Figures such as Fr. Abram Ryan (often referred to as the Poet-Priest of the South), Benjamin J. Keiley (bishop of the Diocese of Savannah and Confederate veteran), and Margaret Mitchell (author of Lost Cause epic *Gone with the Wind*) became examples of how white Catholics could be good patriots, in both American and Confederate senses, and contribute to the formation of white Southern identity. Unlike the parish boundaries definition of organic Catholic community, which was ethnically exclusive by definition, Blacks had a place in the Southern community, but only as a class of permanent serfs to be kept on the periphery of society. The static nature of the post-Reconstruction, pre–civil rights South created what amounted to a closed society, especially in rural areas. Blacks and whites in the South were indeed bound together by paternalistic, familiar, and familial relationships, but these ties were tinged by anger, resentment, and violence, at both individual and institutional levels. The terror imposed on Blacks in the Jim Crow South and the white violence that accompanied the Civil Rights Movement would lay bare the claim of so-called benign white paternalism.[21] Whether in the North or in the South, Blacks were considered a social problem to be neutralized rather than full members of the community (however defined).

Examining Atlanta's pre–Vatican II white Catholic communities reveals a subculture that was separate from yet intimately connected to both white and Black iterations of Protestantism as well as a small Black Catholic presence. The first Catholics in Atlanta were Irish railway workers who opted to settle in the city after the Georgia Railroad was completed in 1845. Two missionary priests based in Augusta, Fr. John Barry and Fr. Gregory Duggan, followed the progress of the Georgia Railroad and traveled around the state to minister to the handful of Catholics scattered throughout the region. Masses were held in private residences, and Barry said the first Mass in Atlanta at the home of Michael McCullough at the intersection of what is now Martin Luther King Jr. Drive and Central Avenue. A congregation began to form around these occasional home Masses, enough to warrant a monthly visit by a priest in 1846, with Masses now being said at the home of Terrance Doonan.[22] The mission based at the Doonan home was simply known as the Catholic Church of Atlanta and lasted from 1846 to 1848. By 1848, the number of Catholics in Atlanta had grown to the point where a permanent parish needed to be erected. A plain wooden church was dedicated by Bishop Ignatius Reynolds of Charleston in 1849 in the name of the Immaculate Conception, making it the first church of any denomination built in Atlanta.[23]

The sacramental records of the Church of the Immaculate Conception reference a number of enslaved persons. However, this does not necessarily mean that slaves were regular attendees at the church. Given the paucity of Catholic churches in Georgia in the antebellum period, Immaculate Conception's territorial boundaries would have extended far beyond Atlanta's city limits. The bulk of the slaves in question most likely lived on plantations in rural Georgia and had their sacraments recorded at the church in whose territory they lived (i.e., Immaculate Conception). Enslaved Blacks were unlikely to have any actual relationship with the Catholic Church in Atlanta during the antebellum period.[24]

Sacred Heart Church (now the Basilica of the Sacred Heart) was the second Catholic church to be built in Atlanta. By the late nineteenth century, Atlanta's Catholic population had increased to the point where establishing a second parish became necessary. In response, Saints Peter and Paul Church was established on Alexander Street (now Ivan Allen Boulevard) in 1880 to serve Catholics living north of Edgewood Avenue. The Marist Fathers were invited to Atlanta in 1897 to staff missions and educational institutions in northern Georgia, and one of their commissions included Saints Peter and Paul. Although the population of the parish was growing quickly, the property of Saints Peter and Paul was run down and unsanitary because of unchecked urban development in the surrounding neighborhood. The Marist Fathers bought a plot of land at the corner of Peachtree Street and Ivy Street (now Ralph McGill Boulevard) for a new church building, while continuing to say Mass at Saints Peter and Paul. When construction was completed in 1898, the congregation moved to the new building, which was rededicated as Sacred Heart Church.[25]

Atlanta's third Catholic church was St. Anthony of Padua, established in the West End in 1903 by women who were tired of walking three to four miles to Immaculate Conception. Essie Chandler, wife of famed writer Joel Chandler Harris, author of the Uncle Remus stories, invited the other Catholic women of the West End to lobby the hierarchy to create a permanent parish in their neighborhood. Bishop Benjamin Keiley of the Diocese of Savannah agreed to their demands, and he celebrated the first Mass under the aegis of St. Anthony's Parish at the home of Mrs. George Corley on June 13, 1903. The congregation acquired a house on Gordon Street (now Ralph David Abernathy Boulevard) that was remodeled into a church and rectory and subsequently dedicated as St. Anthony of Padua Church on September 20, 1903. The foundation for the current church building was laid in 1911, but it was finally finished and dedicated only in 1924.[26] Although the West End had a Black presence in the early twentieth century because of its proximity to the Atlanta University Center, St. Anthony of Padua remained officially segregated until the 1950s. Black Catholics from the Atlanta University Center (a consortium of historically Black institutions that at the time included Atlanta University, Clark College, the Interdenominational Theological Seminary, Morehouse College, Morris Brown College, and Spelman College) would occasionally attend Mass at St. Anthony of Padua during the Jim Crow era because it was closer than Our Lady of Lourdes, although they had to sit in the back of the church and receive Communion after the white parishioners. In the 1950s, St. Anthony of Padua became the first white parish in the Archdiocese of Atlanta to welcome Black families into its membership, and it would become majority Black by the 1980s.[27]

Our Lady of Lourdes became Atlanta's fourth Catholic congregation in 1912, but as it was a "colored mission," the city's white Catholics considered it an afterthought. Unlike Sacred Heart, Immaculate Conception, and St. Anthony of Padua, which were diocesan parishes, Our Lady of Lourdes was owned and operated by the SAM until March 26, 1963, when the Archdiocese of Atlanta bought all of its buildings and property. Our Lady of Lourdes relied on white Catholics to provide for its financial, material, and staffing needs for much of its history, but actual contact with whites was limited to the SBS and whomever the parish priest was at any given time.[28] Our Lady of Lourdes members could and did attend Mass at the white Catholic churches if they missed Mass at their own parish, but they had to sit in the back and receive Communion after the whites. Yet there was a perception on the part of many Our Lady of Lourdes members that the Jim Crow seating arrangements found in Atlanta's white Catholic churches were still superior to what they experienced in the city's white Protestant churches, where Blacks could not attend at all.[29]

The impetus for the establishment of Our Lady of Lourdes came from Fr. Ignatius Lissner, the French-born head of the SAM, rather than from Bishop Keiley. Lissner was already known to Keiley, as he was responsible for building most of the "colored missions" in Georgia. However, the two men did not get along, possibly because Keiley viewed Lissner's zeal for evangelizing Blacks to be counterproductive, given the difficulties the Catholic Church faced in the Jim Crow South. A December 7, 1920, letter from Keiley to Cardinal James Gibbons refers to Lissner in scathing terms, with the former stating, "This man Lissner is personally very distasteful to and is disliked by every priest in my Diocese."[30] The letter indicates that Gibbons and Cardinal Gaetano de Lai of the Roman Curia had written to Keiley, expressing their shared belief that Lissner should be appointed the bishop for all Black Catholics in the Diocese of Savannah. Keiley disagreed, stating that Lissner was a divisive and controversial figure among white Catholics in the diocese and giving him a higher profile would provoke more "anti-negro prejudices." He warned not only that "every priest in the Diocese . . . [would] sign a letter of protest" if Lissner were appointed bishop but also that he himself would be forced to resign because such an act would "overthrow all the work done" for the advancement of the Church in Georgia.

This letter was written nine years after Our Lady of Lourdes was founded, but it illustrates the extent to which the evangelization of

Blacks remained a contentious issue, not just in the South but between Southern prelates and other members of the Catholic hierarchy. According to Lissner's 1948 obituary in the *Bulletin of the Catholic Laymen's Association of Georgia*, there had been only two hundred fifty Black Catholics in the entire state of Georgia prior to Lissner's arrival in the Diocese of Savannah in 1907.[31] By the time of Keiley's 1920 correspondence series with Gibbons, the number of Black Catholics had risen to twelve hundred. As Keiley himself admitted in a February 26, 1920, letter, the SAM in Georgia had raised "a large amount of money, and has labored very hard with some success."[32] However, these very successes among Georgia's Black denizens appear to have been considered counterproductive to the overall mission of the Catholic Church in Georgia since too many Black Catholics would presumably raise fears that the Church was encouraging "race mixing." Thus, Our Lady of Lourdes and other "colored missions" in Georgia mirrored the second-class status of their parishioners in that they were tolerated yet despised by the religious organization in which they claimed membership.

2

Atlanta's Religious and Political Ecology and the Establishment of Our Lady of Lourdes

Our Lady of Lourdes Catholic Church was cofounded by Fr. Ignatius Lissner, the American superior of the Society of African Missions (SAM), and Katharine Drexel, foundress of the Sisters of the Blessed Sacrament (SBS), in 1911 to increase the number of Black Catholics in the Diocese of Savannah, which at the time encompassed the entire state of Georgia. Bishop Benjamin J. Keiley invited the SAM to the Diocese of Savannah in 1907. Incidentally, Lissner had personally overseen the successful planting of Black missions and parochial schools in Augusta, Savannah, and Macon. In addition to planting missions, Lissner also took over Black missions that had been run by other religious orders such as the Jesuits and the Benedictines, "thus relieving the Diocesan and religious priests who were endeavoring to serve both white and colored congregations at the same time." Drexel had been funding projects in the Diocese of Savannah since 1891, when she gave money toward a short-lived community of Black Franciscan sisters. Her patronage of Lissner also began at this same time when she provided him with funds for a mission in Dahomey (present-day Benin). He then shifted his plan for missions to Georgia as an alternative for European missionary priests who were unable to tolerate the climate of sub-Saharan Africa but still felt called to work with "the colored."[1]

In 1911, a Marist priest assigned to Sacred Heart Church, a white parish in downtown Atlanta, encouraged Lissner to build a mission to serve Atlanta's sixty thousand Black residents. After investigating Black neighborhoods across the city and finding "only fifteen Catholics, most of them elderly," Lissner identified a property on Highland Avenue to build a church, school, and rectory. However, when word of Lissner's project reached the attention of the "white area" of Highland Avenue between Hilliard Street and Fort Street, their collective outrage forced Lissner to find a different location for his mission. With the help of Jack Johnson

Spalding, a member of Sacred Heart and a prominent lawyer, Lissner secured a plot of land at 101 North Boulevard (now 29 Boulevard NE) in the Sweet Auburn neighborhood.

Once Drexel pledged sixteen thousand dollars and a cadre of SBS to staff the school, construction on the mission began. Like other SAM missions in the South, the plan for the main structure of the Atlanta plant consisted of a large building that contained the chapel on the first floor, a four-room school on the second floor, and a parish hall on the third floor. Unlike many of the buildings on Auburn Avenue, this one was made of brick and Stone Mountain granite, a detail that would enable it to survive the Atlanta Fire of 1917 that consumed much of the neighborhood. The plant was finished in the fall of 1912 and christened the Archbishop Ryan Memorial in honor of Patrick John Ryan, the deceased archbishop of Philadelphia who had been Drexel's spiritual advisor. Drexel eventually changed the mission's name to Our Lady of Lourdes because Ryan had died on the feast day of Our Lady of Lourdes.

In his 1912 request to Drexel to send SBS to staff the Our Lady of Lourdes School, Lissner stated that he wished it to be "a school in every way Catholic and yet equal or superior if possible to any other city school." The "headsister" would run the school, and the SAM priest assigned to the mission would assist with religious education if necessary. However, Drexel had started three other missions in 1912, and there were not enough sisters to send to Our Lady of Lourdes. Thus, the school began the academic year of 1912–13 on October 1, 1912, with four Black, non-Catholic laywomen as teachers: during that first year, the school consisted of kindergarten to third grade, and a grade was added each year until it went to eighth grade.[2]

On July 29, 1913, the first SBS—Sr. Mary Thomas Aquinas, Sr. Mary Carmelita, Sr. Mary Imelda, and Sr. Mary Mildred—finally reached Atlanta. They arrived to find a sparsely furnished convent, a barebones chapel, and a curious neighborhood. The convent itself consisted of little more than an empty house with a table, some chairs, five beds, and no other furniture or housewares. The chapel contained only an altar that was sent from the SBS Motherhouse. Fr. Rapier, pastor of Sacred Heart, gave Sr. Mary Aquinas a check for twenty-five dollars to compensate for the primitive state of the mission. He also organized a missionary society at Sacred Heart to help provide supplies for the fledgling mission.

Figure 2.1. Sanctuary of Our Lady of Lourdes Mission, circa 1912. Courtesy of the Catholic Historical Research Center.

A white Catholic friend of the sisters, known only in the annals as Mrs. Withers, helped them procure wholesale furniture for the convent and donated household items and food. On August 8, 1913, over one hundred ladies associated with the Sacred Heart Missionary Society, the priests of Atlanta's three white Catholic churches (i.e., Immaculate Conception, Sacred Heart, and St. Anthony of Padua), and Bishop Keiley gave a reception for the SBS, where the sisters received an additional thirty-five dollars. The following week, the sisters held an open house for "the Colored people interested in the work in the auditorium of the school." As we will see, moving between the world of white Catholic patrons and that of the Black Atlantans they served would be an ongoing pattern with the SBS throughout their association with Our Lady of Lourdes.[3]

The SBS began the 1913–14 school year with fifty-eight students, but thanks to word of mouth, by the time Katharine Drexel visited in October 1913, enrollment had risen to over a hundred. Soon the school was

Figure 2.2. Priest and students of Our Lady of Lourdes School, 1932. Courtesy of the Catholic Historical Research Center.

bearing fruit for the Church in the form of conversions among the student body and their families. "A wave of Catholicity seems to be sweeping over the school," reported Sr. Mary Aquinas in a 1914 letter. "So many are anxious to 'join Church' and 'become a member.' I hope and pray it's a genuine wave and not a tidal [illegible] and will land many of them in the True Fold."[4] Six baptisms were performed on Easter Sunday 1914, and a baptized couple took Holy Communion for the first time. When classes ended on June 5, 1914, the school held a closing ceremony that attracted five hundred people.[5]

Our Lady of Lourdes School's early popularity resulted from it being established during a period when Black Atlantans were demanding access to more and better schools for their community. In 1903, there were twenty public schools for whites but only five for Blacks. The schools designated for Blacks were located on polluted grounds with substandard buildings and underpaid teachers. Black residents had attempted to organize to support bond issues to address the problem. Although the Black male vote had been suppressed and excluded from the all-important Democratic primary during the first decade of the twentieth century, it was still possible for Blacks to vote in special elections, including those pertaining to bond issues. They had supported bond issues in 1902 and 1909 with the understanding that preexisting Black schools would be renovated. However, few if any funds were secured. For example, Black schools received only $38,000 of the $600,000 from the 1909 bond referendum. The NAACP would address the Atlanta School Board about the need for improvements for Black schools in 1917, but their requests were ignored by the all-white body. Black schools were both underfunded and insufficient in number; in 1913, the year that the SBS came to Atlanta, only half of the city's Black children had a school they could attend.[6]

As politically active Black men continued to lobby the Board of Education for more and better schools, Black women would occasionally run small private schools out of their homes as stopgap measures to educate children who lacked access to a public school. The schools in the Atlanta University Center also took it upon themselves to teach children who were not being served by the public schools. According to Jay Winston Driskell Jr., "By 1910, Atlanta Baptist (Morehouse), Atlanta University, Morris Brown, and Spelman collectively enrolled 604 high school students and 1,111 grammar school students—a student body that dwarfed the city's entire Black college cohort, comprising only 147.... Between 1898 and 1907, the tuition paid to these four institutions totaled more than $210,000, a significant sum from a population whose financial security was so tenuous. However reasonable they might have been, these tuition payments made education inaccessible to most working class African Americans."[7] In comparison, tuition at the Our Lady of Lourdes School was a mere ten cents a month, and no child was turned away due to an inability to pay. The school building was utilitarian but solidly built and not located near factories or slaughterhouses. It also contained a playground that was open to neighborhood children, whether they were students at the school or not. Given the dire state of Black education in early twentieth-century Atlanta, it is not hard to understand why the Our Lady of Lourdes School would be an attractive choice for Black Protestant families.[8]

The early success of Our Lady of Lourdes School was jeopardized by a bill put forth by the Georgia legislature in 1915 that sought to make it illegal for whites to teach Black students. The legislation may have been proposed in response to the parochial schools the SAM had established in Georgia's major cities. Given that many whites considered Black schools, whether secular or religious, to be an existential threat to the status quo, these schools were considered subversive. Bishop Keiley was able to get the bill withdrawn by negotiating with the legislature, but it was indicative of the ongoing efforts to strip Georgia's Blacks of political and civic citizenship in the early twentieth century. This pervasive atmosphere of racial oppression compelled many of the converts made at Our Lady of Lourdes to emigrate North as part of the Great Migration. There they joined other SBS missions such as St. Cyprian's in Columbus, Ohio, St. Monica's in Chicago, and St. Mark's in New York. Consequently, the membership at Our Lady of Lourdes hovered around one hundred parishioners for much of its early history, not because the SBS were unsuccessful in their work but because the general trend for Southern Blacks to resettle in Northern cities for better social and economic opportunities meant that converts often left for other states shortly after they joined.

Internal migration within the state of Georgia also contributed to instability at the Our Lady of Lourdes School. As Northern cities were inundated by Catholic immigrants from Europe, late nineteenth- and early twentieth-century Atlanta experienced waves of Black emigration from rural Georgia, where they had endured dismal, semifeudal conditions as sharecroppers or tenant farmers. Black sharecroppers were continually in debt to their white landlords and the general store owner (who was usually the same person), leaving them little cash to buy bare necessities. Although they could theoretically grow crops and livestock for their own consumption, Black sharecroppers were forbidden by their landlords to grow anything but cotton. Malnutrition and starvation conditions were rife among Georgia's Black rural population, and there was a real fear that Southern Blacks would be wiped out, not by racist violence or eugenic schemes, but by near-famine conditions. According to Driskell, "Between 1880 and 1910, the fertility of Black women declined by one-third due to disease, overwork, and malnutrition. Due to the high rate of infant mortality, the average life expectancy of Black men and women in the rural South was only thirty-three years. A Black woman who survived to the age of twenty could expect to see one out of every three children die before his or her tenth birthday, and she herself would die in her mid-fifties, well before her youngest child left home."[9] Many Black emigrants were motivated to relocate to Atlanta for the promise of a more settled and dignified existence, but for others, escaping the peonage of sharecropping was a life-or-death decision.

Sr. Mary Aquinas, the first principal of the Our Lady of Lourdes School, reported in an undated letter to Drexel that many children whose families had just arrived from rural Georgia temporarily enrolled in Lourdes because the public schools would not take them once the school year started. "So we get them while they pass their yr [*sic*] of probation and gain a little city polish," stated Sr. Mary Aquinas. "Then they pass in to the great and glorious public school of Ga." Consequently, the school not only had to deal with a transient student body who viewed Our Lady of Lourdes as a temporary stop in their emigration process, rather than joining a particular religious community, but also had to contend with children for whom urban life and institutional education were foreign concepts. In another undated letter, Sr. Mary Aquinas expressed her relief that there were "no bigger boys in the lower grades," which suggests that previous years were marked by older boys with spotty educational records and disruptive behaviors. She did not specify whether these boys were emigrants or not, but it seems likely given that Black educational resources were even more limited in rural Georgia than in Atlanta.[10]

The Sacred and the Profane on Auburn Avenue

The particular history and culture of Auburn Avenue would have a major impact on the identity and culture of Our Lady of Lourdes. Although it may seem inevitable from a modern vantage point that the Southern states would pass legislation to legally enshrine white supremacy, most Jim Crow laws were not passed until the early twentieth century, more than thirty years after the end of Reconstruction; for example, Black males continued to vote in Georgia until a 1908 referendum stripped them of the franchise. Boycotts and protests against segregation in public accommodations occurred in every state of the former Confederacy, to no avail. One of the new societal changes that Jim Crow brought was the imposition of residential segregation.[11]

After the Civil War, many Blacks in Atlanta continued to live in the same manner that they had during the antebellum period (i.e., servants' quarters that were adjacent to the homes of their white employers). By the 1880s, however, Blacks began to create settlements throughout the city that would evolve into distinct Black neighborhoods. These areas tended to be environmentally undesirable, being either near railroad tracks or in flood plains, but they were cheap enough for recently emancipated slaves to afford. According to Alton Hornsby Jr., "By 1883, at least six identifiable African American neighborhoods had developed in the city. These included the 'West Side,' a mostly low-ground area west of the Terminal Railroad Station; 'Pittsburgh' in the southwest quadrant of the city near a railroad roundhouse; 'Summerhill,' to the east and north of 'Pittsburgh' and south of the downtown area; 'Tanyard Bottom,' in the northern part of the city, 'at the bottom of a valley near the city's largest tannery'; and the 'Butler Street Bottoms,' along Decatur Street, east of downtown."[12] The appearance of these Black neighborhoods in the late nineteenth century belied the fact that these areas were characterized by a surprising amount of residential integration; 52 percent of homes in 1880 were either next door to or across the street from a dwelling inhabited by a member of another race. Although this figure had fallen to 20 percent by 1896, the Buttermilk Bottoms neighborhood in the Fourth Ward had both the highest percentage of Blacks living there (46 percent) and the highest rate of integration (26 percent) in Atlanta. Even after the U.S. Supreme Court in *Plessy v. Ferguson* (1896) legalized the principle of "separate but equal," many areas in Atlanta, including Auburn Avenue, remained racial gray areas where whites and Blacks were in close social proximity.

The Atlanta Race Riot of 1906 was the catalyst that led to the development of Auburn Avenue as a haven for Black cultural and political aspirations, about fifteen years before residential segregation was actually enshrined in Georgia law.[13] The genesis of the riot was the sharp increase of anti-Black sentiment caused by the gubernatorial race between Hoke Smith and Clark Howell, both of whom used the specter of "Negro domination" and the necessity of Black male disenfranchisement to inflame the white electorate. In keeping with the yellow journalism of the time, Georgia newspapers regularly tried to outdo each other with sensationalist accounts of Black men allegedly raping white women, all of which was supposedly the result of Black male suffrage. When rumors spread of four separate assaults on white women on September 22, 1906, mobs of armed whites attacked Black-owned businesses and neighborhoods in an assault that lasted almost two days. Officially, the coroner issued only ten death certificates for Black fatalities, but the actual death toll among Black Atlantans was almost certainly much higher.[14]

White reaction to the riot was a mix of horror at the destruction, anxiety that the violence would project a negative image of the city of Atlanta to outsiders, and a firm resolution that "separation of the races . . . is the only logical solution of the Negro problem." Even though the riot was instigated by whites, the prevailing view was that the mob had no choice but to resort to violence to protect "white manhood and womanhood" from the depravity of Black men. Periodic outbreaks of mass anti-Black violence were necessary to keep Blacks "in their place," else they would act with sexual impunity among respectable white women.[15] For Blacks, especially those in the middle class, the Atlanta Race Riot was a shocking and disillusioning event that called into question the goodwill of white elites who were unable or unwilling to constrain anti-Black violence. The combined effects of Jim Crow laws and the fear instilled by the Atlanta Race Riot caused Blacks to be confined to the west side of the city near the Atlanta University Center and portions of the east side around Auburn Avenue.

The commercial district of Auburn Avenue consisted mostly of Black-owned alternatives to the white businesses found in downtown Atlanta. These businesses were smaller than their white counterparts, but they helped Blacks fulfill their daily needs and prevented them from having to patronize white businesses, where they would invariably be treated poorly by the management. It was also home to Black financial institutions, such as Atlanta Life Insurance, Standard Life, and Citizens Trust Bank, which provided loans and other monetary services to Blacks when white institutions refused their business. Other prominent Black-owned financial institutions such as Chatham Mutual Insurance Company, Pilgrim Health Insurance Company, and North Carolina Mutual Insurance Company had branches on Auburn Avenue, which cemented its reputation as a center for Black commerce. Black professionals such as accountants, doctors, lawyers, and dentists had offices on Auburn Avenue, and nightclubs like the Royal Peacock Theater and the Casino Club made Atlanta one of the most important stops on the "chitlin circuit" of the Jim Crow era. Auburn Avenue also contained numerous social and political organizations, including the offices of the *Atlanta Daily World*, the NAACP, the Urban League, the Odd Fellows, and the Prince Hall Masons. Auburn Avenue functioned as a counter-public space for Atlanta's Blacks to gather away from the white gaze and a place to organize against white supremacy.[16]

The Major Churches of Auburn Avenue

Churches were among the most important of the counter-public spaces on Auburn Avenue. They were places of corporate religious expression that also functioned as nonprofits that provided secular activities for the Black community, such as social services, meeting spaces, and educational events. The three largest Auburn Avenue churches in the early twentieth century—Wheat Street Baptist Church, Ebenezer Baptist Church, and Big Bethel AME Church—were particularly active in the realm of political and social activism.[17]

Wheat Street Baptist Church was established in 1869 by members of Friendship Baptist Church (near the Atlanta University campus) who disliked the distance they had to travel to go to church. With the blessing of the pastor, seven ex-members of Friendship established a mission on Howell Street, which was in between Wheat Street (now Auburn Avenue) and Turnpipe Road (now Irwin Street). After a decade of steady growth, the congregation moved to its current location on the corner of Old Wheat Street (now Auburn Avenue) and Fort Street, receiving its definitive name of Wheat Street Baptist Church. The church remained small and relatively insignificant until William Holmes Borders (1905–93) assumed the pastorate in 1937.

Under Borders, who served from 1937 to 1988, Wheat Street became the most socially and politically engaged Black church in mid-twentieth-century Atlanta. Wheat Street offered an unparalleled array of social services, including a nursery school, a credit union, a day care, a medical clinic, an affordable housing complex, and a retirement home.[18] Wheat Street also provided sign language interpretation of Sunday services for the deaf in the 1930s, almost sixty years before the passage of the Americans with Disabilities Act. Its prison ministry worked to obtain jobs for ex-convicts and train fare to send them back to their respective homes. The end of Sunday was marked by a potluck or a formal dinner prepared by one of the church's many auxiliary groups.[19] Wheat Street under Borders also provided a safety net for members who were experiencing economic hardships. Former Wheat Street member Anita Martin recalled, "Once when my mother was out of work, Rev. Borders . . . gave my mother a job to clean up the church, so she would be able to make money to feed us. We were able to go on trips with the church, even though . . . sometimes my mother couldn't afford for us to go, we were still able to go."[20] The extensive outreach ministries at Wheat Street reflected Borders's vision of a church that would be a refuge to all on Auburn Avenue, regardless of their educational attainment or socioeconomic status.

In interviews with those who remember that time, Rev. Borders looms large. According to current Wheat Street member Gwendolyn Elmore, "And he was, Rev. Borders, a leader, and probably was the most prominent Black preacher involved in [the Civil Rights Movement], 'cause, like I said, Dr. King was in Montgomery, but this thing, he was worldwide. As far as Atlanta was concerned, Rev. Borders was one of the leaders in the, the movement. There were several preachers, but he played a very major role."[21] His prowess as a preacher was recognized by Atlanta's Black community, regardless of whether they were members of Wheat Street or not. Dr. Nellie Adams, a member of nearby Big Bethel AME Church, recalled,

> Growing up, this is my impression, that Wheat Street was the leading church during the civil rights era. Everybody wanted to go to Wheat Street and hear Rev. Borders. [Ebenezer] was not the leading church on Auburn Avenue, it was Wheat Street and Rev. Borders. He had [a] full congregation and choir and he was an orator. He had written a poem that was recited on the radio many times, *I'm Somebody, I am Somebody*. And he supported Morris Brown College. He was a friend to Bishop Fountain, who was the chancellor [of] Morris Brown College. His son was the president and it seems to have been some, in my opinion, envy between Ebenezer and Wheat Street . . . and of course, Big Bethel was close to Wheat Street. Rev. Borders and the AME used to get along, but the two Baptist churches, there was some competition there between those two. That was my impression.[22]

Borders was a major influence on Martin Luther King Jr., especially in terms of his oratory skills and his ability to mobilize his flock for political and social causes. The young King Jr. was even known to sneak away from his home church of Ebenezer Baptist to listen to Borders's sermons.

Borders was considered the city's most prominent Black civil rights activist until King Jr. returned to Atlanta in 1960 to copastor Ebenezer Baptist Church with his father. He helped mobilize support for the victims of the 1946 Moore's Ford lynching in Monroe, Georgia, including paying for the funerals of the deceased and organizing a protest committee based out of Wheat Street.[23] Through his contacts in City Hall, Borders was able to double the number of registered Black voters in Atlanta from six to twelve thousand in 1939. Borders led the Love, Law, Liberation ("Triple L") Movement to desegregate Atlanta's mass transit system in 1957, and he, along with five other Black ministers, was arrested for violating the city's Jim Crow ordinance.[24]

Ebenezer Baptist Church is not only the most famous church on Auburn Avenue but one of the most famous churches in the United States because of its connection to Dr. Martin Luther King Jr. It was founded in 1886 on Airline Street by John A. Parker and a group of thirteen congregants. Adam Daniel Williams (1861—1931), the maternal grandfather of Martin Luther King Jr., was Ebenezer's second pastor, and he transformed a struggling congregation of only seventeen into one of Atlanta's leading churches for the Black bourgeoisie. He was both a follower of the social gospel and a believer in the kind of evangelical Christianity that was common to Black churches in the early twentieth century. Williams pioneered the concept of using the Black church as a base for political action, and he was personally active in many civil rights initiatives. In 1906 he started the Equal Rights League, an organization devoted to ending Georgia's white primary and obtaining civil rights for Blacks, was the first president of the Atlanta branch of the NAACP, using both Ebenezer and his own home as a meeting place for the organization, and organized boycotts against businesses that advertised in the *Georgian*, a newspaper known for its frequent use of racial slurs. Like Wheat Street, Ebenezer provided social services to the Auburn Avenue community, a trait that was especially important during the Great Depression, when rural Blacks migrated to Atlanta in search of new economic opportunities and many Black churches struggled to remain open. Williams made sure that food, clothing, and child care were freely provided, regardless of church membership status.

When Williams died in 1931, his position as head pastor of Ebenezer was succeeded by his son-in-law, Michael King Sr., later known as Martin Luther King Sr. or "Daddy King." Like his predecessor, King Sr. challenged Atlanta's Jim Crow status quo while preaching a theologically conservative brand of Black Protestantism. He was a member and president of the NAACP, working with that organization to register Black voters and to organize against a bond issue that failed to provide adequate funds for Black public schools. King Sr.'s other accomplishments during the 1930s included numerous protests, from raising objections to segregated elevators at the Fulton County Courthouse to demanding equal salaries for Black teachers. He vocalized his displeasure with segregation in his personal life as well, verbally objecting to policemen calling him "boy" and to businesses that demanded he sit in their "colored" sections. For King Sr., being a positive agent for social change was as fundamental to the life and mission of a Christian as believing in the right doctrines. King Sr.'s political variant of the social gospel was key to the thought of his son, even as the younger King chafed at what he saw as his father's authoritarianism and fundamentalism.[25]

In an oral history recorded by WRFG's Living Atlanta project, Phoebe Hart, the former dean of women at Clark College (now Clark Atlanta University), gave a firsthand account of King Sr.'s activism on Auburn Avenue:

> Talk about boycotts now, we used boycotts back then at Ebenezer Baptist Church in the early forties. I can remember a business on Auburn Avenue. Pastor King [Martin Luther King Sr.] went into the organization and looked things over. He saw these white girls in there. He said, "I have a number of girls in my church. Would you give one of them a job?" He said he wasn't hiring Negroes. He said, "But you can hire them, you can." The man just shrugged his shoulders. He said, "Oh yeah, oh yeah, you can hire them."
>
> He went back to church the next Sunday, he said, "Let me tell you one thing. That man is employing these white girls here and your son and your daughters could be working in there, and we could be giving *them* help." And there was a boycott. We looked up and the store was closed.

King was riding out here on Martin Luther King Drive, which was then Hunter, and he saw this store just across Ashby. And he told his wife, "You know, I believe that's that same guy come out here." He got out, he went in, and this young lady, colored, said, "May I help you? What would you like to have?" He said, "You clerk here?" She said, "Yes." He said, "Where's your boss?" So he came out, he looked at him and he knew King knew he knew him. He said, "Now you're all right and you're going to get some business."[26]

King Sr. used his position within Ebenezer in particular and the Black community in general to disseminate messages of a spiritual and a secular nature. He was wont to say, "I've got them in this church from *Morehouse* [College] to *no house*. And I've got more from *no house*," and he actively worked to raise the socioeconomic statuses of those in the "no house" group, encouraging parishioners to own homes, sign up for insurance, and patronize and start Black businesses. King Sr.'s constant advocacy on the part of the Black community is what earned him the nickname "Daddy King" on Auburn Avenue.[27]

Big Bethel African Methodist Episcopal (AME) Church is believed to be the oldest Black congregation in Atlanta. It has its roots in the Union Church, a majority-white congregation founded in 1847 that was conceived as a sort of religious "halfway house" for new arrivals to the city, until they could establish their own churches. Slaves were able to worship with whites at the morning service, but in a segregated seating area. They were also allowed to have their own church service in the evening, albeit under the supervision of a white minister. Black congregants grew dissatisfied with their second-class status within the Union Church, and they requested permission to start their own church. The white leadership eventually agreed and gave the slaves seven hundred dollars to start a new congregation. The new church, known at this point as Bethel Tabernacle, was finished in 1855 and was located on Jenkins Street (now Auditorium Way). The Union Church sent two white ministers to oversee Bethel Tabernacle, but the Black membership, including minister James Woods, was in charge of the building and maintenance of the church.

After Emancipation severed the legal links that held Blacks in submission to whites, the members of Bethel Tabernacle sought to free themselves from the control of the whites at the Union Church, who owned the deed to all church property and held veto power over any decision made by the congregation. They found an opportunity when Bethel Tabernacle formally joined the AME Church in 1866, thus officially disaffiliating themselves from the Union Church's denomination, the Methodist Episcopal Church South. At first, the leadership of Union Church was outraged and threatened to repossess the Bethel Tabernacle property. Their intention was to purchase land for slaves to worship under their watchful eyes, not a place for freed Blacks to potentially conspire against whites. In the end, the Union Church backed down and deeded the land to Bethel Tabernacle, but many Black churches established after the Civil War were not so lucky, as the Methodist Episcopal Church South routinely reclaimed Black congregations that dared to affiliate with the AME Church or become independent from white oversight.[28]

Once the congregation established its independence from the Union Church, it changed its name to Big Bethel and quickly established itself as one of the largest and most prestigious Black churches in Atlanta. It was a major contributor to the institutional life of Black Atlanta, as both the Gate City Colored School, the first public school for Blacks in Atlanta, and Morris Brown College, the only college founded by Blacks in Georgia, started in Big Bethel's basement in 1879 and 1881, respectively. Because Big Bethel was the largest church on Auburn Avenue for many decades, it was often used as a meeting place for secular speeches and activities, giving it the unofficial title of "Auburn Avenue's City Hall."[29]

While Wheat Street, Ebenezer, and Big Bethel cast large shadows over Atlanta's Black community, most Black Atlantans in the early twentieth century attended small churches. These congregations ranged from modest-sized assemblages with a few hundred members to small storefronts that often consisted of extended family members worshipping together in a semiorganized fashion. Our Lady of Lourdes was considerably smaller than the Big Three—the typical pre–Vatican II Sunday mass at Our Lady of Lourdes consisted of roughly one hundred people—but the same was true for most religious organizations on Auburn Avenue, all of which had to fight for the attention of a public that faced an overabundance of church options.[30]

The boundaries between churches on Auburn Avenue were porous, and it was the norm for individuals to visit many churches, for both religious and secular events, even if they held membership at one particular

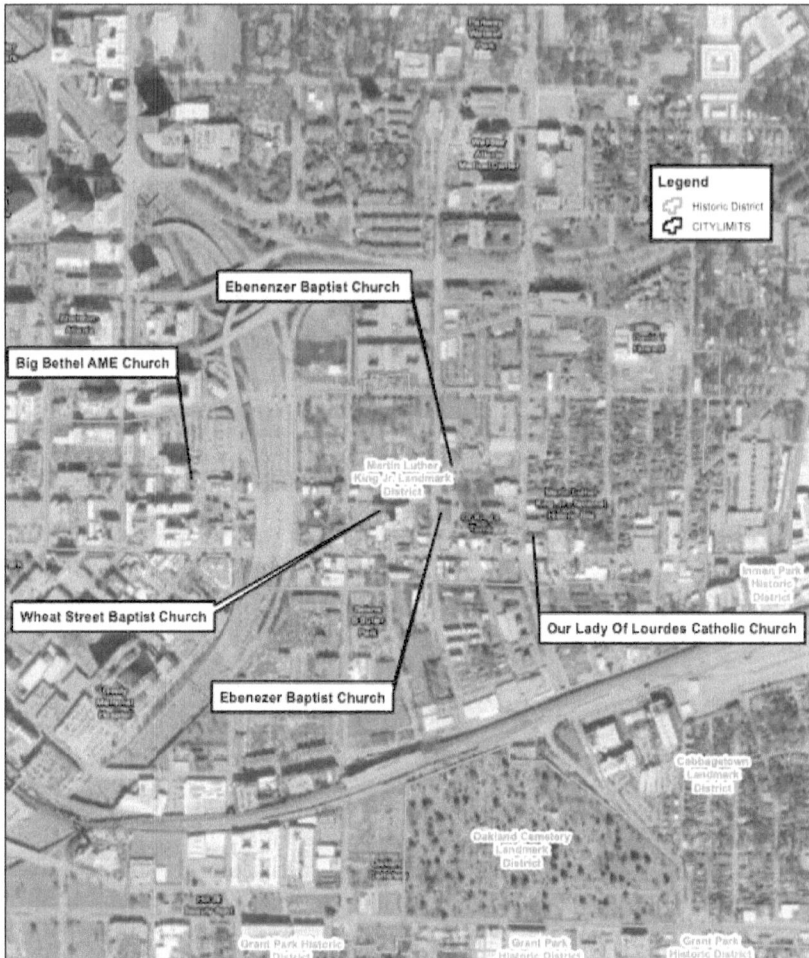

Figure 2.3. Auburn Avenue / Sweet Auburn / Old Fourth Ward Map. Courtesy of the City of Atlanta Planning Department.

congregation or identified strongly with their respective denomination. For example, longtime Big Bethel member Willie Taylor Robinson recalled, "Well, we had members in our church . . . like our bandmaster . . . his wife was Catholic. So we had relations with them, like at Christmas time. I had never been to a Catholic church before. He and his wife carried me to the Catholic church. So I got experience with going to that church during the Christmas holiday. Otherwise, most of the time we just went to our church, but we did go to visit, we'd go to Catholic churches, Baptist churches, and other kind of churches."[31] When Our Lady of Lourdes was built, it became part of this wider network of churches and social/familial ties that linked Auburn Avenue together.

Like other residents of Atlanta's Black community, Our Lady of Lourdes members frequented the various Protestant churches around Auburn Avenue. Sandra Criddell, a longtime member of Our Lady of Lourdes, stated, "We went to church every Sunday at somebody's church, somebody's service on Sunday. That was a rule, wherever it be, whether you went to a Catholic Church or you went to. . . . I was the only Catholic at that time. So I had to go to mass every Sunday, but in the meantime, I could go to other folks' churches too. And we had this young lady my mother raised, she would go down to the Baptist church, so I would go down to the Baptist church with her. But I had to go to Mass on Sunday first." The interactions of Our Lady of Lourdes members with Black Protestantism were not limited to Sunday services. Wednesday night has traditionally been reserved for prayer meetings and Bible study in the Black Protestant tradition. These activities were foreign to pre–Vatican II Catholicism, so it was not unusual for Our Lady of Lourdes members to attend Wednesday night religious activities at Protestant churches. According to Deion Hutchinson, who is Ms. Criddell's niece and a fellow Our Lady of Lourdes member, "We would go to different churches in the neighborhood on Wednesday nights in the neighborhood, because there were a lot of Baptist churches [on Auburn Avenue], but our church was Catholic, Our Lady of Lourdes Catholic Church." Statements like these indicate that there was a generalized Black religious tradition present on Auburn Avenue that influenced the collective outlook of all residents, regardless of their religious affiliation.[32]

Patronizing different churches may have been part of the culture on Auburn Avenue for Catholic and Protestant alike, but it was not technically allowed by the pre–Vatican II Catholic Church. According to *My Catholic Faith*, a college-level religious textbook from 1954, "A Catholic sins against faith by taking part in non-Catholic worship, because he thus professes belief in a religion he knows is false. . . . It is wrong to even be present at Protestant or Jewish *services* even when we do not participate in them, because such services are intended to honor God in a manner He does not wish to be honored in. If He instituted a Church of His own, He must wish to be honored in the ways of that Church. In addition, we then give bad example, and expose ourselves to the danger of losing our faith."[33] The Vatican regarded Protestantism as not only a perversion of "true Christianity" (i.e., Roman Catholicism) but a Trojan horse for socialism, communism, and liberalism, all ideologies that were attacking the influence of the Catholic Church in its post-Reformation strongholds in Continental Europe. From the perspective of the nineteenth-century popes, Protestantism was a sinful rebellion against the God-ordained authority of the Catholic Church, and socialism, communism, and liberalism were the natural byproducts of the antiauthoritarian attitudes unleashed by the Reformation.[34] The fundamental problem with Protestantism was not so much that it fostered incorrect theological positions (which could be cured through proper instruction by the Catholic authorities) but that it entailed rejecting the authority of the Catholic Church, which was akin to rejecting God.[35]

Avoiding Protestant churches was a simple matter for white Catholics in the North, the vast majority of whom lived in monoethnic and monoreligious neighborhoods where "neighborhood, parish, and religion were constantly intertwined."[36] Staying entirely within the Catholic institutional orbit would have been possible, although not quite so easy, for Atlanta's white Catholics, since all of the city's Catholic institutions were built with them in mind. However, for the Black Catholics of Our Lady of Lourdes, Protestant churches were a ubiquitous presence, both in the neighborhood itself and in the lives of their friends and family members. According to Andrew Hill, "There weren't very many Black Catholics, so there was a strong sense that [Black Catholics and Black Protestants] were in this segregation thing together. . . . I don't know if there was a sense of separateness . . . we understood that their churches were different, and we noticed that there was, and that's the key thing, a lot more emotion."[37] This same sentiment is echoed by Anita Whatley, who spent her childhood at Our Lady of Lourdes: "You know, all our good friends went to the other churches. Like I said, if they didn't go to Catholic church, they went to Wheat Street or West Hunter [Baptist Church]. They went to Zion Hill down the street, they went to Mount Zion, they went to First Congregational Church. Our world was so small. We all interacted."[38] A third interviewee, Cassandra Peters-Johnson, said of the relationships between Auburn Avenue's Catholics and Protestants,

We had a great relationship ... we had a lot of Protestants who attended the Catholic school, people that were students that were not Catholic came to the Catholic school for various reasons. And also because there were so few of our families whose children were actually in Catholic school, we, the families were friends with people in all of the other churches, the Protestant churches, so we had good relationships with the Protestant churches, and as I mentioned, I had come out of a Protestant church, so we all had friends still in those different churches in our neighborhood. Our friends went to the different churches, and the parents, the families, were all friends. So we would sometimes go to events at those Protestant churches, and people who were in the Protestant churches would sometimes do events at Our Lady or the Catholic churches. And when St. Paul of the Cross [Atlanta's second Black Catholic parish, established in 1954] opened the same thing you know. We would have events, the Protestant folks would come to our events, because the kids were friends, and the parents were friends. So we'd go back and forth between the churches and the family events. So I don't think there was any conflict among the churches at that time. The Baptists didn't hate the Catholics or anything like that.[39]

This sentiment (i.e., all Blacks were united against segregation, regardless of class, education level, or religion) stands in stark contrast to the dynamics between the various white ethnic neighborhoods described in *Parish Boundaries*, in which ethnic balkanization tended to trump the need for pan-Catholic solidarity contra Protestant nativist chauvinism.[40]

Although the churches on Auburn Avenue competed for members and resources, they also cooperated with each other, advertising the social and political events that were held at the neighboring congregations. This is confirmed by longtime Wheat Street member Gwendolyn Elmore:

When I was a little girl, I can remember very distinctly I used to read the Emancipation Proclamation every New Year's Day. Wheat Street had a relationship, not necessarily with the Catholic church [i.e., Our Lady of Lourdes], it was with Big Bethel AME Church. And they would always ask me to read the Emancipation, it was like a New Year's, New Year's Day celebration, not Watch Night, but New Year's Day. And I would go to this service and read the Emancipation Proclamation just to kind of renew our belief in our, I guess our commitment to being free from slavery. That was happening for every year I can remember at Wheat Street for at least twenty years. Then we had another thing we did sometimes with Liberty Baptist Church and sometimes with Ebenezer, and it was called Watch Night. Would be, um, New Year's Eve, where you prayed about what you want for that year.[41]

When Our Lady of Lourdes was built, it was absorbed into the larger religious network on Auburn Avenue. Since Black audiences were completely excluded from attending high cultural events at venues such as the Municipal Auditorium, the churches sponsored concerts to bring classical artists to the Black community. For example, First Congregational Church, another large church in the Auburn Avenue neighborhood, sponsored a national music festival every August, and Big Bethel hosted Marian Anderson concerts.[42] Refusing to patronize Black Protestant churches would have cut off the members of Our Lady of Lourdes from social and recreational opportunities that they would not have been able to get anywhere else. Thus, Protestants were not an unknowable "other" for the members of Our Lady of Lourdes, as it might be the case for white ethnic Catholics in the North. On Auburn Avenue, their relatives, friends, and neighbors just happened to attend different churches.

Such close religious intermingling posed problems, however, for any attempts to prevent intermarriage. The Catholic Church officially forbade marriages between Catholics and "heretics" without a dispensation because it was believed that such unions encouraged religious indifferentism, especially among any potential offspring.[43] However, the combined effects of segregation and the small size of Atlanta's Black Catholic community meant that it was impractical if not impossible for the members of Our Lady of Lourdes to restrict their marriage prospects to those of their own religion. Since Our Lady of Lourdes was classified as a mission in a territory where Catholics in general were a distinct minority, mixed marriages were probably not perceived to be subversive by the clergy or the laity in the same way as they might have been at a white ethnic parish in the North. In some cases, the non-Catholic spouse would eventually convert to Catholicism. This was the situation with Anita Whatley's father, who was originally a member at Wheat Street but joined Our Lady of Lourdes in the 1960s.[44]

Aside from its small size and all-Black congregation, Our Lady of Lourdes during the pre–Vatican II period was normative for Catholic parishes of the era. Parish life was characterized by following the liturgical year and partaking of the sacraments, especially the Eucharist and Confession. Devotions, such as the rosary, May Day processions, and the Forty Hours, also played a large role at Our Lady of Lourdes. Most of the organizations at Our Lady of Lourdes during this era focused on fostering particular devotions or encouraging the cults of certain saints. Sunday Mass consisted of a single Low Mass held at ten o'clock in the morning. High Masses were held only on the most significant feast days, such as Easter, Christmas, and the feast day of Our Lady of Lourdes. Sometimes a High Mass would be sung in honor of important visitors, such as a bishop or Katharine Drexel. Our Lady of Lourdes parishioners who missed Mass at their own parish could attend an afternoon Mass at Immaculate Conception, the white parish whose boundaries in which most of Atlanta's Black Catholics resided. However, Blacks attending Mass at Immaculate Conception had to sit in the back and receive Communion last, so as not to offend Jim Crow sensibilities.

Our Lady of Lourdes lacked the coffers and size of its more famous neighbors on Auburn Avenue, but it was still active in various uplift activities for its congregation and the wider community. At the beginning of the 1924–25 academic year, the sisters established a music room in the school where children and adults could receive low- or no-cost music lessons. According to a 1941 document written by the SBS for the Jubilee of Our Lady of Lourdes, Catholic Action organizations and projects at the parish included "St. Vincent de Paul Society, a Tabernacle Society, a Venetian Club, an Ave Maria Club for little girls, a Tarcisius Club for small boys, and a thriving Blessed Martin Club. Eight centers for religious education have opened in various homes of the parish where teachers, both white and Colored, guide the little ones to the 'Light of Faith.'"[45] The Our Lady of Lourdes Mission and Clinic was established in February 1940 at a house on 348 Forrest Avenue (now Ralph McGill Boulevard) by a group of Atlanta-area white Catholic women to "reach the large Negro population of Atlanta with spiritual and material assistance." It initially offered job training and placement, along with religious instruction for Blacks interested in Catholicism. As the name suggests, the Our Lady of Lourdes Mission and Clinic was considered to be a natural outgrowth of the Our Lady of Lourdes mission parish, and the priest in charge of the latter oversaw the activities of the former.

Within a year, the mission had also established a free clinic, which was staffed by the Medical Mission Sisters, a women's order that provided health care for the sick in areas deemed "mission territory." Like everything else in Jim Crow–era Atlanta, health care was separate and unequal for the city's Black population. The only Atlanta hospital that admitted Blacks in the early and mid-twentieth century was Grady Memorial Hospital, a public hospital that tended to patients of both races, albeit in segregated wings. Grady offered good care for Blacks, but its Black wing was chronically overcrowded and understaffed. The Catholic Colored Clinic was one of several small, private hospitals that served Atlanta's Black population. While it lacked the capacity of a large public institution like Grady or a private white hospital like Crawford Long, by its fifth year of operation the Catholic Colored Clinic had "treated 104,265 medical patients, 977 surgery cases (200 yearly for capacity), 11,000 outpatients, with the total visits to the clinic numbering some 36,217."[46]

Unlike the social programs offered at other Auburn Avenue churches like Wheat Street or Ebenezer, which were controlled by and were for the Black community, the Our Lady of Lourdes Mission and Clinic was possible only through the assistance and patronage of white Catholics. From a practical perspective, this was not necessarily a problem since the Mission and Clinic did not have to rely upon a relatively small, Atlanta-based population for its funding. Not only could the Mission and Clinic utilize the time and talents of white doctors and female volunteers from the Atlanta area, but it could also rely upon Catholic contacts that went beyond the state of Georgia. For example, many of the mission's medications were donated by the Catholic Medical Mission Board of New York, and the Medical Mission Sisters were based out of London.[47]

However, the fact that Black doctors were not allowed to work at a clinic designated for the Black community was a recurring problem for the Catholic Colored Clinic and its successor institution, Holy Family Hospital. Sister Mary Clare of the Medical Mission Sisters stated in a 1947 letter to Monsignor Joseph Moylan, "One ever-recurring big question zoomed up again with the negro group: Will negro doctors be allowed to bring in patients? As you probably know, [Black doctors] are quite antagonistic to us for not permitting them on staff." Moylan's response to Sister Mary Clare indicated that since charity institutions like the Catholic Colored Clinic were sustained by white money, it made sense that whites would be the ones to decide how said funds would be used and who would be hired. According to Moylan, it was more important for the Catholic Colored Clinic to have an all-white staff, which would ensure continued white patronage, than to provide employment for Black doctors: "As to admitting one or two Negro doctors to the Staff, one is sufficient to overturn the entire setup, and if one is admitted then the entire faculty will have to be Negro. The moral law does not require that we sacrifice the entire institution. Neither are we required to build a hospital for the benefit of Negro physicians."[48] Moylan's attitude was typical of the Jim Crow–era white paternalism that interpreted Black demands for self-determination and representation as ungratefulness toward the charity of whites at best and senseless "agitation" at worst. Blacks were to be the objects of charity, not subjects who were able to decide what kind of partnerships they wanted from prospective white benefactors.

At midcentury, Black Atlanta continued to evolve. In response to the increased migration of Black families into Southwest Atlanta, a second parish for Black Catholics, St. Paul of the Cross, was established in 1954 on Harwell Road. Like Our Lady of Lourdes, which was classified as a SAM mission until 1962, St. Paul of the Cross was and continues to be run by a religious order, specifically the Passionists, who at the time ran Black missions in North Carolina, Texas, and Alabama. Unlike the Auburn Avenue area, which was a more economically mixed neighborhood, Southwest Atlanta had become the preferred location for Black professionals, including scholars and intellectuals at the Atlanta University Center. Fr. Ernest Welch, the Passionist Provincial, described the affluence of the neighborhood surrounding the proposed St. Paul of the Cross campus to the majority-white readership of the *Bulletin*, the official newspaper of the Diocese of Savannah-Atlanta: "This is something entirely new and entirely unexpected to anyone accustomed to seeing the poor conditions in which [Blacks] usually live, and it is certainly indicative of the betterment of the social position of the Negroes in the Deep South. Among the colored citizenry are numerous highly educated leaders, successful in many professions and business enterprises. Atlanta University for Negroes with its several affiliated colleges draws students from all over the United States."[49] St. Paul of the Cross was built on a hundred-acre property that was once known as Clarke Estates. The parish itself covered forty acres, while Holy Family Hospital, the successor institution to the Catholic Colored Clinic, was built on the other sixty acres in 1958.

St. Paul of the Cross was created by bisecting Our Lady of Lourdes; members of Lourdes who lived in Southwest Atlanta were assigned to the new parish, while those who resided in Northwest Atlanta would continue attending Lourdes. The first masses organized under the aegis of St. Paul of the Cross were held at the Blacks-only McClendon Hospital in 1955. The school and convent on Harwell Road were dedicated in 1958. The Sisters of St. Joseph and the SBS staffed the St. Paul of the Cross School. Segregation during the 1950s and 1960s was such that St. Paul of the Cross was the only Catholic parish in Atlanta with which the members of Our Lady of Lourdes had sustained contact.

For the members of Our Lady of Lourdes and later St. Paul of the Cross, "neighborhood, parish, and religion were intertwined," as was the case with their white coreligionists in the North, but Protestantism was always a factor in how they interpreted and experienced being a Black Catholic. It was a given that most of Auburn Avenue was Protestant, but all Blacks, regardless of religious affiliation, were affected by Jim Crow, and they all had an interest in ending it. Similarly, Atlanta's white Catholics saw themselves primarily as whites first, with an interest in maintaining the Southern way of life, even if doing so was against Catholic social teachings. When white Southern anti-Catholicism increased sharply after the Civil War, vocally supporting white supremacy was a way for white Catholics in the South to gain political and social acceptance from otherwise disapproving white Protestants.

The continued growth and power of the Catholic Church in Atlanta during the postwar period seemed to provide validation that the hierarchy's strategy of accommodation to Jim Crow was beneficial. Pope Pius XII created the Diocese of Atlanta out of the Diocese of Savannah-Atlanta in 1956, as an acknowledgment of the Church's growth in northwest Georgia. Atlanta had already reached co-cathedral status with Savannah nineteen years earlier in 1937, with the yet-to-be-built Church of Christ the King designated as the bishop's second seat. Francis Hyland, the auxiliary bishop of Savannah-Atlanta since 1949, was appointed bishop of Atlanta. White Catholics from non-Southern states also began to move to Atlanta during this time, which led to an increase in the total Catholic population. This in turn necessitated the construction of new Catholic parishes in towns and cities on the outskirts of Atlanta. While some of the new transplants were appalled by Jim Crow norms, most either tacitly accepted segregation or became enthusiastic defenders of the status quo. However, by the 1960s, the societal and religious changes wrought by the Civil Rights Movement and the Second Vatican Council would end the segregationist accommodations found in the Catholic Church in Atlanta.[50]

3

Our Lady of Lourdes, the Civil Rights Movement, and School Desegregation

White Catholics, especially self-described conservatives and traditionalists, often interpret the 1960s negatively as the period in which the perceived unity of American Catholicism was shattered because of the moral and liturgical uncertainty ushered in by the Second Vatican Council as well as the simultaneous breakup of the white Catholic ghettos in Northern cities. This sentiment is not shared by Black Catholics, who interpret this same period as a time of hope and creative change, both in the Church and in secular society. Tempering this optimism is the fact that de facto racism continues to limit the extent to which social relations can be reshaped for the better in the post–Jim Crow era.[1]

When white leaders spearheaded the desegregation process throughout the South, their definition of what constituted "progress" on racial issues was often at odds with the interests and desires of Black communities. Formerly all-Black institutions were often closed under the guise of fighting against segregation without considering whether it was feasible or desirable for Blacks to patronize white alternatives. This was the case when the Archdiocese of Atlanta was faced with the issue of desegregating its parishes and schools during the 1950s and 1960s, when the city's only Black Catholic high school was shuttered after only five years of existence and Our Lady of Lourdes was threatened with closure. Although the approach the archdiocese took toward desegregation was considered progressive for the period, especially when compared to other Southern dioceses, it did not take into account what Atlanta's Black Catholics actually wanted in a post–Jim Crow society.[2]

Atlanta's Black Catholics and the Civil Rights Movement

When examining the extent to which Our Lady of Lourdes participated in the Civil Rights Movement, one must separate out the contributions of the laity versus those of the Sisters of the Blessed Sacrament (SBS) who were assigned to the parish school. Members of Our Lady of Lourdes were involved in the Civil Rights Movement, but their activities were generally coordinated not through the parish itself but through various indigenous institutions and organizations that existed in Atlanta's Black community as a whole. Aldon Morris posits that mass protest movements are the product of a "well-developed indigenous base" that consists of "the institutions, organizations, leaders, communication networks, money, and organized masses within a dominated group." The indigenous base also consists of cultural elements, such as music, oratorical styles, and modes of speaking that reinforce group identity and help mobilize the masses within the group in question. Because the cultural elements of the Civil Rights Movement drew heavily from Black Protestant churches, the presence of Black Catholics in the movement tends to be overlooked. Using Morris's framework of an indigenous base turning its resources into power allows one to see how Black Catholics existed in a movement that seemed on its surface to have a very Protestant identity.[3]

Unlike many places in the Deep South, Atlanta possessed a sophisticated indigenous base that included large Black churches, a cluster of historically Black colleges and universities at the Atlanta University Center (AUC), civil rights organizations, social clubs, and unions that all operated within a subculture that was artificially closed due to segregation. This created a social ecology of intertwined social and communication networks that simplified the mobilization process of the masses. Consequently, even individuals who were not involved in the more visible forms of civil rights participation (e.g., protests and marches) could support the movement in less visible ways, including donating money to civil rights organizations, listening to lectures by leaders in the movement, and refusing to patronize businesses that were being boycotted.[4]

The Atlanta Student Movement of the early 1960s effectively mobilized the entire student population of the AUC, including students with ties to Our Lady of Lourdes and St. Paul of the Cross. This phase in Atlanta's civil rights history began when Morehouse students Julian Bond and Lonnie King (no relation to Martin Luther King Jr.) read about the sit-in movement to desegregate public spaces in Greensboro, North Carolina, which was led by students from North Carolina A&T University. Inspired by the success of their peers at North Carolina A&T, Bond and King decided to use sit-ins to desegregate public spaces in downtown Atlanta. Bond, King, and a third student, Joe Pierce, canvassed the AUC for like-minded people, and within several weeks of its inception, seventy-seven members of the Atlanta Student Movement had been arrested for violating segregation laws at white-owned businesses located in taxpayer-funded institutions in downtown Atlanta, including the cafeterias at the State Capitol, City Hall, and the Fulton County Courthouse.[5]

The proximity of the AUC meant that many students who graduated from Our Lady of Lourdes School and later St. Paul of the Cross attended a college there. The momentum of the Atlanta Student Movement mobilized into action students from all five schools, and this enthusiasm for social change cut across denominational lines. One of these students was Marshall Thomas, a graduate of the Our Lady of Lourdes School and Drexel High who attended Morehouse College in the 1960s and participated in the Atlanta Student Movement and the Student Nonviolent Coordinating Committee (SNCC). Thomas primarily participated in marches and demonstrations aimed at forcing retailers in downtown Atlanta to desegregate their facilities. He described his experiences as an activist as follows:

> I would go and we would always outline what we were going to do and how many people would actually go to jail based on the budget for that day. In other words, it may have been $25 to bail people out, it would have been high in those days, $15–25. . . . I would just be part of the, uh, I called it, group picketing. I would be, if we took 100 people out there, we would only allow 20 or 10 people to get arrested. Those were the ones who would stay until the police arrested them, we would just keep moving. And we had something called "Super SNCC" and the SNCC Juniors and they would help by adding more people to the, uh, thing we do. And I assisted my brother, who was a local SNCC person, when he was at Fort Valley [State College].[6]

Thomas's experiences working with SNCC and the Atlanta Student Movement were normative for students across the AUC, where a culture of mass protest flourished.

The Atlanta Student Movement inspired Blacks across Atlanta, far beyond those who were directly associated with the AUC, to participate in sit-ins and protests. Much of Atlanta's "old guard" civil rights establishment—lawyers from the NAACP, presidents of AUC institutions, older ministers—disapproved of direct action because they believed it was "undignified" and might alienate white moderates. However, the Black masses supported the sit-in movement in overwhelming numbers.[7] Local Black businesses supported the movement in a variety of ways; the Atlanta Life Insurance Company gave its employees time off to protest, while restaurants around the AUC, including Frazier's and Paschal's, gave protesters food, money for bail, and rooms in which to meet to plan future actions.[8]

Older Black Catholics were involved in other aspects of the Civil Rights Movement through participation in the NAACP, unions, and other neighborhood groups. The best evidence for the widespread presence of Black Catholic adults in Atlanta's Civil Rights Movement is a December 1961 letter that seven parishioners at St. Paul of the Cross, five men and two women, sent to Bishop Francis Hyland. The letter informed Hyland not only that Atlanta's Black Catholic community supported the Civil Rights Movement but that they "actively support and participate in, the peaceful demonstrations which have transpired here in recent weeks." The letter requested "an interpretation of diocesan policy with regard to ethnic groups," a roundabout way of demanding action on the desegregation of Atlanta's Catholic school system. There is no evidence that Hyland directly replied to the letter, but he did address the concerns raised by the missive in the joint pastoral letter he signed along with Paul J. Hallinan of Charleston and Thomas J. McDonough of Savannah that defended the Catholic Church's position on segregation.[9]

Members of the SBS at Our Lady of Lourdes were also involved in Atlanta-area protests, but the dynamics of their participation were different from those of Black Catholic laypeople. Clergy and churchgoers who wanted to take part in demonstrations or other political actions had to seek permission from the superior of their order and the local bishop. Since the members of the pre–Vatican II hierarchy, especially those in the South, believed in a "law-and-order" approach to social problems, having habited nuns involved in marches and protests, especially for Black civil rights, would make the entire Church appear politically suspect to white Protestants. Mother David, the superior general of the SBS from 1964 to 1970, allowed her sisters to take part in nonviolent protests if they received permission from their local bishop first. She was aware that many bishops in the Deep South, where most SBS missions were located, were unlikely to agree to allow nuns to publicly advocate for Black civil rights, so she reminded the sisters that marches were one form of Christian witness and the SBS had proven their commitment to Southern Black communities by their decades of service.[10]

However, by the early 1960s, Southern prelates found it increasingly difficult to oppose priests and religious who wanted to be active in the Civil Rights Movement. They were under pressure to desegregate from Black Catholics, secular civil rights groups, Catholic interracialists, the federal government, and the Vatican. There was a rapid evolution in the Catholic Church's philosophy on racial issues in 1963 in particular. Pope John XXIII's 1963 encyclical *Pacem et Terris* stated that "no form of approval is being given to racial discrimination" and that "truth calls for the elimination of every trace of racial discrimination." In August, the American hierarchy issued a joint pastoral letter, titled "On Racial Harmony," that implored Catholics to ensure that "voting, jobs, housing, education and public facilities are freely available to every American." A week after the release of "On Racial Harmony," Archbishop Patrick O'Boyle of Washington, D.C., gave the invocation at the March on Washington, which provided an implicit endorsement of the philosophy, if not the means, of the Civil Rights Movement. Even if they were indifferent to the concerns of civil rights groups or even Catholic interracialists, Southern prelates could not ignore the pressure that was being exerted on them by their brother bishops in other parts of the United States and the Vatican. Although prelates in particularly conservative areas continued to bar clergy and churchgoers from being involved in protests, it was becoming increasingly common for pro–civil rights priests and nuns to simply ignore these dictates.[11]

The seven SBS at Our Lady of Lourdes joined a 1963 march headed by Martin Luther King Sr. at the Atlanta Federal Courthouse to protest the brutality Birmingham police had unleashed on civil rights protesters. On March 16, 1965, the SBS assigned to Drexel Catholic High School, along with students and other faculty members, participated in a protest at Atlanta's Old Post Office to demand federal troops intervene to protect civil rights marchers in Selma, Alabama. When Martin Luther King Jr. was killed on April 4, 1968, the SBS were among the few whites who participated in the funeral procession. The annals described the event as follows: "A great tragedy for our people and our nation, indeed for all mankind, took place when Rev. Martin Luther King was assassinated in Memphis, Tenn. His body was returned to Atlanta where it lay in state at Spelman College. We were privileged to be among the thousands who viewed it there. The funeral brought over 200,000 people to Atlanta, including Sr. M. Marie Stella, Sr. M. Veronica, Sr. M. Juliana, Sr. Marie Monique and about 40 Xavier [University of Louisiana] students. All the Sisters participated fully in the funeral services, which were profoundly moving."[12] The presence of the SBS was significant because Atlanta's white community studiously ignored King's funeral and the masses of angst-ridden Black humanity it attracted in favor of Easter shopping at Lenox Square Mall. It also illustrated their solidarity, not just with the members of Our Lady of Lourdes but with the Black community that they and their order had embedded themselves in for half a century.[13]

The civil rights activism exhibited by the sisters and parishioners at Our Lady of Lourdes occurred at other SBS plants with a vibrant civil rights protest culture. For example, at St. Vincent de Paul Catholic Church in Nashville, Tennessee, a number of the members attended the March on Washington in 1963. The SBS at St. Vincent de Paul taught workshops on interracialism to white Catholics and provided hospitality for participants in the 1968 Poor Peoples' Campaign. Sr. Ruth Phillips, the local SBS superior during the 1960s, was not only the treasurer for the aforementioned Poor Peoples' Campaign but also a member of the boards of the Nashville Opportunities Industrial Center and the Nashville Community Relations Council.[14]

Xavier University of Louisiana, the Black university started by the SBS in New Orleans, was involved in the Civil Rights Movement both at an institutional level and through the protests of students, faculty, and administrators. Prior to the Civil Rights Movement, Xavier was involved in Catholic interracial activities, such as the Southeastern Regional Interracial Commission, which sought to improve race relations between Black and white Catholics through nonconfrontational meetings. In 1961, Xavier allowed Freedom Riders who were passing through New Orleans to stay at the university, despite threats of violence from the local White Citizens

Council and other segregationists. A number of Xavier students joined the Freedom Riders during that same year, and they were soon arrested in Jackson, Mississippi, for violating that state's segregation laws.[15]

Direct involvement in civil rights activism was less prevalent at the SBS missions in the rural South, where the sisters and the parishioners lacked the institutional and organizational base to challenge the status quo and had to spend much of their time raising money for bare necessities. At some rural missions in Louisiana, such as Our Lady of the Assumption Mission in Carencro, Louisiana, most of the students did not even speak English as their primary language and the school day had to be modified to accommodate the reality of the children having to work in the fields. Given the reluctance of local governments in the South to provide even the most basic public services for Blacks, especially in rural areas, and the chronic indifference of Southern prelates toward "the Negro apostolate," SBS schools and churches were often the only source of institutionalized education for these impoverished communities until the mid-1960s. In these isolated, governmentally underserved areas, just providing formal education and suggesting the idea that there was a life beyond sharecropping was a subversive act.[16]

Although the SBS annals for Our Lady of Lourdes do not directly mention the topic of civil rights until 1962, they do show that the sisters were very much aware of segregation within the Catholic Church in Atlanta. For example, when all of the seventh- and eighth-grade Catholic school students were supposed to meet Francis Hyland, then the newly elected auxiliary bishop of Savannah-Atlanta, at the train station on January 18, 1950, the SBS were informed that only white children had been invited to the event. When Fr. McKeever, the priest at Our Lady of Lourdes at the time, drove three SBS to the dedication of the all-white St. Pius X High School on November 2, 1958, the annals remarked, "Very nice, but still nothing in sight for our children."[17]

There were no Catholic high schools in Atlanta during the immediate postwar period that would accept Blacks; Our Lady of Lourdes graduates who wanted to continue their education in a parochial school had to attend an out-of-state high school such as the St. Francis de Sales School in Rock Castle, Virginia, or St. Jude's in Mobile, Alabama, both of which were boarding schools run by the SBS. Most, however, attended Booker T. Washington High School, the only public Black high school in Atlanta until the 1960s. In comparison, by 1960 two regional coeducational diocesan high schools had been built for whites, the aforementioned St. Pius X in northern Atlanta near the suburbs and St. Joseph's in downtown Atlanta. White Catholics also had the option of sending their children to two private Catholic high schools, Marist College High School, a Catholic military school for boys near Sacred Heart, and D'Youville Academy, a girls' school in Chamblee, Georgia.[18]

Since it was still unclear whether Atlanta's schools would integrate as the 1950s ended, the diocese began planning a third diocesan high school for Blacks on the St. Paul of the Cross campus. Called Drexel Catholic High School after the recently deceased SBS founder Katharine Drexel, the school was the idea of Bishop Francis Hyland, who saw the building of a Black Catholic high school as a way to nullify Black Catholic criticism about St. Pius, especially its segregated admission policies and its geographical distance from the Black community.[19] Drexel was built to accommodate only three hundred students. The religious orders that staffed Our Lady of Lourdes and St. Paul of the Cross—the Passionists, the Sisters of St. Joseph, and the SBS—also provided personnel for Drexel, presumably because they were already accustomed to serving Atlanta's Black population. Drexel began with a freshman class of thirty-three and added a grade a year until it was a full four-year high school in 1965. However, by the time Drexel opened, the educational landscape in Atlanta had changed to the point where its existence was a point of embarrassment for the archdiocese.[20]

Public and Parochial School Desegregation in Atlanta

The controversy over school desegregation was the first major civil rights issue to directly affect the Catholic Church in Atlanta in the 1950s and 1960s. While the Catholic hierarchy might have been able to claim that matters such as equal accommodations in public facilities or fair housing were tangential to their religious mission, school desegregation directly affected the Church's extensive network of parochial schools in the South. White bishops in the South had traditionally supported the racial status quo to avoid confrontations with the white Protestant majority, but this strategy was no longer viable when the Jim Crow social order began to collapse in the 1950s. Like the majority of white

Southerners, whites in Georgia considered *Brown v. Board of Education* to be an attack by the federal government on states' rights and the Southern way of life. Several hours after the Supreme Court's decision became publicly known, Georgia governor Herman Talmadge proclaimed to the news media, "We're not going to secede from the Union, but the people of Georgia will not comply with the decision. Even if federal troops were sent down . . . they wouldn't be able to enforce it."[21] Talmadge and his successor, Marvin Griffin, created an extensive plan for privatizing Georgia's public schools in case the federal government tried to force school desegregation. Ernest Vandiver was elected as governor in 1959 with the promise that not a single Black child would attend a white school during his tenure. Although Vandiver would later soften his stance on the issue, his "No, not one" slogan echoed the feelings of many whites in late 1950s Georgia who were prepared to end public education in the state, rather than accept even token desegregation.[22]

While Atlanta's public schools were threatened with closure rather than desegregation, parochial schools remained untouched by the controversy during the 1950s, as they remained segregated. Hyland had suggested desegregating Atlanta's Catholic schools in an October 1957 meeting with the Board of Consultors, by allowing the eighty-seven Black Catholic school students of high school age to enroll at the soon-to-be-finished St. Pius X High School. If his idea had been implemented, the Diocese of Atlanta not only would have been the earliest Southern diocese to desegregate its schools but would have done so earlier than the city's public schools. Instead, the bishop's advisors told him that desegregating even one school would bring public censure on the Catholic Church, which would in turn lead to state action, including substantial fines, the removal of teaching licenses, and the possible closure of parochial schools. When Hyland dedicated the school at St. Paul of the Cross on February 23, 1958, he tried to justify his seeming inaction on school desegregation by "expressing to the Negro people his support and sympathy in the situation in Georgia which so often ties his hands when he wants to help them." The conflict between Hyland's personal desire to desegregate Catholic institutions and his anxiety about negative repercussions for doing so would typify his response to the issue throughout his tenue as bishop.

Had Hyland decided to desegregate Atlanta's Catholic schools, his actions would have been backed up by "Discrimination and Christian

Conscience," a 1958 pastoral letter issued by the American hierarchy that explicitly identified racism and segregation as a moral problem that the Church was obliged to address. According to the letter, segregation was wrong because it "imposes a stigma of inferiority" upon the affected groups and "has led to oppressive conditions and the denial of basic human rights for the Negroes." In keeping with Catholic social teachings' emphasis on maintaining social harmony, the letter urged a program of gradualism that would not "sacrifice the achievements of decades in ill-timed and ill-considered ventures." The document ended by calling upon Americans of goodwill to "seize the mantle of leadership from the agitator and the racist." Although "Discrimination and Christian Conscience" contained an acknowledgment that segregation was harmful to individuals and society, it was unable to speak positively of the Civil Rights Movement because of the Leonine strategy's fundamental distrust of civil disobedience and grassroots social movements. Despite this, Hyland was conflicted between his moral responsibility to end a practice that he and his brother bishops had acknowledged was wrong and his practical need to avoid alienating white Catholics.[23]

Hyland regarded himself as a racial moderate and believed that desegregation was inevitable, but he did not want it accomplished with violence or public disorder. He did manage to speak out in favor of the peaceful desegregation of Atlanta's public schools in December 1959 when there was a real possibility that they would be closed. At the time, a federal district court was demanding that the Atlanta Board of Education commence with the immediate desegregation of its schools. Since Georgia's "massive resistance" laws stated that any white school that admitted Blacks would be immediately closed, complying with the court's decisions would cause the entire Atlanta public school system to be shuttered. Hyland said of this situation, "As Christians and Catholics we would deplore most earnestly the severe handicap under which the children of our fellow citizens, and some of our own children as well, would labor were their education to be interrupted even temporarily or curtailed or impeded in any way. . . . We would deplore with equal earnestness the inevitable harm and disrepute which would come to the state of Georgia through the closing of the public schools."[24] Hyland appealed to a sense of "Christian justice" and a love of "law and order" among his fellow white Georgians to prevent the chaos that would inevitably follow if the public schools were closed en masse.

The Atlanta Board of Education finally submitted a desegregation plan that was approved by the federal courts in 1960, although it amounted to little more than tokenism; a grade a year would be desegregated, beginning with twelfth. The desegregation process did not begin in Atlanta until 1961, during which time the University of Georgia in Athens became the first public school system in the state to be desegregated when two Black Atlantans, Hamilton Holmes and Charlayne Hunter, were allowed to attend the school under court order. Hunter, whose family belonged to Big Bethel, had converted to Catholicism as a high school junior and had been a member of St. Paul of the Cross before going to Wayne State University as an undergraduate. An entry from the SBS annals dated February 19, 1961, described a visit Hunter made to St. Paul of the Cross on Ladies Appreciation Day, during which she effused to the SBS and the Sisters of St. Joseph over the University of Georgia's Newman Club.

The desegregation of Atlanta's public schools began on August 30, 1961, when nine Black twelfth graders were admitted to four local high schools: Brown High, Henry Grady High (now Midtown High School), Northside High, and Murphy High. One of the students who integrated Grady was Mary J. McMullin, an Our Lady of Lourdes graduate who chose that school when her request to attend St. Pius was denied. Despite the obvious tokenism of adding just nine Blacks to the student bodies of four large white high schools, this first fitful attempt at desegregation indicated that the days of "massive resistance" were over.[25]

As Atlanta's public schools grudgingly accepted the inevitability of desegregation, the city's Catholic schools remained segregated. Hyland sent out a pastoral letter that was read during Mass in all of the parishes in the diocese regarding the Church's response to racism. The letter was a joint project between Hyland, Bishop Thomas J. McDonough of Savannah, and Bishop Paul J. Hallinan of Charleston. The letter appealed to the erstwhile patriotism and piety of white Catholics, stating that "hatred is neither Christian nor American" and that it was natural for the Church to be proactive about racism because it was a moral issue that affected all of society. It quoted from the bishop's and archbishop's 1958 condemnation of segregation, perhaps as a way to remind white Catholics that the

American hierarchy had already decided that the practice was immoral and the topic was not open to further debate. The three-point plan for the desegregation of Catholic schools consisted of (1) allowing any Catholic student, regardless of race, to enroll in a Catholic school "as soon as this can be done with safety," (2) continuing to operate Catholic schools that were formerly designated for Blacks for as long as necessary, and (3) devoting 1961 to teaching white Catholics about the Church's position on racial justice through "pastoral letters, sermons, study clubs and school instruction." The letter emphatically stated that the Church was not changing any of its previous teachings, only that "changing times" required new applications for long-standing doctrines.[26]

On April 10, 1961, a pastoral letter written by Hyland was read during Mass at Our Lady of Lourdes and St. Paul of the Cross in which he tried to justify his reluctance to desegregate Catholic institutions. The impetus for the letter may have been the missive Hyland received earlier in the year from seven St. Paul of the Cross members asking for "an interpretation of diocesan policy with regard to ethnic groups." After spending the bulk of the letter acknowledging that Atlanta's Black citizens were right to be impatient about the slow pace of civil rights in both secular and religious realms, he explained the difficult position he was in as a bishop who must serve Black and white Catholics:

> There are approximately 33,000 Catholic people in our diocese; of these 33,000 Catholic people, less than 2,000 are members of the Negro race. Mathematically, our problem does not seem to be a great one—bringing less than 2,000 Negro people into the full Catholic life of 33,000 people. But, of course, it is not a simple mathematical problem at all. It is a problem which requires a change of heart and mind on the part of some. It is a moral and a spiritual problem. It is the problem of bringing all our Catholic people together in the great Christian virtue of love—a love which manifests itself not in words but deeds—deeds which embrace all the implications of Catholic social justice.[27]

Part of the conflict Hyland was experiencing was rooted in the breakdown of pre–Vatican II strategy of deferring to "law and order" to guide how the Catholic Church should interact with a white Protestant supermajority society. With the Supreme Court and various federal courts mandating school desegregation while state governments in the South attempted to tighten Jim Crow laws in defiance, it was no longer clear what following "law and order" meant. If segregation was indeed a moral issue, the archbishops and bishops were obliged to be proactive about it, yet few were willing to do anything that would offend the white community.

While Hyland tried to chart out the best path for Catholic school desegregation, he oversaw the construction and dedication of a permanent church building for Our Lady of Lourdes. He was initially reluctant to approve construction, believing that the congregation had more pressing projects that were in need of funding, such as an $84,000 renovation of the school. Undeterred, the community launched a fundraising drive to achieve their goal. The capital campaign to raise money for the Our Lady of Lourdes church was reminiscent of the fundraising efforts to build the school in that it relied heavily on the charitable donations of Atlanta's white Catholic parishes. The Cathedral of Christ the King donated $3,600, while Sacred Heart gave $1,000. Our Lady of Lourdes itself provided $7,000, in addition to $1,000 that the children of the parish's school were able to raise. An additional $1,000 was donated by "Mr. Dolan and Mrs. J. Dolan and family," a household whose race and parish affiliation are unknown. As a result of these fundraising efforts, Fr. Michael McKeever was able to present Bishop Hyland a check for $13,000. This was far less than the $90,000 that was necessary to pay for the construction costs in full, but the funds indicated to Hyland that the membership of Our Lady of Lourdes was serious in their desire to help defray construction costs.

Despite this significant shortfall in funds, Hyland gave permission for the DeGive Construction Company to begin work on the church in March 1960. Construction of a solid red brick structure with a concrete foundation that matched the adjoining school building was finished in the fall of 1960. Our Lady of Lourdes's new church was modest in comparison to the majestic Romanesque and neo-Gothic facades that characterized Atlanta's white Catholic parishes, but it was a visual representation of the growth and prominence of the congregation within the Auburn Avenue area.[28]

Hyland's sermon during the church's dedication ceremony on February 12, 1961, focused heavily on the legacy of Katharine Drexel, who had died in 1955, and her role in the founding of the Our Lady of Lourdes

Figure 3.1. Sister Louis Marie with students in Our Lady of Lourdes's sanctuary, circa 1961. Courtesy of the Catholic Historical Research Center.

community. He alluded to the contemporary Civil Rights Movement: "If Mother Katharine were alive and active today, she would surely be an valiant supporter of the just aspirations of the Negro people to acquire the full rights to which they have every claim and title as members of the one human family, as children of the same God and as citizens of the United States of America." Hyland ended his sermon by stating, "Fifty years ago [establishing Our Lady of Lourdes] was a notable victory and I hope and pray that it foreshadowed the ultimate victory of the aspirations of our good Colored People of the present day." Hyland's sermon retained the paternalistic attitude common to whites of the time, with its singular focus on Drexel as "the greatest benefactress of the Negro people." However, he was clearly trying to link the Catholic Church with Black struggles of the past and present.[29]

In the end, Hyland did not have to decide on Catholic school desegregation because he resigned from his bishopric on October 11, 1961, after suffering a nervous breakdown from anxiety caused by the "racial issue." For several months, Atlanta had no bishop, and the question of whether or when the city's Catholic schools would desegregate had no certain answer. By March 1962, Paul Hallinan, the former bishop of Charleston, had been chosen to replace Hyland. The changing of the ecclesiastical guard coincided with the elevation of the Diocese of Atlanta to that of a Metropolitan See consisting of the Dioceses of Charleston, Atlanta, Savannah, Miami, and St. Augustine, thus making Hallinan not only the first archbishop of Atlanta but the first archbishop in the entire Deep South.[30]

The SBS from Our Lady of Lourdes attended Hallinan's installation at the Cathedral of Christ the King, where they were encouraged to hear "how very fond he was of the Colored" during his tenure in Charleston. Hallinan spoke of his concern for racial justice during the installation ceremony, saying, "Neither in the North or in the South can [the Catholic Church] bear the ugly blemish of prejudice and fear. Small in numbers but great in loyalty, our Catholic people are trying to reflect the unity of Christ's Mystical Body as they move towards the reality of full racial justice—with prudence, with courage and with determination." Unlike the moderate Hyland, Hallinan was liberal, on both racial and liturgical matters, and he used the momentum of the Civil Rights Movement to push for changes.[31]

The notion of the Mystical Body of Christ that Hallinan referred to throughout his installation speech was a theological and Catholic social teaching concept developed by Continental theologians during the interwar period and then subsequently embraced by Black Catholics and white Catholic interracialists in the United States. According to John T. McGreevy, the Mystical Body of Christ doctrine meant that "the Church was Christ's Mystical Body on earth. All Catholics, therefore, were united through both this Mystical Body and Christ's literal body and blood as present in the Eucharist." The Eucharist dissolved the man-made divisions that kept humanity separated, such as race, nationality, and ethnicity, and united them, not just in the act of physically taking Communion but under the authority of the triune God and the papacy. Racism and other forms of prejudice and bigotry went against the mystical, universal brotherhood that the Eucharist created and caused harmful divisions within the Mystical Body of Christ. For advocates of the Mystical Body of Christ, the emergence of genocidal nationalism during the interwar period was the logical end, not just of detaching Continental Europe from its collective roots in Latin Christendom but of trying to find societal consensus in values other than a universal commitment to Catholicism.[32]

As Hallinan's installation speech indicated, the Mystical Body of Christ provided him a way to justify the desegregation of Atlanta's Catholic schools in a way that was consistent with Catholic tradition. To prepare white students and staff for the inevitable desegregation of Catholic schools, Hallinan distributed copies of *A Syllabus on Racial Justice*, a guide to teaching racial justice from a Catholic perspective for students from seventh to twelfth grade. The *Syllabus on Racial Justice* was originally commissioned by Hallinan in 1961 when he was bishop of Charleston. The document had an impeccably Catholic background. It was written by Fr. Leo Crogan, a teaching priest at Bishop England High School, and Sr. Mary Bernard, the diocesan supervisor of Charleston. Hallinan's accompanying letter addressed to teachers stated that the *Syllabus on Racial Justice* was part of the educational process that had been promised in the February 19, 1961, pastoral letter that had been distributed in the dioceses of Atlanta, Charleston, and Savannah. Although Catholic schools had always taught about "the Universality of the Church, the Mystical Body of Christ, and the virtue of Justice," it was necessary to present these concepts in new ways to address contemporary concerns over Black civil rights in general and school desegregation in particular.[33]

By September 4, 1962, the opening of the parochial school year, the schools at St. Anthony of Padua, Immaculate Conception, Sacred Heart, and St. Joseph's High School had begun the desegregation process with no disturbances reported. The annals of the SBS describe the reaction to Catholic school desegregation at Our Lady of Lourdes:

> This morning in all the Churches of the Archdiocese the enclosed letter of Archbishop Hallinan was read. Open admission to all Catholic schools in the Archdiocese for Catholic children regardless of race or color was announced. There was little immediate comment on the part of our people as it had been expected. It must have been received with great relief by many of our parents, both Catholic and non-Catholic, who had been upholding the Church in the face of sharp criticism from co-workers,

especially in the field of education. . . . We do not expect to lose many of our pupils through transfer however. As the Archbishop said, the thing our people really want is the freedom of choice.

Seven former Lourdes students enrolled at St. Joseph's, and the other schools had an unspecified number of Black first graders on their rolls. The annals report that one family, the Fraleys, transferred their membership to St. Anthony's, a foreshadowing of the many former Lourdes members who would migrate to the West End parish by the end of the decade. When Hallinan visited Our Lady of Lourdes for the parish's Silver Jubilee celebration on September 23, 1962, he considered it to be a testament to the SBS and the Our Lady of Lourdes School that so few of the students had left for white schools.[34]

The archdiocese also arranged for student exchanges to foster interracial understanding between the students of the Black and white Catholic high schools. The *Georgia Bulletin*, the official newspaper of the Archdiocese of Atlanta, listed a number of these encounters. One such encounter occurred when members of the St. Pius school newspaper team visited their counterparts at Drexel. The white visitors were treated to a tour of the St. Paul of the Cross School and Drexel High before they "exchanged ideas and gave many hints on journalism." An April 15, 1965, article describes how Barbara Williams, daughter of civil rights leader Hosea Williams and a senior at Drexel, provided a firsthand account of the Selma to Montgomery march to white students at D'Youville Academy.[35] Once Drexel High had established a twelfth grade, its seniors attended graduation exercises at the famed Fox Theatre with the white Catholic school graduates, albeit in a separate section. Presumably, the intent was to accustom white and Black Catholics to coexisting in the same physical space, even if said space remained segregated by default.[36]

The desegregation of Atlanta's Catholic schools was faster and more total than that of the city's public schools, which saw only token desegregation in the upper grades. In some cities within the archdiocese, such as Marietta and Athens, the public schools remained segregated, while the Catholic schools were desegregated. From the perspective of Hallinan and the other officials of the archdiocese, the desegregation process had been accomplished with little to no violence or ill will between the races. Although Our Lady of Lourdes School did not experience any attrition after Jim Crow ended, Drexel High would become a casualty of desegregation, and its closing would jeopardize the relationship that the SBS had nurtured for so long between the Catholic Church and Atlanta's Black community.[37]

The Controversy of the Closing of Drexel High

The question of whether to close Drexel was precipitated by the fact that the school was supposed to seek accreditation in November 1967. If Drexel became accredited, the archdiocese would be "seek[ing] to make permanent its status" as a lasting institution it had an interest in sustaining over the long term. Achieving accreditation for Drexel would require improvements that would add an estimated $15,000 to the preexisting operating deficit of $27,205. Another issue was the small size of the student body, which at its highest consisted of 155 pupils, with 53 percent coming from the St. Paul of the Cross School, 11 percent from the Our Lady of Lourdes School, and 34 percent being non-Catholic.

As the city's only Black Catholic high school, Drexel should have been the school Our Lady of Lourdes graduates attended, but it was on the other side of Atlanta, making it too far for many Lourdes members to reach. Since St. Joseph's was desegregated the same year as Drexel, it was more convenient for Our Lady of Lourdes's Catholic graduates to enroll there rather than at Drexel. However, the small size of Atlanta's Black Catholic community was such that the majority of parishioners of Our Lady of Lourdes and St. Paul of the Cross had a personal, community, or family connection to Drexel.

To become accredited, Drexel would also need to be classified as an integrated school, something that archdiocesan officials did not think was possible because it was a "colored school." Although none of the *Georgia Bulletin* articles about Drexel explicitly describe it in racial terms as a "colored school" or a "Negro school," readers would have known that it was for Black students because of its location and the presence of the SBS, a religious order famed for educating "the colored and the Indian." Since all of the Catholic schools in the archdiocese were now open to Catholic children, regardless of race, Drexel should have theoretically been the high school of choice for white Catholics living in the southern part of Atlanta. However, white Catholics were wary of sending their own children to Drexel because of its status as a "colored school," even if they had grown to begrudgingly accept small numbers of Black students in formerly white parochial schools.

At first glance, consolidating Drexel's student population with that of St. Joseph's was a logical solution. The costs of operating Catholic schools, especially at the secondary level, were increasing and the elimination of Drexel, the newest and weakest of the schools, would help keep St. Joseph's, which was also operating at less than full capacity, solvent. Closing Drexel and reassigning the sisters and priests who had worked there to St. Joseph's would have the added bonus of balancing the ratio of religious teachers to lay teachers, and it would further reduce the deficit at the latter school. Similarly, sending the remaining Drexel students to St. Joseph's would enable that school to function at full capacity and maximize the archdiocese's limited resources. Despite all the logistical advantages, the archdiocese realized that closing Drexel would have negative repercussions for the image of the Catholic Church among Atlanta's Blacks. Closing the only Catholic high school in the heart of the Black community would create the appearance that the Church was abandoning its "negro apostolate," subjecting the archdiocese to the charge that it had never made a serious attempt to integrate Drexel and relieve it of its reputation as a "colored high school."[38]

Indeed, when the Black community learned that Drexel might be closed, the reaction was a sense of outrage that surprised Hallinan and other archdiocesan educational officials. Consequently, Hallinan announced that he would defer a decision on the closing of Drexel until after engaging in further discussion with the school community. Both sides agreed that it had been a mistake for Drexel to be built, albeit for very different reasons. Hallinan thought that Drexel was inherently inferior to St. Joseph's and St. Pius in terms of its offerings in academics, athletics, and the arts. He was convinced that no amount of fundraising, physical improvements, or student recruitment could improve it. The archdiocese would be doing the students at Drexel a favor by ensuring them a seat at a better school, rather than have them continue their education in an inferior one. Black families at Drexel, on the other hand, felt that the school had been built only as a way for the archdiocese to avoid having to desegregate its schools, even though it should have been apparent when Drexel first opened in 1961 that continuing to build separate faculties for Blacks would no longer suffice in a post–*Brown v. Board of Education* educational landscape. On a more personal level, Drexel families objected to the archdiocese ignoring the spirit and community they had built around the school. If the archdiocese was now claiming that Drexel had been a fatally flawed school from its inception, the logical question to ask was why Drexel had not been designed at the outset to make it competitive with other public and private schools in the city.

Even if Drexel was weaker in some aspects than St. Joseph's and St. Pius, its students did not perceive that they were getting an inferior education. In fact, Drexel students won a number of awards, including scholarships to colleges and universities and honors for drama, debate, and athletic contests, including contests sponsored by the archdiocese itself. The only trouble Drexel alumni reported in their transitions to other high schools or colleges was related to the archdiocese's own incompetence in failing to release transcripts from Drexel after it closed. Black families resented the implication that the archdiocese was somehow doing them a favor by closing their school and forcing them to travel to the other side of town if they wanted to send their children to a Catholic high school, especially when white Catholics would never be asked to make such a sacrifice.[39]

The inability or unwillingness of the archdiocese to integrate Drexel would become a major point of contention between it and the Black community. Theoretically, the school could have operated to its original capacity of three hundred pupils if students from the feeder schools in south Atlanta such as St. Anthony of Padua, Blessed Sacrament, St. Joseph (Marietta), and Holy Spirit had been willing to attend. The Drexel community believed that the school could be integrated and filled to capacity and beyond if Hallinan used his authority as archbishop to ensure that white Catholic families did not bypass it in favor of St. Joseph's or St. Pius. They saw a future for Drexel that involved accreditation and improvements to its facilities and personnel. Rather than seeing Drexel as an embarrassing relic of segregation, they thought that it was a good school with potential that was being prematurely strangled because of the prejudice of white Catholics against anything deemed "colored." The archdiocese's claim that Drexel had to be closed because it could not be integrated seemed especially hypocritical, given that St. Pius remained de facto segregated.[40]

Despite pleas from the Drexel community, Archbishop Hallinan determined that the school was not viable, and it closed in the summer of 1967. The remaining students at Drexel were provided automatic enrollment at either St. Joseph's or St. Pius, with most choosing the former, as it was much closer to Atlanta's Black communities. To help facilitate the transition for Drexel students, two SBS taught at St. Joseph's for the 1967–68 academic year, although none were assigned to St. Pius. Archbishop Hallinan considered the closing of Drexel and the absorption of its students into the white Catholic high schools to be a success, but the sense among Black Catholics in the wake of Drexel's closing was that they had to sacrifice their own institutions, so the archdiocese would not have to worry about making white Catholics, especially those moving to the suburbs, uncomfortable.[41]

Although the archdiocese insisted that closing Drexel was the logical result of good administrative practices and a genuine desire for Black students to have the best Catholic education possible, there is evidence that white public opinion was a major factor. Drexel graduate Andrew Hill recalled a private conversation he had with Hallinan that suggested that placating white Catholics was indeed a major factor in closing the school:

> Shortly after I graduated from Drexel Catholic High School, I believed it was shut down, because they couldn't get enough white students to attend the school. . . . I would later learn, from the archbishop himself, because I went to him to ask him not to close [Drexel], and he said to me, "We have to close it, because there are white Catholics in this city who will take their children out of Catholic schools altogether rather than send them to a school in a Black neighborhood." And when I understood the truth of that, it was one of the most upsetting things that's ever happened to me, and it stays with me to this day.[42]

In fact, it does not appear that most of the Drexel community considered it to be a "colored high school," even though it was located in a Black neighborhood and had an entirely Black student body. For them, it was simply another Catholic high school option in Atlanta. They thought that white students would eventually enroll there because of its proximity to the interstate and because of the seeming inevitability of desegregation. From the perspective of the Drexel community, a true commitment on the part of Hallinan to integrating the school would have solved most of its perceived weaknesses vis-à-vis St. Joseph's and St. Pius.[43]

Similarly, the minutes of a meeting held at Hallinan's residence with members of the Drexel Home School Association indicate that the parents repeatedly asked the archbishop whether money was the motivating factor behind the suggestion that Drexel should close. Hallinan denied this charge, which contradicted the insistence of the archdiocese that the school had to be closed because its small size made it financially unsustainable. The parents also brought up the possibility that they could embark upon a major recruitment and funding drive in the Black community, suggestions that Hallinan rejected. If the real issue with Drexel was its status, real or perceived, as a "colored high school," then increasing the number of Black students or Black funding would not help it survive.[44]

At the time of Drexel's closing, whites were fleeing Atlanta, causing formerly white schools and neighborhoods to become majority Black. By the end of the decade, an estimated sixty thousand whites had resettled in the northern suburbs and a hundred thousand would follow in the 1970s. Enrollment at St. Pius, which was located in a white suburban area that was geographically inaccessible for most Blacks, was surging, while St. Joseph's in downtown Atlanta struggled to retain students. Despite the continued insistence from the archdiocese that it had an obligation to serve Catholics of all races, the suburbanization of white Catholics fundamentally changed the dynamics and priorities of the Church in Atlanta, in terms of both its institutional priorities and where its white Catholic population situated itself.[45]

The "integration" of Atlanta's white Catholic schools was seen very differently by archdiocesan officials and by the Black students who actually had to attend them. White officials who made the decision to close Drexel deemed the integration of former Drexelites into St. Joseph's to be a success in the sense that no riots or physical violence occurred, but the students in question were put off by the racist attitudes exhibited by white teachers and students. White Catholics had theoretically been preparing for school desegregation for the previous five years through various educational endeavors sponsored by the archdiocese, but the recollections of former Drexelites who attended St. Joseph's and St. Pius indicated that white Catholics were unwilling to accept Blacks as peers. As Drexel graduate Anita Whatley put it, "The kids that were left at Drexel had to either go to [St. Pius], the juniors had to finish at St. Joseph's and it just killed them to have to finish there, because there was, it was just racist to the max, downtown Atlanta right there."[46] An anonymous account of a junior from Drexel who had to finish her senior year at St. Pius also reported a nonstop stream of microaggressions from white students and staff. While this account does not mention any acts of overt racism, there was a pervasive sense that the former Drexel students were being tolerated, not accepted into the St. Pius community.[47]

The demise of Drexel High was illustrative of the nationwide trend during the mid-1960s and early 1970s of closing "inferior" Black institutions, ostensibly to eliminate the vestiges of Jim Crow and facilitate desegregation. However, this view failed to take into account what Blacks wanted from desegregation and the extent to which they had identified with the institutions in their communities. Blacks also assumed that desegregation would be a two-way street, in which whites would enter institutions once designated for Blacks, just as Blacks were now allowed to be in institutions that were once labeled all-white. Instead, Blacks were expected to travel long distances to desegregate white facilities and abandon their own institutions, while it was enough for whites to merely tolerate their presence. Black Catholics were being "planned for, not planned with" in Atlanta's desegregation process, and this trend would not stop with Drexel's closing.[48]

White Flight, Black Migration, and Our Lady of Lourdes

While the desegregation of Catholic institutions did not directly affect Our Lady of Lourdes, white flight and changing Black residential patterns caused a dramatic decrease in the membership of the parish by the end of the 1960s. Severe housing shortages combined with the desegregation of public facilities caused previously white, working-class neighborhoods in Southwest Atlanta—West End, Mozley Park, Adamsville, Grove Park, and Center Hill—to become Black enclaves, virtually overnight. White flight was not limited to the working classes, as middle- and upper-class whites who had lived in areas of northern Atlanta that were already too difficult for most Blacks to access via public transit fled further north into suburbs such as Sandy Springs and Roswell.[49]

Once the heart of Atlanta's Black community, Auburn Avenue became depopulated toward the end of the 1960s as its middle-class Black residents fled for more desirable locations. Accordingly, the number of parishioners at Our Lady of Lourdes who actually lived in close proximity to the parish plummeted and tuition for the school became cost prohibitive for the children who did live in the neighborhood. School desegregation, of both public and private institutions, meant that the Our Lady of Lourdes School was no longer the only or even the best educational option for upwardly mobile Black families, as it had been in the Jim Crow era.[50]

These new residential patterns—Blacks moving into previously restricted areas of Atlanta and whites leaving the city altogether—led to a corresponding realignment in the racial composition of Atlanta's Catholic parishes; the two downtown white parishes, Sacred Heart and Immaculate Conception, lost members to new suburban parishes, while many Our Lady of Lourdes parishioners migrated to the west side of Atlanta, where they joined St. Anthony of Padua in the formerly white West End or St. Paul of the Cross. As white Catholics left Atlanta, the archdiocese faced the reality of having too many urban parishes relative to the number of Catholics who continued to reside in the city. Our Lady of Lourdes became a particular point of contention, not only because of the unseemliness of continuing to maintain a personal "Negro parish" when the archdiocese had publicly announced its commitment to desegregation, but also because it was situated in the middle of Sacred Heart's territory. The archdiocese had purchased all of the land and buildings associated with Our Lady of Lourdes from the Society of African Missions in March 1963, meaning that it should have had the same status as any other diocesan parish, including permanent, distinct borders. These overlapping boundaries had not been a problem during the Jim Crow era, when white and Black Catholics lived in separate but unequal worlds, but now that Blacks were welcome and encouraged to attend the parish closest to their respective homes, there was no logical reason for the continued existence of Our Lady of Lourdes. Although St. Paul of the Cross was also designated a "colored parish," it did not pose the same existential threat, presumably because its boundaries did not intersect with those of any other parish and because it had a larger membership than Lourdes.

Auxiliary Bishop Joseph Bernardin held a meeting at Our Lady of Lourdes on January 11, 1967, with the pastors of Sacred Heart, St. Anthony of Padua, Our Lady of Lourdes, and Immaculate Conception to discuss the challenges faced by the inner-city parishes in general, but more specifically "what we intend to do with OLL Parish." Fr. Dale Freeman, the priest at Our Lady of Lourdes, stated that the parishioners at Our Lady of Lourdes, especially the elderly, felt that the parish "gives them a sense of community and identity . . . eventho [sic] it is defact [sic] segregated." However, Freeman also said that the younger members could acquire "educational, social, and economic gains" by attending the other urban parishes, although the specifics of these supposed benefits were not described. The minutes imply that the attendees thought that if the members of Our Lady of Lourdes went to the parishes in the neighborhoods in which they resided, the other urban parishes would gain members to replace the white Catholics who had moved to the suburbs, as Freeman estimated "there were from 40 to 50 addresses in each of the other down [sic] parishes of Negro Catholics attending OLL Parish." While discussing the necessity of redrawing Our Lady of Lourdes's boundaries, Bernardin, Freeman, and the other priests also debated what the parish's future held. Several suggestions were brought forth, such as turning the school into an adult education center or another facility that would serve all of the downtown parishes. It seems clear that none of the attendees, not even the priest assigned to it, envisioned Our Lady of Lourdes continuing to exist as a functioning parish.[51]

Two weeks later, on January 26, 1967, another meeting was held between Bernardin and the pastors of Sacred Heart, Immaculate Conception, and Our Lady of Lourdes. They determined that "no decision be made at this time regarding the closing of Our Lady of Lourdes." Instead, parishioners at Our Lady of Lourdes would be encouraged to attend the parishes nearest to their homes, by convincing them that

> they truly belong to the territorial parishes in which they live (their membership in a personal Negro parish is by way of exception to the general policy of the Church) and that they will be welcome in those parishes. This would be accomplished by Negroes (at Mass or at meetings), by put-

ting them on their mailing list so that they will know what is going on in the territorial parishes, and by trying to establish some contact between the white and Negro Catholics (e.g., through Mass in the home). All the while the pastors of the territorial parishes would be conditioning their own parishioners for this change. At the same time, Father Freeman [of Our Lady of Lourdes] would be encouraging those who wished to join the territorial parishes.

The minutes stated that a final determination about Our Lady of Lourdes's future status was dependent on the speed at which Black Catholics left it to attend territorial parishes, with the underlying assumption being that Lourdes's closing was inevitable. This is perhaps why the contentious issue of territorial boundaries was often discussed, but never resolved, because the assumption was that the subject would be a moot point once the parish closed.[52]

Since the controversy over the closing of Drexel was occurring at the same time these meetings were taking place, there may have been a reluctance to shutter two Black Catholic institutions in rapid succession. The unexpected blowback the archdiocese received over the closing of Drexel High was such that preemptively closing Our Lady of Lourdes would further discredit the Catholic Church in the Black community. Our Lady of Lourdes and the SBS were regarded favorably as an integral part of Auburn Avenue, even if the Church as a whole was still regarded with suspicion. The minutes for the January 11, 1967, meeting indicate that Our Lady of Lourdes's pastor, Dale Freeman, pleaded that "before any solution could be reached as to the future struction [sic] of OLL Parish the Negro community itself must [be] consulted and seriously considered." Unspoken was the implication that this was not how the Drexel affair was handled. This would explain why both of the letters from January 1967 suggest mounting a campaign to persuade Black Catholics to join their respective territorial parishes, so Our Lady of Lourdes would die a natural death, rather than being shut down unexpectedly by episcopal fiat.[53]

As with the case of Drexel, the archdiocese also considered consolidating Our Lady of Lourdes with a larger, white Catholic institution in downtown Atlanta, in this case Sacred Heart. However, the findings of a master's thesis by Rev. William Headley, a Black priest of the Con-

Figure 3.2. Drexel Catholic High School, undated. Georgia Bulletin Photograph Collection, Office of Archives and Records, Roman Catholic Archdiocese of Atlanta.

gregation of the Holy Spirit doing graduate work at Atlanta University, suggested that combining the two parishes would provoke negative reactions among both white and Black Catholics. Headley's research consisted of data pulled from a survey of 205 members from both parishes, with roughly half of the participants coming from each. Headley concluded that "stimuli to alignment on a racial basis seemed so natural and strong that other stimuli such as religious affiliation are somewhat overlooked." While Blacks were more generally accepting of desegregation than whites, there was more acceptance of the idea among young adults of both races (defined as those between fourteen and twenty-one) than among older adults. However, as the anger over the closing of Drexel indicates, many Blacks who supported desegregation in terms of opening up public facilities did not believe that this should entail the automatic closure of Black institutions. The findings of Headley's thesis convinced the archdiocese that consolidating Sacred Heart and Our

Lady of Lourdes would be imprudent, and the topic, like that of the latter's territorial boundaries, was shelved for future study.[54]

The demise of Drexel High and the threatened closing of Our Lady of Lourdes in the late 1960s vividly illustrate the failure of the Catholic Church in the United States to understand or appreciate the Black Catholic subculture. From the perspective of the Archdiocese of Atlanta, the best way to achieve desegregation was to simply shutter "inferior" Black Catholic institutions and encourage the use of "superior" facilities that had once been reserved for whites. This view assumed that Blacks would naturally gravitate toward formerly whites-only institutions, without taking into account that Black Catholic institutions possessed a unique history and culture. As the case of Drexel High demonstrates, Black Catholics in Atlanta wanted their respective parishes and schools to receive the same access to resources as white parishes and to be treated as equals should they visit or join a majority-white parish. The tendency of the archdiocese to relegate Black Catholic institutions to second-class status would only intensify as all of the city's urban parishes struggled to survive in an environment characterized by increasing suburbanization and white flight.

4

Liturgical Renewal and the Second Vatican Council in Atlanta

Exactly one month after Paul J. Hallinan, archbishop of Atlanta, desegregated the city's Catholic schools, he left his see to attend the opening of the Second Vatican Council (i.e., Vatican II) in Rome on October 4, 1962. The council had been convoked on December 25, 1961, by Pope John XXIII as a means of "bringing the modern world into contact with the vivifying and perennial energies of the Gospel," and it was set to formally open in mid-October 1962. Hundreds of Catholic schoolchildren, including students from Our Lady of Lourdes, who had up until that point been excluded from mass archdiocesan events, saw Hallinan off at the airport. Upon seeing the crowd of children, Hallinan announced that the opening day of the council, October 11, 1962, would be a school holiday. He also made sure to say a personal goodbye to Joey Moore, a fifth grader and altar boy at Our Lady of Lourdes who was suffering from terminal cancer. After a brief vacation in New York, Hallinan embarked on a transatlantic ship to his final destination of Rome.[1]

Once the council began in earnest, Hallinan was unexpectedly thrust into the role of liturgical reformer, and he had a crucial role in the debates surrounding the composition of *Sacrosanctum Concilium*, the Constitution on the Sacred Liturgy. The documents of Vatican II covered a wide range of issues, from the status of the Oriental Churches to the proper use of the mass media, but for many lay Catholics the changes to the Mass that were caused in the wake of *Sacrosanctum Concilium* were the most important outcome of the council. Relatively few outside of academic or clerical circles might understand the meanings of *aggiornamento* (i.e., updating) or *ressourcement* (i.e., return to the sources), but it was plain that something dramatic was occurring when the words, symbols, and rubrics of the supposedly immutable Mass began changing. Once approved, changes to the liturgy were implemented rapidly, with the transition from the Tridentine Latin Mass to the Missal of Paul

VI happening within five years after *Sacrosanctum Concilium* was approved. Some parishes or dioceses tried to delay liturgical renewal, but once it was clear that the Vatican intended for the reformed liturgy to be the new status quo, rejecting the changes was not an option.[2]

From a modern conservative or traditionalist perspective, the Tridentine Latin Mass was and continues to be "the eternal Mass," the most perfect form of worship that, by definition, is never in need of renewal. Thus, Vatican II in general and liturgical renewal in particular were not only unnecessary but dangerous, as they acted as Trojan horses for oft-condemned modernist ideas to infiltrate the Church's previous impenetrable ideological fortress. In comparison, liberals consider Vatican II's calls for liturgical renewal to be the Holy Spirit breathing fresh air into an otherwise moribund institution. The renewed liturgy, with its emphasis on "active and intelligent participation," was indicative of the laity outgrowing the "Father says" mentality of the post-Tridentine era and growing into spiritual adulthood. However, at the time Vatican II was occurring, the Council Fathers who favored liturgical reform did so not because they wanted to self-consciously break with Tridentine Catholicism but because they saw a more streamlined liturgy as a pragmatic response to a number of problems facing mid-twentieth-century Catholicism, especially the phenomenon of the disengagement of the laity from the Mass.[3]

Like the majority of American Catholics, the parishioners of Our Lady of Lourdes followed the proceedings of the council with interest. The timeline of the Second Vatican Council overlapped with the tail end of the Southern phase of the Civil Rights Movement, creating a moment when social change and religious renewal had the potential to revolutionize Black Catholic life. As the Civil Rights Movement challenged white supremacy in American life, the principles found in *Sacrosanctum Concilium* inspired Black Catholics to envision Catholicism beyond the Eurocentric confines of the pre–Vatican II Church.[4]

Catholic Devotionalism and the Liturgical Movement

The vituperative nature of the post-councilar "liturgical wars," at both official and grassroots levels, belies the fact that the liturgy was largely tangential to the spiritual lives of the Catholic laity until quite recently.

Although lay Catholics in the pre–Vatican II era had to attend weekly Mass to fulfil their "Sunday obligation," they were essentially spectators watching a private dialogue between the priest and God. The lack of connection that lay Catholics had to the Mass was not necessarily a problem because Catholicism was a "total lifestyle" in which the liturgy constituted only one aspect. Pre–Vatican II life at Our Lady of Lourdes, for example, was characterized by numerous bodily practices such as fasting, performing Confession, participating in processions, and wearing distinctive clothing (e.g., cassocks, habits, Catholic school uniforms). Time was organized according to the rhythms of the liturgical year and feast days. All of these practices were mediated and interpreted by a strict hierarchical chain of command of bishops, priests, and sisters. At Our Lady of Lourdes and other parishes throughout the United States during the pre–Vatican II era, the liturgy was an element of being Catholic, but it was not necessarily the most important in terms of shaping their personal spirituality.[5]

The group of practices that most constituted "religion" for non-cleric, non-monastic Catholics before the council was popular devotions. The 1911 *Catholic Encyclopedia* defined popular devotions as "external practices of piety by which the devotion of the faithful finds life and expression." The Mass, on the other hand, was the official public worship of the Church. Ann Taves divides devotions into two general categories, the first being prayers in vernacular tongues to accompany participation in the Mass and other sacraments and the second being spontaneous lay activity directed toward various aspects of the faith (including holy places or holy persons) that manifests itself through oral traditions and observances. Many devotions, such as the rosary, the scapular, the Seven Dolors of the Virgin Mary, and Books of Hours, originated as monastic practices that filtered down to the laity in modified forms. Others, such as the Stations of the Cross, were initially intended to re-create pilgrimage experiences for ordinary Catholics who lacked the means and ability to engage in long-distance travel. Devotions associated with specific people, including saints, Marian apparitions, and various aspects of the person of Jesus Christ (e.g., the Sacred Heart, the Holy Blood, the Divine Mercy), are also common objects of devotion.[6]

The roots of Catholic devotionalism as a lay parallel to the liturgy lie in the late medieval period, when what would be later known as Corpus Christi processions gave rise to the concept of "ocular communion." During the thirteenth century, the practice of parading the Blessed Sacrament in a monstrance outside the church building to bless onlookers and passersby became increasingly common, as it was believed that the Eucharist was so holy that merely looking upon it conferred blessings of grace. These parades were organized in response to a number of heretical groups, such as the Cathars and the Free Spirits, that denied the Real Presence in the Host. Infrequent Communion among the laity had also caused a withering of Eucharistic piety, and these proto–Corpus Christi processions allowed ordinary people to be blessed by the Blessed Sacrament, even if they did not feel they could physically partake of it. These same factors also led to the development of Benediction (i.e., services focused on a blessing by the Blessed Sacrament) and the Exposition of the Blessed Sacrament during the same time period, as churches left the Host on the altar so laypeople could look and be blessed by the Host while they attended Mass. The elevation of the Host, and later the chalice, during the Mass was also introduced as a way for laypeople to experience the "saving gaze" of ocular communion.

The assumption that lay participation in the Mass extended only to ocular communion was reflected and reinforced by subsequent architectural trends during the Counter-Reformation. High altars became thrones where Christ could either look down on the congregation in the monstrance or exude unseen authority from the tabernacle where the reserved Hosts were stored. Although the laity was supposed to unite their thoughts and intentions with those of the priest celebrating Mass, their collective attention was necessarily divided between adoring the physical presence of Christ in the monstrance as a tangible object of devotion and Christ's liturgical presence, which was largely inaccessible to them. Louis Bouyer argued that until the early twentieth century most lay Catholics thought that the liturgy was something to be performed, but not understood, not even by priests. While the laity could appreciate the splendor and theatricality of the Mass as a sort of grand royal court for Christ, there was no connection between the actual Communion of the priest at the altar and the ocular communion / visual participation of the congregation.[7]

Eucharistic devotions were controlled by the hierarchy, but some of the most popular devotions were disseminated by certain religious orders—the Jesuits promoted the Sacred Heart, the Dominicans had the rosary, and the Franciscans introduced the Stations of the Cross. Until the mid-nineteenth century, most devotions were very local in their scope, oftentimes found only in a single region, town, or even parish. These local devotions did not require literacy for participation, and they were spread through oral traditions and by the continual practices of successive generations of devotees. Carl Watkins claims that these community-based devotions "provided a range of preventive and remedial strategies ranging from processions, votive Masses and invocations of special saints to searches for signs in the weather and prognosticatory lotteries, all shaped to the needs of the immediate community." While "official Catholicism" was based on universal concepts like sacred Scripture, sacred tradition, the sacraments, canon law, and the Mass, "local Catholicism" was based on beliefs and practices specific to local conditions and experiences.[8]

During the nineteenth century, the Vatican sought to "Romanize" liturgical and devotional practices, that is, to make Catholic practices found in the city of Rome normative across the Roman Rite. While many aspects of Romanization were directly taken from local Roman customs, such as the use of the honorific "monsignor" and the adoption of cassocks as normative priestly attire, in other cases it simply meant that Rome had approved something for use throughout the universal Church, regardless of whether it had originated in Rome or not. The Romanization of Catholicism created the illusion of a global Church united under the authority of the pope and celebrating a common liturgy, but it also imposed a particular way of being Catholic onto localities that had their own, preexisting ways of being Catholic.[9]

The drive to Romanize Catholic practices stemmed from the rise of ultramontanism as a strategy for the Church to strengthen and consolidate its power, especially in its post-Counter-Reformation strongholds where its traditional authority was being challenged by industrialization and modernity. The reasoning behind pushing a Roman approach to lay spiritual life at the expense of local customs not only gave more power to the institutional Church but also promoted a more uniform concept of what Catholicism was vis-à-vis other worldviews. In the face of Protestantism, liberalism, and socialism, Roman devotions focused on uniquely Catholic concepts, such as the Sacred Heart, the Immaculate Heart, and the Blessed Sacrament, further differentiated Catholicism from other forms of Christianity and socialized lay Catholics into Tridentine ultramontane orthodoxy.[10]

The emergence of mass literacy and the rise of print culture not only facilitated the dissemination of Roman devotions throughout the world but also changed the ways in which lay Catholics embodied their devotions. Catholic devotional life began moving away from those that were based on oral traditions and communal practices and shifted toward those that could be written down in books and performed as individual prayers or meditations. Although reactionary popes such as Gregory XVI and Pius IX often complained about how the mass media disseminated anticlerical and anti-Catholic literature, this same industry was also responsible for the explosion in the sales of Catholic books for adult lay readers during the nineteenth century. In the United States, for example, improved printing technology and the growth of the common school movement in the Northeast meant that even recent immigrants could be expected to read and possess several volumes of Catholic prayer books and devotional literature.[11]

While the content of these prayer books differed from edition to edition, all of them shared the same general format: prayers for waking and going to bed, devotions to be said during Mass, prayers to be said before, during, and after receiving the Eucharist, prayers before eating, instructions for saying the rosary, and prayers for the sick and the dead. Taves notes that prayer books published after 1840 contained significantly more devotions than those published prior to that point. While this increase can be partially explained by the fact that it was much cheaper to print large prayer books after 1840 than in previous years, it was also due to the proliferation of indulgenced prayers and devotions, especially during the pontificate of Pope Pius IX. Compilers of prayer books dutifully translated and transcribed the new prayers and devotions and used their indulgenced status as selling points to prospective buyers. The increase in indulgenced prayers was also a tactic used by the Counter-Reformation papacy to assert more control over devotions in general, especially those that were perceived to be too "superstitious" or of dubious provenance. Attaching an indulgence to a prayer was a not-so-subtle way of steering the laity away from local devotions and toward "universal devotions" containing papal imprimaturs.[12]

Prayer books also contained "devotions for Mass," which were prayers for the users to silently recite while the priest celebrated the Mass. However, the push among some advocates of the Liturgical Movement for hand missals in the early twentieth century caused many later editions to include translations of the Mass rubrics. Intelligent lay participation as defined by nineteenth- and early to mid-twentieth-century prayer books consisted of having a general idea of what the priest was doing, especially during the Offertory, Consecration, and Communion, and uniting one's intention with that of the celebrant. For example, *My Pocket Prayerbook* from 1922 contained a section titled "A Devout Method of Hearing Mass," which lists prayers to be said for each of the specific points in the Mass. These prayers did not correspond to what the priest read in his missal but were instead intended to create a prayerful mood that corresponded to the priest's own intentions as he offered Mass. However, until the liturgical changes caused by Vatican II were enacted in the 1960s, reciting the rosary remained the most common lay activity during the Mass, especially among women. The centrality of the rosary to lay Catholics is attested by the fact that the most famous Marian apparitions of the pre–Vatican II period, such as Lourdes and Fatima, had much to say about the necessity of saying the rosary and barely anything about the Mass or the Eucharist.[13]

In this devotional-centric model of Catholic piety, the Mass was tangential, rather than central, to the spiritual lives of lay Catholics. At best, the Mass was background noise for individuals saying the rosary or other prayers, and at its lowest, it was little more than a magical ceremony that had little relevance for the audience witnessing it. The average Catholic parish had become a gathering place for individual prayer, rather than a congregation united in communal worship. Given how alienated average Catholics were from the Mass, it should not be surprising that devotions were the primary vehicle that shaped how they thought about and embodied their faith. It was for this reason that many members of the hierarchy were hesitant to encourage a more Mass-centric faith among the masses, since de-emphasizing devotions would be akin to destroying Catholicism as many people understood it.[14]

Nevertheless, the Liturgical Movement arose in the early twentieth century to restore the liturgy to its place as "the source and summit of

Christian life" by enabling the laity to be "intelligent participants" at Mass. Like most trends in the Catholic Church, the Liturgical Movement had its origins among a group of reform-oriented clerics in the nineteenth century who had become dissatisfied not only with the devotional-based spirituality of lay Catholics but with the state of Catholic liturgy in general. Chief among these reformers was Dom Prosper Guéranger (1805–1875), a French diocesan priest. Guéranger's work was largely theoretical, focusing on the restoration of "pure Gregorian chant" and the reopening of the monastery of Solesmes, which had been closed during the French Revolution. Guéranger envisioned that Solesmes would become the epicenter of Catholic renewal in post-revolutionary France, especially in terms of propagating the "correct" version of the Roman Rite that was free of the errors that he believed had crept into the French liturgy via the influence of Gallicanism and Jansenism. The rites and rituals performed by the bishop of Rome would be used as the model for liturgical norms, rather than local customs or tastes. Modern scholarship has invalidated many of Guéranger's findings, such as his belief in a singular "pristine" medieval liturgy and his dismissal of the liturgies of the Eastern Rite Churches as aberrations in need of Romanization. Despite these shortcomings, Guéranger's work inspired the development of modern liturgical studies and persuaded Catholic thinkers to envision how a liturgy-centric Catholicism might look. Although Guéranger's reforms were designed specifically for those in the clerical and monastic life, his ideas spread far beyond the cloister.[15]

The most important individual to be influenced by Guéranger's ideas was Pope Pius X (1835–1914), whose reign was marked not only by his doctrinal and theological conservatism but also by his commitment to increasing liturgical piety and literacy among the laity. For Pius X, "active participation" for the lay Catholic during Mass consisted of the laity and priest being united in the singing of Gregorian chant (which he believed to be the most reverent form of music for Catholic worship) "so that the faithful may again take a more active part in the ecclesiastical offices, as was the case in ancient times." As a young parish priest, Pius X had successfully taught his congregations how to sing Gregorian chant, and these experiences convinced him of the necessity and possibility of having a schola in every parish. To achieve this end, he encouraged seminaries to have classes in Gregorian chant so priests could learn how to sing it properly and in turn teach their congregations. Not surprisingly, this goal was never achieved in the pre–Vatican II period.

After becoming pope, Pius X outlined his vision for the liturgy in his 1903 motu proprio, *Tra Le Sollecitudini*. The document stated, "In order to restore the true Christian spirit the faithful must be brought back to the first and indispensable source of that spirit, the active participation of the faithful in the holy mysteries and in the public and solemn prayer of the Church." However, Pius X's understanding of what constituted "active participation" was very conservative; he did not think the laity needed to understand exactly what they were singing, as he believed it was more important for them to embody the spirit of the liturgy rather than dwell upon the meaning of specific words. Furthermore, *Tra Le Sollecitudini* banned women from singing in church choirs, as Pius X considered scholas to have a quasi-clerical function. Despite Pius X's reputation for theological and political conservatism, his vision of a singing, liturgy-centric parish was in many ways progressive for the time, and his endorsement of "active participation" would inspire the Liturgical Movement for decades to come.[16]

The point at which the Liturgical Movement transitioned from clerical intellectual current to popular movement is usually attributed to the Liturgical Week held during the 1914 Holy Week at Maria Laach Abbey in Germany, the first such event that was open to the laity. Would-be lay intellectuals in the professions and academia left Maria Laach with an interest in promoting "intelligent lay participation," and soon scholarly and popular publications on the liturgy began proliferating in Catholic Europe. The Liturgical Movement came to the United States with the establishment of *Orate Frates*, a magazine founded by Dom Virgil Michel of St. John's Abbey in Collegeville, Minnesota, in 1925. *Orate Frates* contained a mix of articles about liturgical theory and reports about experiments in "active participation" in the United States and abroad.[17]

One way liturgical reformers hoped to get the laity "intelligently involved" in the Mass was through the proliferation of lay missals, books that detailed the rubrics of the Mass and provided translations of the priest's Latin prayers in vernacular languages. Missals for the laity were a new innovation at the time because the Catholic Church had banned translations of the prayers of the missal into vernacular until the mid-nineteenth century. The earliest mention of a lay missal that the author was able to find was from an 1846 edition of the *Dublin Review*, in which a brief review of *The Missal for the Laity*, published by Derby Press, is provided in the "Notices of Books" section. Interestingly, while the anonymous reviewer states that the missal "will be a treasure to all classes" and a useful reference for learning the deeper meaning behind the rubrics of the Mass, he does not wish for it to replace more traditional devotional prayer books at Mass, perhaps because he was cognizant of the importance of such devotions in the spiritual lives of the laity.[18]

It is not clear when or why the Catholic hierarchy authorized translations of the missal, but by the early 1920s there were at least two lay missals available in the American marketplace. Over the next three decades, sales and use proved brisk. One of the two initial missals, *My Sunday Missal* by Rev. Joseph Stedman, sold three million copies in less than three years, evidence of a hunger among many American Catholics to better understand the Mass. During World War II, over three million missals of varying editions were distributed to members of the armed forces by Catholic chaplains. So not owning a personal missal would not be an impediment to understanding the Mass, Rev. Paul Bussard edited and distributed *The Leaflet Missal*, small booklets with translations of the prayers and explanations of the rubrics, to parishes across the United States. Still, the use of lay missals was not considered to be an ideal situation for proponents of the Liturgical Movement since it was regarded as trading in one set of private devotions for another. Reformers believed that if the laity at least understood what was going on during the Mass, they would desire to have a greater role in the liturgy.[19]

The Liturgical Movement's insistence on "intelligent participation" at the Mass to the exclusion of traditional prayers and devotions was controversial among many members of the Catholic hierarchy. Many believed the concept placed lofty expectations onto the laity—especially for poor, illiterate Catholics—that they could not possibly achieve. No less an authority than Pope Pius XII echoed these concerns in his 1947 encyclical *Mediator Dei*:

> Many of the faithful are unable to use the Roman missal even though it is written in the vernacular; nor are all capable of understanding correctly

the liturgical rites and formulas. So varied and diverse are men's talents and characters that it is impossible for all to be moved and attracted to the same extent by community prayers, hymns and liturgical services. Moreover, the needs and inclinations of all are not the same, nor are they always constant in the same individual. Who, then, would say, on account of such a prejudice, that all these Christians cannot participate in the Mass nor share its fruits? On the contrary, they can adopt some other method which proves easier for certain people; for instance, they can lovingly meditate on the mysteries of Jesus Christ or perform other exercises of piety or recite prayers which, though they differ from the sacred rites, are still essentially in harmony with them.[20]

However, Pius XII would eventually authorize a number of changes in keeping with the aims of the Liturgical Movement, including the establishment of an official Vatican commission on liturgy in 1948 and easing the rules on the Eucharistic fast so more people could partake of Holy Communion. He was also responsible for an extensive reform of the Holy Week liturgy, including the addition of a foot washing ceremony on Maundy Thursday, the inclusion of a Communion service on Good Friday, and the restoration of the Easter Vigil to the evening of Holy Saturday rather than the morning.[21]

Pius XII was not the only highly ranked church official to have doubts about the necessity of lay missals and the "intelligent participation" of the laity during the Mass. Roughly ten years earlier, in 1937, Monsignor Johannes Maria Gföllner, bishop of Linz, Germany, denounced the Liturgical Movement's desire to end the common lay practice of reciting the rosary during Mass, invoking Pope Leo XIII's endorsement of the activity. Liturgical experiments performed by the more radical liturgical reformers, such as saying Mass in the vernacular and moving the altar *pro populo* (i.e., facing the congregation), practices that would become the norm after Vatican II, caused the conservative German bishops to sour on the entirety of the Liturgical Movement. The controversy over liturgical reform in World War II–era Germany was so bitter that the German bishops ended up taking over the leadership of the Liturgical Movement to ensure that any reforms would originate from within their ranks.[22]

Another reason for the Catholic hierarchy's hesitancy about accepting the Liturgical Movement was that it had implications for the social and political order. Although it helped to develop the field of liturgical studies and spearheaded the Gregorian revival, the aesthetical aspects of the liturgy, such as church architecture, vestment design, or even music, were tangential to the concerns of the Liturgical Movement. Rather, the primary interest of the Liturgical Movement was the renewal of Christian life through the liturgy, which would inspire Christians to engage in practical social engagement to construct "the Kingdom of God." A liturgy marked by full participation would emphasize the common humanity of everyone involved as they profess the great truths of the Christian faith (i.e., ecumenism). The liturgy should not consist of mere rubrics to be followed or a place to perform private devotions, but it should rather be a dynamic ritual "which taught the individual faithful (of any age) to live as a Christian in the world and, secondly, formed these same faithful into a corporate identity through sacramental and liturgical participation in the Mystical Body of Christ." For proponents of the Liturgical Movement, the liturgy should be a place for the "intellectual and sacramental formation" of socially engaged Catholics for the modern era.[23]

The social aspect of the Liturgical Movement was particularly discernable in its American iteration, especially in *Orate Frates*, a publication started by Benedictine monk Dom Virgil Michel in 1926. *Orate Frates* was founded during the interwar period, a time characterized by the rise of fascism, economic uncertainty, and the seeming inadequacy of liberal democracy to resolve deep-seated societal issues. For Dom Virgil Michel, the doctrine of the Mystical Body of Christ as embodied by the liturgy could address the social and political malaise of Western life in a way that secular ideologies such as fascism, communism, and laissez-faire capitalism could not. He wrote that the nationalist was interested only in individuals who were part of the "racial community" and the capitalist humanitarian helped others as a means of self-aggrandizement, but the Mystical Body of Christ indicated that only loving others for God's sake could create true brotherhood.[24] According to Katherine Harmon, "Liturgical movement advocates argued that the human condition was social and humans had a responsibility for the welfare of those around them, and that this social premise found its theological and spiritual formation in the person of Jesus Christ. Active participation in Christ's Mystical Body on earth, or Catholic Action, was most radically realized in the corporate worship of the church, especially the Mass." The Mass empowered the individual to be a receptacle of grace, while uniting them in solidarity with the rest of the Church Militant. After Mass ended, these regenerated individuals would be ready to reconstruct society according to Catholic social teachings because they understood how the teachings of the liturgy needed to be applied to every aspect of life.[25]

The implications of the Liturgical Movement and social engagement were best articulated in the Catholic Worker Movement, founded by Dorothy Day and Peter Maurin, which combined a radical personalist philosophy with anticapitalistic, pacifist, and interracialist politics. Day and Maurin were both inspired by the works of Dom Virgil Michel, especially his emphasis on the unity between liturgical action and social action. Day believed that liturgical prayer was the antithesis of private prayer and the individualistic spirit that was characteristic of liberal democratic societies. According to Day, when Catholics participated in the Mass (as opposed to reciting private devotions),

> When we pray with Christ (not to Him) we realize Christ as our Brother. We think of all men as our brothers then, as members of the Mystical Body of Christ. "We are all members, one of another," and, remembering this, we can never be indifferent to the social miseries and evils of the day. The dogma of the Mystical Body has tremendous social implications.
>
> All the work of the Campion Propaganda Committee [a bookstore owned by Catholic Workers in St. Louis, Missouri], its study and its activities against extreme nationalism, against racial hatreds, against social injustice has its basis in an understanding of the liturgical movement and a participation in it.[26]

The ethos and praxis of the Catholic Worker Movement was to combat the individual and structural ills of the day with the vast repository of Catholic spiritual practices: the Benedictine emphasis on work and prayer contra the "Protestant work ethic," the poverty of St. Francis as a response to consumerism and materialism, the works of mercy as an antidote to the class war, and the liturgy to rebuke the atheism of the modern world. The direct action of the Catholic Workers against racism, war, and the exploitation of labor was part of a larger mission to remake society according to Catholic social principles, with the liturgy as its foundation.[27]

The success of the Liturgical Movement before Vatican II, then, was decidedly mixed. The dissemination of missals helped lay Catholics understand what was happening during the Mass, but missal ownership became an end unto itself, rather than a catalyst to enhancing lay participation, as Liturgical Movement proponents had hoped. When the average American Catholic thought about the Liturgical Movement at all, they tended to assume its objective was popularizing Gregorian chant or bringing back medieval vestments, according to liturgical reformer Ernest Koenker. Despite the efforts of liturgical reform advocates to educate the laity on the possibility of renewing self and society through participating in the liturgy, performing private devotions during Mass was still the norm in American Catholic parishes until the late 1960s. Writing shortly after the Council had ended, Koenker said, "The inattention in the majority of parishes, the use of manuals of prayer during the Mass, the recitation of the rosary—these conditions are appalling. How many offer more than the minimum of 'implicit attention' during Mass? Lethargic and elderly people cannot learn to use the missal, it is perhaps true. It has been through the insistence of the Liturgical Renaissance that this rift in piety has been made apparent and is presented as a vital issue."[28] The Liturgical Movement's goal for "intelligent participation" in the Mass was an ideal that was never realized in the pre–Vatican II era, as the clergy and laity regarded devotionalism as the traditional and default form of lay Catholicism, a situation that would change only after the reforms to the Roman Rite wrought by Vatican II were enacted in the late 1960s.

If the results of the Liturgical Movement at the popular level were mixed, it made a much bigger impression in clerical and scholarly circles. This was reflected in the work of the preparatory commission on the liturgy that Pope John XXIII formed in early 1962, just prior to the opening of the council, to study questions related to liturgical reform. The consensus of the preparatory commission was that Latin should retain its place of primacy for the training and prayers of the clergy, while the languages of the people would be used only during unspecified occasions. Still, the suggestion that vernacular tongues had any place in the liturgy outraged the group's more conservative members. For example,

Monsignor Ignio Anglés Pamiés, dean of the Pontifical Institute of Sacred Music and the head of the commission, deliberately sabotaged the work of the group he was supposed to be chairing because it was "the number one enemy of Latin." Of particular concern to Anglés Pamiés was the possibility of congregational singing during the Mass, which he felt threatened the body of sacred music that had been composed throughout the centuries with the choir, not the congregation, in mind. Rita Ferrone notes that there was not yet an equivalent of Catholic traditionalism or any kind of organized opposition to liturgical reform in 1962. However, the fact that the possibility of using the vernacular in the liturgy was up for debate at all indicated to conservatives that the concept of extensive liturgical reform was moving out of the academy and niche liturgical subcultures and toward institutionalized practice. By the end of the 1960s, the changes in the Roman Rite—the replacement of Latin by vernacular languages, the use of nontraditional musical styles, and the decline of popular devotions—would go beyond what even the most radical liturgical reformers in the 1950s could have imagined.[29]

Paul J. Hallinan and Sacrosanctum Concilium

On October 20, 1962, Hallinan was elected as the North American representative for the Liturgical Commission by a large majority, and he attended the first meeting the following day. In many ways, Hallinan was an unusual choice for the Liturgical Commission; at fifty-one, he was the youngest archbishop in the American contingent, and he had been a member of the hierarchy for only five years. His Latin skills were poor, and he tried to keep up with the verbose speeches given by the other Liturgical Commission members by focusing on the endings of nouns and verbs. Hallinan had a limited understanding of the more esoteric aspects of liturgical studies and relied on Fr. Frederick McManus, a close personal friend and *peritus* during the council, for guidance. Despite these shortcomings, especially in terms of language, Hallinan proved to be adept at maneuvering the international and interpersonal politics that dominated the workings of the council behind the scenes.[30]

Most significant in terms of the final outcome of the Liturgical Commission, Hallinan's clerical background as a Newman Club chaplain and as the archbishop of an area where Catholics constituted less than 5 percent of the population gave him a unique perspective about the relationship between the laity, the Mass, and wider society. His work with the Newman Clubs during the immediate postwar period convinced him of the need for the Mass to be more understandable to the average Catholic. He believed that the organization's primary function should be to provide college-level religious education for university students attending secular institutions, rather than having them be social clubs for students to find a prospective Catholic spouse. During Hallinan's tenure as head of Cleveland College's Newman Hall, he sponsored apologetic lectures, semester-long courses on moral theology, advanced lectures on scholastic and modern philosophy, and study groups about the works of John Henry Newman. Hallinan viewed the Newman Clubs not as Catholic ghettoes in the midst of secular universities but as training grounds to produce well-informed Catholics who could respond to the questions and criticisms levied against the Church by Protestants and atheists.[31]

Shortly after becoming bishop of Charleston, Hallinan formed a liturgical committee to help improve the quality and extent of lay participation in the Mass. He invited noted liturgical experts, such as close friend Fr. Frederick McManus and Fr. Godfrey Diekmann, to speak at diocesan clerical conferences. Hallinan also organized several well-attended outdoor Dialogue Masses in Latin to demonstrate the possibilities of "intelligent lay participation." Although he would later become a vocal advocate for Mass in the vernacular during Vatican II, Hallinan's liturgical views during his time in Charleston appear to have been cautiously conservative; according to Thomas J. Shelley, he opened the first meeting of his liturgical committee by stating his support for traditional lay devotions at Mass: "These practices of piety are not to be changed or discontinued, but they must be influenced by the spirit and principles of the liturgy." At this point, Hallinan seems to have thought that the practice of lay devotions during Mass could be reformed to make them more in line with the Eucharistic spirit expressed by the liturgy itself. Once Hallinan was on the Council's Liturgical Commission, his views on the liturgy would become significantly more radical.[32]

Hallinan's liturgical activities during his first year in Atlanta appear to have been minimal, presumably because the issue of Catholic school desegregation absorbed the bulk of his attention, but they became one of his main priorities once Vatican II began. Although he did not view himself as being particularly "progressive" prior to his arrival in Rome, he was quickly won over to the progressive cause after being exposed to new ideas and possibilities from his brother bishops from across the globe, especially those from the self-identified reform camp (*aggiornamento*) that originated from the countries bordering the Rhine: France, Belgium, the Netherlands, Austria, the two Germanys, and Switzerland. This was not an unusual occurrence, as many of the American Council Fathers experienced similar epiphanies during the council. The ghetto mentality and knee-jerk ultramontane of pre–Vatican II American Catholicism kept the members of the hierarchy from the United States ignorant of the theological and liturgical developments that were occurring among the more daring European prelates and theologians. Although some members of the American contingent, most notably Cardinal Francis Spellman of New York, remained opposed to changes in the status quo, for others like Hallinan, exposure to Continental ecclesiastical trends was an exhilarating and eye-opening experience.[33]

The writing of *Sacrosanctum Concilium* unfolded in two stages, first in the Liturgical Commission, where the appointed committee members composed the basic outline of the document, and later on the council floor, where the particulars were clarified by all of the bishops in general and plenary sessions. The floor debates on *Sacrosanctum Concilium* began on October 22, 1962, continued until November 14, 1962, and consisted of "fifty hours of debate, 387 oral interventions, and 297 interventions submitted in writing." Early in the negotiation process, Hallinan was dismayed that Cardinal Francis Spellman, the de facto leader of the American contingent, and Cardinal James Francis McIntyre of Los Angeles voiced their opposition to vernacular liturgies in particular and approving the schema on increasing lay participation (chapter 2) in general. In response, Hallinan gave an intervention of his own on October 31, 1962, in which he urged the council to approve the schema in question.[34]

Hallinan's intervention weaved together the insights he had gained as a Newman Club chaplain on secular campuses and as a bishop in the Protestant supermajority American South, along with the new ideas about *aggiornamento* he had absorbed at the council. He began by alluding to Spellman and McIntyre's opposition to liturgical change by emphasizing that he spoke for most but not all of the American bishops when he stated his desire for a more participatory role in the Mass. The problem with Catholics in general and American Catholics in particular was "an excessive spirit of individualism" that was reinforced by the practice of performing individual devotions during the Mass. The individualism and atomization of devotions was contrasted by the public character of the Church's public prayer, the liturgy. However, the liturgy could not be public until the laity could truly understand and take part in it. Catholics, lay and clerics, should be united with the whole Church with Christ as its head, not engaged in private devotions as isolated individuals.

Hallinan also argued that a more accessible, streamlined liturgy would also facilitate "Church Unity" (i.e., the conversion of Protestants to Catholicism) by making the Mass more understandable to "separated brethren" from other Christian traditions. As a Catholic prelate in an archdiocese where Catholics constituted barely 2 percent of the population and low church Protestantism was the default form of Christianity, Hallinan felt that the Tridentine Latin Mass was of limited comprehensibility to those who were not "equipped by learning or formed by habit." A reformed liturgy stripped of unnecessary medieval trappings and more reflective of the Scriptures would open new avenues for communication among the "separated brethren." Common prayer in a common language between the people, whether inside or outside of the Church, was the first step toward Church Unity.[35]

At a press conference held immediately after his intervention, Hallinan further elaborated upon his vision for how liturgical renewal would manifest itself at the grassroots level. The very publicness of the liturgy was an antidote to both the extreme individualism that characterized modern life as well as the assertion that religion was a private matter that had nothing to do with any other aspect of life. As the Church's public worship, the liturgy had a pedagogical function that could enable it to make complex doctrinal issues comprehensible to the masses, assuming the liturgy was in a form intelligible to the average lay Catholic. Hallinan admitted that the progress of the Liturgical Movement in the United States was slow compared to that of its Continental counterparts, yet there were encouraging signs that the laity wanted a more robust role in the life of the Church, including "the deepening interest in spiritual retreats and reading and contemplation and especially in the self-evaluation that is going on in Catholic educational, cultural, and welfare circles." While there would still be a place for the traditional devotions in Catholic life, what Hallinan called "the public concept of the Mass and Sacraments" demanded that all Catholics, regardless of their state in life, enter into a fuller Christian life as members of the Mystical Body of Christ.[36]

While he was in Rome, Hallinan sent missives back to Georgia about the proceedings of the council and how the reforms would manifest themselves in the parish setting. These writings included pastoral letters, columns in the *Georgia Bulletin*, and a booklet titled "How to Understand Changes in the Liturgy." Upon returning to Atlanta after the first session of Vatican II ended in December 1962, Hallinan created a diocesan liturgical committee that controlled the pace and nature of liturgical changes in a top-down, uniform fashion. Despite his enthusiasm for liturgical reform, he remained fundamentally conservative in his approach to changes in the Mass; he expected that liturgical experimentation would be micromanaged by the clergy, not organically developed among the laity. Hallinan's vision for a reformed, post–Vatican II Roman Rite liturgy was of one that was still uniform across racial and cultural lines and reflective of Eurocentric aesthetic tastes.[37]

Hallinan's commitment to advancing a renewed yet somehow traditional liturgy was tested when he became the chairman of the Bishops' Commission on the Liturgical Apostolate (later called the Bishops' Commission on the Liturgy), shortly after the end of Vatican II's second session in 1966. Although Hallinan was considered a progressive by the standards of his fellow Council Fathers, he discovered upon returning to the United States that there were radicals who wanted to engage in liturgical experiments that were far more sweeping than what he had envisioned. Unlike many of the American bishops, who considered liturgical experiments to be irreverent at best and anarchical at worst, Hallinan was not opposed to liturgical experimentation per se, but he believed that such innovations needed to occur with the guidance and permission of the hierarchy. He urged—to no avail—that his brother bishops petition the Consilium ad Exsequendam Constitutionem, the liturgical commission Pope Paul VI established in February 1964, for permission to form "controlled communities" where liturgical experimentation could occur under the supervision of the local ordinary. Hallinan's second request for officially sanctioned liturgical laboratories was rejected in January 1968. Three weeks later, Hallinan died of hepatitis and diabetes at the archbishop's mansion in Atlanta.[38]

Liturgical Renewal at Our Lady of Lourdes

The liturgical changes ushered in by Vatican II were gradually phased into the Mass at Our Lady of Lourdes, as was the case at parishes all over the United States. Our Lady of Lourdes had had dialogue Masses sporadically during the early 1960s, but these were still within the rubrics of the Tridentine Latin Mass. The first change occurred on March 1, 1964, when Fr. Michael McKeever, the priest of Our Lady of Lourdes, celebrated the Mass *pro populo* (i.e., facing the congregation) rather than *ad orientum* (i.e., facing the High Altar). According to the SBS annals, "The

Figure 4.1. Fr. Michael McKeever at the new wooden altar he constructed himself for Our Lady of Lourdes to be used for Mass under the new liturgy set by the Second Vatican Council (Vatican II), 1964. Annabella Jones Collection, Office of Archives and Records, Roman Catholic Archdiocese of Atlanta.

Congregation seemed to like it, if we can judge by the intense concentration, and Father McKeever liked it very much." Mass in English was first introduced to the Archdiocese of Atlanta during a Liturgical Conference that was held from October 22 to 25, 1964, at the Cathedral of Christ the King. The first English Mass was said at Our Lady of Lourdes about a month later on November 29, 1964. The annals describe the event as follows: "At last we have the Mass in English. The people of the parish had been prepared gradually for the transition. Both Father McKeever and Father Calhoun are enthusiastic about the changes. Father McKeever had invited Father MacDonough (our confessor) to sing a High Mass to celebrate the new liturgy. The congregation had been taught the new English Mass by Father Calhoun so everyone participated." There is no mention in the annals of what happened when the Missal of Paul VI completely replaced the Tridentine Latin Mass in 1969, presumably because the previous changes overshadowed missal changes that would not have been immediately obvious to non-clerics.[39]

As the SBS annals indicate, the changes in the Mass were generally received well by the laity at Our Lady of Lourdes. In an interview conducted by Andrew S. Moore, Our Lady of Lourdes parishioner Janis Griffin recalled how she became involved with the folk Mass movement when she was a college student at Howard University's Newman Center. Upon returning to Atlanta in 1967, Griffin wanted to bring the folk Mass format to Our Lady of Lourdes, but she discovered that the only instrument at the parish was still the organ and there was considerable resistance to the concept of guitars in the sanctuary. However, Griffin and several other folk Mass proponents were persistent, and they were allowed to play guitar during the Saturday Mass. Sandra Criddell recalled that one woman was so outraged by the liturgical changes that she switched her membership to Sacred Heart, which still offered a Latin Mass at the time. However, after the initial liturgical paradigm shift at Our Lady of Lourdes in the late 1960s, there does not seem to have been any major dissension about the meaning of Vatican II at the parish.[40]

The brief controversy at Our Lady of Lourdes about guitar music illustrates how music, not language, would become the most contentious liturgical issue in the post–Vatican II era. *Sacrosanctum Concilium* did not specify what kind of music should be used during the liturgy, only that it should be "God oriented" and create a reverent atmosphere for worshippers. While the document reinforced Gregorian chant's status as the best form of music for the Roman Rite, *Sacrosanctum Concilium* also stated that "other kinds of sacred music, especially polyphony, are by no means excluded from liturgical celebrations, so long as they accord with the spirit of the liturgical action." Similarly, the organ retained its preeminent status in *Sacrosanctum Concilium* as "the traditional musical instrument which adds a wonderful splendor to the Church's ceremonies," but "other instruments also may be admitted for use in divine worship, with the knowledge and consent of the competent territorial authority." The document added that instruments could be used in the liturgy only if they were "suitable" or had the potential to be "made suitable," but it failed to elaborate on what the difference between "suitable" and "unsuitable" instruments was.[41]

Another problem was the Catholic Church as a whole had abandoned congregational singing to the Protestants in the wake of the Counter-Reformation, which meant that there was little preexisting music in the Catholic tradition that could be sung by the laity. Prior to Vatican II, Liturgical Movement members had advocated for teaching laypeople Gregorian chant as a way to resurrect congregational singing at the parish level within the context of the Catholic musical patrimony. When Mass in the vernacular and congregational singing became the norm during the mid-1960s, priests and liturgists suddenly had to fill a musical void.[42]

This confusion about what constituted sacred music at the parish level in post–Vatican II Catholicism is reflected in a 1968 letter from Joseph Bernardin, then the auxiliary bishop of Atlanta, to Fr. John J. Mulroy, the pastor of Sacred Heart about the archdiocesan Music Commission. Bernardin said that his travels throughout the Archdiocese of Atlanta indicated "that our music needs much improvement." He recognized not only that there were "a number of very valid and meaningful musical forms," but also that "this will normally mean the use of different forms for different groups." In this instance, Bernardin was specifically referring to folk music played on guitars, but he stressed that "it would be wrong . . . to give the impression that this is the only type which really fits the renewed liturgy and to emphasize it unduly." However, he did not elaborate on which other music styles would be appropriate for the liturgy or which demographics said music would attract. Bernardin ended the letter by stating that the new emphasis on congregational singing should not be used as an excuse to neglect the choirs, noting that Protestants seemed to have been successful in balancing the roles of the choir and the congregation. The sentiments expressed in Bernardin's letter are a microcosm of the conflicting feelings many Catholics experienced in the post–Vatican II period—discontent about the state of liturgical music, coupled with confusion about what would constitute an improvement.[43]

By the early 1970s, the guitar Mass format seems to have become the default liturgical format at Our Lady of Lourdes. An undated article from the early 1970s titled "Lourdes on the Move since Vatican II" provides some insight on how liturgical change affected Our Lady of Lourdes immediately after the council. Guitar masses, led by head priest Fr. Matthew Kemp, appear to have been the norm during this period, as was the case in many parishes across the United States.[44] Another article from *SBS News and Views* from January 1972 provides more details about Our Lady of Lourdes's liturgy during this time: "Men and women lectors are splendid and read with a dignity that is edifying. Parents, who were a bit retiring or shy, now serve on committees or the school board and offer great hope as they meet problems. Baptisms are conducted within the Eucharistic worship and all parish members welcome the newly baptized with a round of applause."[45] These articles suggest that the Liturgical Movement's goal for "intelligent lay participation" in all facets of liturgical life had been accomplished quickly at Our Lady of Lourdes. This process led to a slightly more egalitarian command structure, as some duties that had been the sole responsibility of priests and sisters were now delegated to lay members (e.g., performing the readings during Mass, serving on parish council boards, planning the shape of liturgical celebrations). While a softening of authoritarianism was not the intention of liturgical reformers, increasing lay participation in the liturgy at the parish helped to bolster the Vatican II concept of the Church as the "People of God."[46]

Our Lady of Lourdes experimented with Home Masses and guitar music during Mass like many parishes did post–Vatican II, but it does not appear to have engaged in the more extreme forms of liturgical experimentation that sometimes occurred during that time, such as the "Beatles Mass" former priest Matthew Fox recalls attending in the Netherlands. But neither did the immediate post–Vatican II liturgy at Our Lady of Lourdes have any characteristics that distinguished it from the majority-white parishes in the archdiocese. To many Our Lady of Lourdes parishioners, the music of the "New Mass" was not Black but also not immediately identifiable as traditionally Catholic. Guitar masses may not have been a source of perpetual conflict at Our Lady of Lourdes, but neither were they a point of pride or inspiration.[47]

The glue that held Our Lady of Lourdes together during its period of contraction that lasted from the late 1960s until the early 1990s was the commitment that its members had to each other and their community. However, the dwindling size of its congregation meant that it struggled to pay its bills and maintain its existing property. A crucial part of this community was the SBS, which had founded the parish and staffed the school since 1912 and also acted as a bridge between Atlanta's Black Catholics and the larger white Catholic community. However, after the conclusion of the 1973-74 academic year, the SBS withdrew from Our Lady of Lourdes School, causing further distress to a parish that was already suffering from demographic and financial distress.[48]

5

The Withdrawal of the Sisters of the Blessed Sacrament from Our Lady of Lourdes

The demographic changes to the Auburn Avenue neighborhood that led to a decrease in Our Lady of Lourdes's membership also negatively impacted the parish's school. The school's enrollment plummeted from 370 students in 1960 to 189 by 1973. Furthermore, most of the students traveled to school via car or bus, meaning they did not live in the immediate Auburn Avenue area. Of those students who remained, less than a third were Catholic, and even fewer students attended Sunday Mass at

Figure 5.1. Faculty at Our Lady of Lourdes School. Left to far right: Mrs. Dyer, Mother Sheila, S.B.S., Sister P. Thomas, S.B.S., Sister Lucy, S.B.S., Sister Marianna, S.B.S., and Mrs. Adele Summerhour, 1955. Annabella Jones Collection, Office of Archives and Records, Roman Catholic Archdiocese of Atlanta.

Our Lady of Lourdes. Faced with a social, political, and religious landscape that was very different from when the school and parish were founded some sixty years earlier, the SBS questioned whether they were making a difference among Atlanta's Black poor. The order ultimately decided to withdraw from Our Lady of Lourdes School at the end of the 1973–74 academic year to refocus their efforts on other apostolates.

The withdrawal of the Sisters of the Blessed Sacrament from Our Lady of Lourdes School was another blow to the parish community during an already tumultuous post–Vatican II / post–Civil Rights Movement, leading to a time of contraction and uncertainty. To a certain extent, the decision for the SBS to leave Our Lady of Lourdes was illustrative of larger trends in American Catholicism, such as a precipitous drop in the number of teaching sisters after Vatican II, religious and priestly orders reevaluating their charism in light of the council's demand for the renewal of religious life, and the insolvency of the parish school model. What distinguished the withdrawal of the SBS from Our Lady of Lourdes from other instances in the late 1960s and early 1970s of teaching sisters abandoning some of their schools to realign their resources elsewhere was the unique charism of the order and the relationship between Atlanta's Black community and the sisters that had developed since the founding of the parish in 1911.

The Crisis of American Catholic Schools

When Fr. Ignatius Lissner of the Society of African Missions (SAM) helped to establish Our Lady of Lourdes in the early twentieth century, he did so with the belief that "a church without a school is like a family without children."[1] This assumption was based in the parish school model of Catholic education that flourished within American Catholicism from the late nineteenth century until the mid-twentieth. There had been Catholic schools in the United States since the colonial period, but it was not until the Third Plenary Council of Baltimore of 1884 that the American hierarchy mandated that every Catholic child should attend a Catholic school under pain of mortal sin. This decree was a response to endemic anti-Catholic sentiment in the public schools, which included mandatory Protestant catechism classes, compulsory Bible readings from the King James Version, and anti-Catholic sentiments presented as fact in textbooks and lessons. Catholic parents and prelates rightly saw these as attempts to undermine the religious values their children were learning at home and in the Church. Thus, the bishops and archbishops decided to build a network of private religious schools that they believed would be equal if not superior to the offerings of the public schools, from both academic and moral standpoints.[2]

To ensure that every Catholic child had a Catholic school to attend, the Third Plenary Council ordered each parish in the United States to have a grammar school, staffed by teaching sisters, attached to it. The American hierarchy considered women religious to be the ideal teachers for these schools, not just because they were believed to have superior morals but also because teaching sisters could be paid considerably less than their lay counterparts, which in turn kept tuition low. Parish schools were financed entirely by whatever was received in the Sunday collection, although some parents tithed a certain amount of their income in lieu of tuition. Since each parish school was financially dependent on whatever funds the congregation could donate, they were heavily reliant on the labor and sacrifices of the teaching sisters for their day-to-day operations. The fact that each sister received only a monthly stipend of approximately fifty dollars and no health or retirement benefits kept operating costs and tuition low for the parish that administered the school in question.[3]

The push to build a corresponding school for every parish in the United States created a demand for teaching sisters that far outstripped the supply that the convents could produce, which was reflected in the dubious quality of many of the teaching sisters. The brief period of formation the novices experienced at the motherhouse (about two or three years) emphasized the cultivation of religious vocations, not pedagogical training. Particular attention was paid to socializing novices into the particular customs of their order, teaching them how to live in the community and how to structure their lives according to the monastic schedule of communal prayer. When this initial period of religious formation ended, the novices were assigned to a school, where they learned how to teach from an experienced sister-teacher in a sort of master-apprentice relationship.

The apprenticeship model of sister-teacher formation was popular because it allowed motherhouses to deploy teachers quickly to the continuous expanding network of parochial schools, but it meant having young women barely out of their teens with no teacher training in charge of classrooms consisting of dozens of children. The hierarchy and the heads of religious teaching orders themselves worked to improve the quality of teacher training through a variety of initiatives: holding summer teaching institutes and encouraging the sisters to seek college degrees and obtain teaching licenses. However, there was an inherent contradiction between the need to have as many sisters as possible in Catholic school classrooms and the desire to have said sisters be as qualified as their secular counterparts since increased teacher training meant delaying when new teaching sisters could be deployed to a school.[4]

The continuous need for more Catholic schools meant that there was also a need for more teachers to staff them, which often meant hiring lay teachers to fill the gap left by an insufficient number of teaching sisters. When discussing the sharp decline in the number of sisters that occurred after Vatican II's call for the renewal of religious life, it must be remembered that the number of American women entering religious life, especially the teaching orders, during the twenty-five-year period before the council was abnormally high; in 1965, at the peak of membership in the women's religious orders, there were 104,314 teaching sisters serving at 113,446 Catholic elementary schools in the United States. This unusually high number of vocations to teaching orders suggested to prelates that they should increase the construction of schools in their territories to meet the ever-growing demand for Catholic schools. After this boom period ended abruptly in the late 1960s, the number of women religious returned to historic averages, which left thousands of understaffed Catholic institutions that had to either transition to lay management or be closed. Even if Vatican II and religious renewal had never happened, it would have been impossible for the Catholic Church to maintain the postwar level of women religious indefinitely.[5]

Despite the aggressive campaigns to encourage Catholic women to embrace vocations as teaching sisters in the late nineteenth century and early twentieth, there were never enough schools or teaching sisters to make parochial schools a realistic alternative to the public schools for all Catholic children. This was particularly true when the postwar baby boom strained the capacity of even the most enthusiastic "builder bishops" in the North to make the supply of Catholic schools equal to the demand. For example, Cardinal Francis Spellman was responsible for building over two hundred elementary schools in New York during the 1950s, and by 1960 there was one Catholic school student for every two public school students in the city. However, even after Spellman's ambitious building campaign, the majority of Catholic children in New York still attended public schools. As the number of parochial schools increased in the postwar period, so too did the reliance on lay teachers to fill crucial personnel gaps. More lay teachers meant that Catholic schools had to spend more of their budgets on wages and benefits, which strained the already limited resources of dioceses and archdioceses.[6]

The SBS was never as large as some of the more famous women's orders such as the Sisters of the Immaculate Heart of Mary or the Sisters of Charity, and it did not benefit from the postwar vocations boom; at its peak in 1967, the SBS consisted of 563 professed, living sisters, with about 9 sisters joining each year. The largest band to enter the SBS was when 22 sisters made their vows in 1939. The periods that saw the fastest growth for the SBS were 1914–19 and 1924–29, in which the order grew a total of 176 percent. This period of growth during the second quarter of the twentieth century enabled the SBS to expand their mission territory from isolated reservations in the rural West into Northern cities and the South. However, there were never enough SBS or priests interested in ministering to Blacks to meet the demands of archbishops and bishops who wanted to build "colored missions."[7]

For example, a 1928 document by Sr. M. Regina related how Mass was temporarily suspended at Our Lady of Sorrows, the SBS mission in Biloxi, Mississippi, during Lent and Holy Week because the priest "had suffered a stroke of apoplexy" and there were no other priests in the area willing to minister to Blacks. There were two white parishes close to Our Lady of Sorrows, but Blacks were not permitted to enter them, even if they sat in the back. The sisters kept the parish going during this period by organizing community devotions, such as the Forty Hours, the Holy Hour, the Way of the Cross, and the rosary. The document ends with, "It seems from what has just been related that much can be done [for the Black apostolate] if we had many more generous souls willing to undertake the cultivation of this neglected portion of the Lord's vineyard." The nature of the SBS's charism and work meant that potential recruits to the order not only had to be able to spend the bulk of their time embedded in Black communities but also had to interact with them in a respectful manner that was generally alien to many whites. Hence, the type of woman who would have been attracted to SBS would have had to have been unusually progressive on racial issues by definition, thus limiting the number of potential applicants.[8]

In Atlanta as well, the number of SBS versus the number of lay teachers at Our Lady of Lourdes School reflected the general reliance of Catholic schools on lay teachers. During Our Lady of Lourdes School's first year of existence during the 1912–13 academic year, there were no teaching sisters at all on the staff because the SBS had started three other missions that same year (St. Monica in Chicago, St. Mark in New York, and St. Cyprian in Columbus, Ohio) and the motherhouse in Cornwells, Pennsylvania, did not have enough sisters to send to Atlanta. Once the sisters did arrive the following year, the teaching staff consisted of four sisters and four Black Protestant lay teachers. At the school's period of peak enrollment in the early and mid-1960s, there were six sisters and four lay teachers. However, by 1973, the last year the SBS were at Our Lady of Lourdes, there were four sisters, five lay teachers, and three lay Title I teachers.[9]

Drexel, St. Joseph's, and St. Pius also had substantial numbers of lay teachers on their respective payrolls. Drexel had five sisters from the SBS and the Sisters of St. Joseph's and six lay teachers during the school year before it closed in 1967, whereas St. Joseph's had nine sisters and fourteen lay teachers during that same time period. "Arguments for the Consolidation of St. Joseph's High School and Drexel Catholic High School" estimated that roughly 55 and 45 percent of the budgets of St. Joseph's and Drexel, respectively, was spent on salaries for lay and religious teachers. The document went on to state that any additional faculty hired for St. Joseph's or Drexel, should the latter stay open, would have to be lay teachers, which would further exacerbate operating costs. When St. Pius first opened in 1958, its staff consisted of fifteen sisters from four orders (Grey Nuns of the Sacred Heart, Sisters of Notre Dame de Namur, Sisters of St. Joseph of Carondelet, and the Religious Sisters of Mercy) and six lay teachers. By 1969, there were a combined total of twenty-five sisters and priests on staff at St. Pius, but the number of lay teachers had ballooned to twenty-four.[10]

As Catholic school enrollment peaked in the 1960s, there was increasingly a debate as to whether parochial schools were even the most desirable or necessary option for American Catholics. The parish school movement had begun during a time when anti-Catholicism was pervasive throughout public school curricula and white ethnic Catholics were impoverished and socially marginalized. By the 1950s, many white Catholics had moved to the suburbs, where Catholic parishes were increasingly being built without schools. The demand for Catholic education remained high among suburbanites, but the inability of the hierarchy to supply enough parochial schools caused Catholic families to patronize the public schools. The phenomenon of American Catholics sending their children to public school had always been more common than the hierarchy had wanted to admit, but by the 1960s there was an increasing sentiment among the laity that parish schools were unnecessary. With white Catholics becoming more affluent and assimilated into American life, the need to shelter their children from an aggressively Protestant public school system was waning, as was the intimate connection between neighborhood, ethnicity, and the local school/parish.[11]

Documents from the archdiocese regarding the future of Drexel High alluded to this crisis within the American Catholic education system. St. Joseph's High School, the regional high school for whites located in downtown Atlanta that the archdiocese had considered consolidating with Drexel, had originally been the St. Pius annex to accommodate students whom the latter could not take. The fact that St. Pius had many more applicants than available seats in the late 1950s suggested to archdiocesan officials that a second standalone high school would be necessary to handle the extra students. However, St. Joseph's always operated under capacity, though not to the same extent as Drexel. When discussions about the future of Drexel began in late 1966, the question of how to revitalize St. Joseph's was also raised.

St. Joseph's enrollment woes stemmed from what "Arguments for the Consolidation of St. Joseph High School and Drexel Catholic High School" called "a static situation" in Atlanta's Catholic grammar schools, meaning that no new schools would be built in the archdiocese in the foreseeable future. The number of eighth graders graduating from parochial primary schools who planned to go to Catholic high schools was also starting to decrease, which made operating large regional high schools increasingly inefficient from a financial perspective. While the fate of Drexel was being debated in 1966 and 1967, the Immaculate Conception School was already slated to close at the end of the academic school year. Sacred Heart had closed its school in 1964, and in 1962 the Marist Military College that had been located on its property moved to suburban Atlanta, where it was renamed the Marist School and became a coeducational, nonmilitary college preparatory school. In comparison, St. Pius was experiencing "an influx of students from the public schools," presumably because of white flight, which had caused all of the formerly all-white in-town parishes—Sacred Heart, Immaculate Conception, and St. Anthony's—to lose parishioners during the 1960s and 1970s. Patterns of white flight benefitted St. Pius at the expense of St. Joseph's, especially as its student population became increasingly Black as the decade progressed.[12]

By the end of the decade, the Archdiocese of Atlanta was having increasing difficulty funding its remaining Catholic schools. A month before Drexel High School closed, Auxiliary Bishop Joseph L. Bernardin admitted in an April 17, 1967, letter that the Archdiocese of Atlanta may be forced to close some of its currently existing educational institutions and refrain from relocating or making improvements to those facilities that it chose to retain because of "the increasing cost of construction, the decreasing availability of sisters, [and] increasing salaries for lay teachers." Bernardin's reference to schools that would need to be closed referred to Drexel High, while the one that might need to be renovated or relocated was St. Joseph's, which was later closed in May 1976. A letter, dated January 10, 1969, from Daniel J. O'Connor to Rev. Noel C. Burtenshaw, chancellor of the Archdiocese of Atlanta, stated that the archdiocese would have to subsidize its high school programs and that the Our Lady of Lourdes School was already receiving additional financial aid. The subsidy that Our Lady of Lourdes School received to stay open would later become a point of contention among the SBS as they debated whether to withdraw.[13]

Religious Renewal and the SBS

Although the renewal of religious orders wrought by Vatican II caught many Catholics by surprise, the concept appears to have originated with a solidly traditional pontiff, Pope Pius XII. In 1950, Pius XII told the Sacred Congregation for Religious that orders should liberalize "excessively strict" levels of cloisteration and eliminate outdated customs that were nonessential to the work of their respective apostolates. He reiterated this call for updating religious life the following year at an international meeting of teaching sisters by emphasizing the need for them to have professional credentials that equaled or surpassed those of teachers in secular schools. According to Patricia Wittberg, Pius XII felt that "it was the strangeness of outdated costumes and customs and the strain of being sent into ministry without proper training . . . that was behind the alarming drop-off of religious vocations in Europe after World War II." Addressing the International Congress of Major Superiors in 1952, Pius XII implored the superiors of women's orders to provide their sisters with the training necessary to make them competitive with their secular counterparts. To further this goal, he established the Regina Mundi Institution in Rome to train women religious in theology. Pius XII issued missives about how to reform religious life on an almost yearly basis until his death in 1958, but he remained convinced that the fundamental ideological underpinnings of pre–Vatican II religious life should remain unchanged. He believed there should continue to be a clear division between the consecrated and lay state, the superiority of virginity to marriage should continue to be the ideal for achieving holiness, and women religious should maintain total obedience to the hierarchy.[14]

The superiors of the women's teaching orders in the United States attempted to implement Pius XII's suggestions for reform, with varying degrees of success. Like the pontiff, they had no intention of undermining the institutional or ideological foundations of religious life, and their main interest was improving the educational and professional training of teaching sisters. At a 1952 meeting of the National Catholic Education Association in Kansas City, a committee was formed to investigate what prevented superiors from implementing the pope's reforms. The committee produced a survey that was sent to the members of various religious orders. The responses indicated that the major barriers to reform were that (1) the amount of time needed to complete advanced degrees clashed with the desire among priests and bishops to maximize the number of teaching sisters at their disposal, (2) the cost of educating sisters was prohibitive for religious orders, especially given the extreme poverty said sisters endured, and (3) an anti-intellectual attitude persisted among the clergy and laity, who failed to understand why sisters needed additional education. In light of these findings, American women religious established the Sister Formation Conference, which would later become one of the primary institutions advocating for religious renewal and the increased intellectual formation of teaching sisters in the United States.[15]

Substantive reforms to the religious life would not occur until Vatican II issued *Perfectae Caritatis* (Decree on the Renewal of Religious Life) on October 28, 1965. The document called on religious orders throughout the world to rediscover their distinctive charisms by adhering more closely to the original intentions of their founders. When the council ended, religious were commanded to hold Special Chapters where the members would discuss how to make the spirituality, disciplines, and practices of their orders conform to the dictates of Vatican II. An order such as the SBS that had had a General Chapter when the council was occurring was permitted an extension, but as the SBS worked on planning their Special Chapter for 1968, the sisters studied the documents of Vatican II and queried members of other orders to learn how they had carried out religious renewal. Mother David, the superior general of the SBS, put out a call for the sisters to send in recommendations about what should be discussed at the Special Chapter, and she ended up receiving over thirteen hundred responses.

Before the first session of the Special Chapter commenced, Mother David made significant changes in discipline that pleased sisters excited about religious renewal and concerned those who wanted to keep the customs originally established by Katharine Drexel. Shortly after her election as superior general in 1964, Mother David had already loosened some of the rules regarding the degree of isolation the sisters experienced. She ended the practice of superiors reading the mail the finally professed (sisters who had taken their final vows) and junior professed (novice sisters who had taken temporary vows) received from their immediate family members. Sisters were also allowed to watch the Huntley-Brinkley news at night, and those who resided at the Motherhouse in Cornwells, Pennsylvania, could socialize after the Midnight Mass at Christmas. Perhaps most importantly for the future welfare of older sisters, Mother David not only helped those older sisters who qualified apply for Social Security in 1966 but also arranged for the order to pay into the system for those sisters who had retired since the passing of the Social Security Act. Mother David's realization of the need to consider the welfare of aging sisters would be a prescient decision as the century wore on, when many religious orders faced financial ruin due to their failure to plan for the retirement of the many women who joined during the boom years of recruitment.[16]

This period was also characterized by the first SBS withdrawals (i.e., removing sisters from a particular mission or apostolate) in December 1964. Mother David decreed that the SBS would no longer send sisters to parishes to instruct altar boys, play the organ, or serve as sacristans, not only because said sisters could be reassigned to classroom duty, but also because Vatican II decreed that these tasks could now be done by the laity. Sisters who staffed non-SBS schools were also withdrawn so they could provide much-needed personnel in institutions run by the order. Other early withdrawals stemmed from schools with low enrollment, a desire for children at SBS schools to attend integrated Catholic schools if they were available, or "where the ratio of teaching SBS to lay teachers was 'less than the community wide ratio' of 3:1." Unlike the withdrawals that would occur later in the decade, where lack of personnel was a major factor, these departures were based on a need for SBS to focus on teaching at preexisting SBS teaching missions.[17]

Mother David spent the bulk of 1966 to 1968 planning for the Special Chapter. To ensure that the SBS were prepared, Mother David gave each sister a copy of *The Documents of Vatican II* in September 1966 and mandated that they also read *Katharine Drexel: A Biography* to better comprehend what the intentions and spirit of the SBS's foundress had been. Each convent was to host its own discussion group about the contents of both books as well as other works on religious renewal. Questionnaires about what should be discussed at the Special Chapter were distributed not only to the sisters themselves but also to the various groups in the SBS orbit, including parishioners of SBS institutions, parents and alumni from SBS schools, and clergy.[18]

There were two sessions of the SBS Special Chapter, the first opening on July 22, 1968, and the second on June 1969. At the close of the first session on August 22, seventy-nine of eighty-four proposals passed, and all but five of these were cleared with two-thirds of those present voting in favor. The proposals enabled experimentation in a wide range of areas, including allowing sisters to visit their families once a year, use their baptismal rather than religious name, and wear modified habits. The use of the honorific "mother" would be given only to the mother superior of the order as a means of recognizing the decentralization of power within the SBS. Approved changes to the spiritual practices of the SBS included the typical Vatican II emphasis on encouraging the individual study of theology, Scripture, and Catholic social teachings. However, nonviolent social actions, such as boycotting racist institutions and supporting Black- and Native American–owned businesses, were also recast as spiritual practices that were the logical extension of Katharine Drexel's belief in uplifting Blacks and Native Americans. The second session saw the preliminary steps in the production of a revised set of constitutions that would be titled *Total Gift of Self*.[19]

The annals of the SBS at Our Lady of Lourdes began reporting renewal-related changes at the beginning of 1968. In January, they decided on "the silent times and places for our community." The places themselves did not actually change, but the sisters determined that the Great Silence would not begin until ten at night, and talking would be permitted during Sunday breakfast and when there were visitors to the convent. In February, they began experimenting with their habits because "permission was received from the Motherhouse to experiment with the headpiece publicly and the habit inside the convent. Much excitement was the result and scissors and patterns began to come into view." An entry from the following month concerning a visit the sisters from Atlanta and Montgomery made to the Macon SBS revealed that "there were a great variety of headpieces and habits," indicating that this experimentation was occurring throughout SBS missions in the Deep South. By the time the Atlanta and Montgomery SBS visited the Macon sisters again for Thanksgiving, "all had on the new modern styles except Sr. Edward Marie and Sr. Mary of the Holy Family." On October 11, 1968, the SBS had dinner with the Sisters of St. Joseph who staffed the St. Paul of the Cross School, and the annals reported that the latter were "living in experimental community and they love it."[20]

The 1970 General Chapter instituted more changes to the structure of the SBS, the most significant being a restructuring of the leadership. The position of mother superior was replaced with that of president, reflecting the trend among religious orders in the post–Vatican II era to adopt the terminology of business management. The president was elected to a four-year term, and she was to be assisted in her work by a council of six, each of whom had specific tasks delegated to them. The chapter invested the president and her council with the power to sanction further experimentation, while at the same time giving local SBS communities enough autonomy to make their own decisions pertaining to their specific conditions. Mother Mary Elizabeth Fitzgerald was elected the first president of the SBS during the Special Chapter, and she would later make the decisive resolution to withdraw the sisters from Our Lady of Lourdes School.[21]

As the SBS prepared for the 1970 General Chapter, a sense of hope and anxiety pervaded the order due to a dramatic drop in the number of vocations to the order. According to Sr. Patricia Lynch,

> In the nearly seventy years from 1895 until the Tenth General Chapter in 1964, only ten Sisters in perpetual vows had left the congregation. Seventy-seven had not renewed temporary vows, two-thirds at the decision of the Council. In the six years between the 1964 General Chapter until the opening of the 1970 General Chapter, twenty-seven Sisters of perpetual vows had requested and received Indults of Secularization from the Holy See and twenty-two Sisters did not renew temporary vows, only one of them at the decision of the Council. In addition, the Novitate which had shown signs of growth earlier in the same period, now had only four novices and three postulants.[22]

Since the SBS were a modestly sized order even before Vatican II, the vocation crisis of the late 1960s and early 1970s hit the order particularly hard. Like many orders, the SBS had to make difficult decisions about how to best utilize their limited resources, which often meant withdrawing sisters from one location and moving them to another place where their labor value could be maximized.

The personnel shortage that the SBS faced in the 1970s was not unique, as the disintegration of the women's teaching orders after the council made the already faltering parish school model completely unworkable. Many sisters left religious life in the late 1960s and early 1970s, and the number of women seeking entry to these orders as novices dropped off sharply. Those women who remained sisters often completely changed their approach to being religious in keeping with what they believed to be a rediscovery of the intentions of their respective founders. This process entailed discarding the internal disciplines that had not only prevented sisters from leaving in the past but prevented the ideology of the orders from being "contaminated" by outside ideologies.[23] The loss of so many sisters in such a short period of time compounded the pre-existing problems within the parish school system, which further sped up the closure, consolidation, or transition to lay leadership of those schools that remained. Majority-Black Catholic schools like Our Lady of Lourdes were particularly affected by the vocations crisis because they tended to be dependent on a handful of missionary orders for their staffing needs. However, the changing nature of the area surrounding Our Lady of Lourdes would be the final impetus behind the SBS's decision to withdraw from Atlanta.[24]

The SBS Debate Withdrawing from Our Lady of Lourdes

Our Lady of Lourdes was negatively impacted by the demographic changes to the Auburn Avenue area during the 1960s. Many former Our Lady of Lourdes members joined St. Anthony of Padua in the formerly all-white West End to follow Fr. Michael McKeever, the popular Our Lady of Lourdes pastor who had been reassigned there in 1969. Other former Our Lady of Lourdes parishioners moved to Southwest Atlanta, where they joined St. Paul of the Cross, a result of middle-class Black residents fleeing Auburn Avenue for more desirable locations. Accordingly, the number of parishioners at Our Lady of Lourdes who actually lived in close proximity to the parish plummeted, and tuition for the school became cost prohibitive for the children who remained in the neighborhood. School desegregation, of both public and private institutions, meant that the Our Lady of Lourdes School was no longer the only or even the best educational option for upwardly mobile Black families, as it had been in the Jim Crow era.[25]

At this time, all the archdiocesan schools were working toward accreditation with the Southern Association of Colleges and Schools, and Our Lady of Lourdes School found it increasingly difficult to meet the standards. Certain practices that had been taken for granted in Catholic schools—overcrowded classrooms, unsafe buildings, dubious teacher training, and disorganized curriculums—could no longer be tolerated, and many parochial schools across the country closed because of a mix of safety concerns, poor quality, and rising operating costs. While some Catholic schools in affluent areas had the resources to transition into elite private institutions that just happened to be affiliated with the Catholic Church, as was the case with the Christ the King School attached to Atlanta's cathedral, poorer parish schools like Our Lady of Lourdes struggled to meet both the accreditation standards and their mission to provide an affordable education to the children in their respective communities.[26]

Our Lady of Lourdes School had always been the poorest school in the archdiocese due to its status as a "colored mission" within a neighborhood with a low socioeconomic status, but it had managed to get by through donations from white Catholics and the ingenuity of the sisters and the community. For example, a February 20, 1943, entry in the annals described an incident in which "Mother M. Carmelita, the principal of Sacred Heart School, and one of the Sisters with a group of their girls paid us a visit. They visited each classroom and were amazed [sic] the work our children could do. For the past couple of months a group of these girls have visited us and have brought us all kind of school supplies which they have purchased with their own money."[27] While parish schools in general were heavily reliant on the sacrifices of the sisters and the presence of an engaged community willing to make sacrifices for said school, the poverty of Our Lady of Lourdes School was such that it relied on white benefactors for its day-to-day needs.

The material poverty of the school was not considered problematic in the pre–Vatican II era, but new midcentury educational standards combined with urban decay in the Auburn Avenue area made the SBS assigned to the school feel like they were ill-equipped to address the complex needs of their student body. Evidence for this attitude can be found in a May 7, 1973, letter from Sr. Loretta McCarthy to Mother Mary Fitzgerald: "I don't feel that we have adequately staffed [Our Lady of Lourdes School]. (I don't think that we have ever had more than four Sisters assigned to the school. I was the first free principal in 1967–68 and 68–69. I had no previous training in administration and feel sure that the school did not progress as it would have under an experienced administrator. And, forgive me if this sounds like a judgement, I do not feel that the present principal is an effective administrator.)"[28] Sr. Loretta's concerns about the ability of a handful of sisters to effectively administer a modern elementary school were echoed by Sr. Maureen Immaculate in a May 6, 1973, letter, in which she said that she did not feel like the administration of Our Lady of Lourdes School met *Total Gift of Self*'s dictate that SBS schools have "qualified, efficient, and adequate staff." In the pre–Vatican II period, a less organized approach to Catholic school administration was tolerated and even expected, but postwar educational standards—and the revised SBS constitution—demanded a more professional approach.[29]

By 1972, a convergence of critical issues prompted Mother Mary Fitzgerald to consider whether she needed to withdraw the SBS from Our Lady of Lourdes School. The old parish school model had collapsed. There were chronic personnel shortages and a decline in enrollment. Demographic changes had hit Auburn Avenue and the parish hard, and an existential crisis within the SBS itself questioned whether the order fit in a post–civil rights era. The SBS spent roughly two years debating internally whether they should withdraw from Atlanta. An undated document by Sister M. Judith, the final SBS principal of Our Lady of Lourdes School, that was probably composed around 1972 outlined the pros and cons of withdrawal. The reasons for staying included the ongoing revival of the parish, including the addition of young white couples and an increased number of baptisms, the number of Black families who lacked trust in the public schools, and the possibility of using Title I funds (i.e., federal support for schools of which low-income families composed 40 percent or more of the student body) to serve poor families in the Auburn Avenue area. However, the grounds for leaving were more numerous: the percentage of non-Catholic children at the school was continuing to increase. Most of the children who did attend had to travel across town, often passing other parochial schools to do so; tuition had doubled within the previous three years, leading to a decrease in enrollment and rendering the school inaccessible to the poorest children. Sister M. Judith wrote that she felt that the order was "continuing segregation by accepting such a great subsidy from the archdiocese [$25,000] to keep the school open. I would rather request funds for the parish to pay tuition for children who wish to attend another Catholic school in their area." Her conclusion was a reflection of the fact that many of the SBS who worked in Atlanta had lost faith that the Our Lady of Lourdes School was in keeping with Katharine Drexel's vision for evangelizing and uplifting Blacks through education.[30]

The previously mentioned May 7, 1973, letter from Sister Loretta McCarthy also argued in favor of withdrawal. She did not feel that Our Lady of Lourdes School was providing a quality education because the school had never been adequately staffed and the sisters had to work in administrative roles that they were ill-suited to perform. This, combined with the school's deteriorating physical state, meant that it was impossible for Our Lady of Lourdes School to meet the new educational standards expected of a high-quality school. The uncertainty the SBS had among themselves about whether the school would remain open had trickled down into the congregation, leading to a loss of confidence in its future. McCarthy believed that those families that could afford to pay full tuition should be encouraged to choose a Catholic school other than Our Lady of Lourdes, where their children could be assured of having the best education possible. She ended the letter by asking if there was some way for the SBS to continue to have a presence in Atlanta serving the Black poor aside from teaching at Our Lady of Lourdes School.[31]

In comparison, a letter from Sister M. Patrick Thomas Lynch, who had taught at Our Lady of Lourdes School from 1958 to 1968, argued in favor of remaining in Atlanta. Lynch noted that most of the order's withdrawals thus far had been in areas where there was a Catholic presence among Blacks apart from the SBS, such as New Orleans, New York, and Philadelphia. In Atlanta, the SBS were the Church as far as the Black community was concerned. Although the student body of Our Lady of Lourdes School seldom was more than 51 percent Catholic and the percentage of Catholic parents was even less, she argued that families eagerly supported the sisters' work, whether religious or educational. She also recalled that this had helped break down suspicion and fear about the Catholic Church in a heavily Baptist community and that the SBS had helped Atlanta's Black Catholic community deal with the lingering resentment caused by the closure of Drexel High and the racism their high school students had experienced at St. Joseph's High School.[32]

Sr. Carole Eden, who was stationed at Our Lady of Lourdes School for three years, put forth a compromise between complete withdrawal from Atlanta and attempting to maintain the school in its current form. In an undated letter to Fitzgerald, she stated that the SBS were "both needed and wanted by our Black brothers," but she felt that they were not ministering to Atlanta's underserved Black population as effectively as Katharine Drexel had intended. She mentioned that the current Our Lady of Lourdes pastor, Fr. Matthew Kemp, was seeking grants from unnamed foundations to increase the parish's capacity for neighborhood outreach. Eden's letter concluded by suggesting that the SBS maintain a presence in Atlanta, either by continuing to staff the Our Lady of Lourdes School or as Confraternity of Christian Doctrine teachers. She mentioned the possibility of a small group of SBS serving the Black community in an "inter-community of sisters" from other religious orders, so as not to exacerbate the SBS personnel shortage.[33]

Although the letter does not appear to be extant, Fitzgerald wrote to Thomas Donnellan, the archbishop of Atlanta, in late January or early February 1972 to inform him of her intention to withdraw the SBS from Our Lady of Lourdes at the end of the 1971–72 school year. Donnellan wrote back to Fitzgerald on February 9, 1972, pleading for the SBS to remain in Atlanta. He wrote that he was sympathetic to the situation of the SBS, especially with regard to the vocations crisis that was affecting all religious orders, but the need in the Archdiocese of Atlanta was such that the continued presence of the sisters was crucial. The loss of Our Lady of Lourdes would be catastrophic because "Our Lady of Lourdes is not one of many institutions serving Blacks. It is just one of two . . . and the one that is oldest by far." Donnellan said that the fact that so many families made a point of traveling to Our Lady of Lourdes School when they had other educational options was a testament to how well regarded the SBS were among the Black community. Similarly, the rising socioeconomic level of many Our Lady of Lourdes families was also indicative of how the quality of education that the SBS were providing was helping Blacks achieve social mobility. Donnellan also praised the SBS for being a bridge between the Black and white Catholic communities, including organizing a program for Martin Luther King Jr.'s birthday that brought over three hundred white Catholic children from the suburbs to Our Lady of Lourdes in 1972. He feared that Our Lady of

Lourdes School would have to close if the SBS left because he doubted that he could secure another group of sisters to fill their positions.[34]

Fitzgerald canceled her original plans for withdrawal in 1973, but on October 12 of that year she informed Donnellan of her final decision for the SBS to leave Our Lady of Lourdes School at the end of the 1973–74 school year. Although she was moved by his letter from the previous year imploring the sisters to stay in Atlanta, Fitzgerald felt that the current circumstances in Atlanta indicated that the SBS were no longer needed at Our Lady of Lourdes. She reiterated her reasons for the withdrawal— namely decreasing enrollment, rising tuition that was out of reach for poor Blacks, the fact that many of the remaining students traveled across town to reach Our Lady of Lourdes, and a decrease in vocations that necessitated reassessing how the SBS used its limited human resources. Fitzgerald ended the letter by stating, "We hope and pray that our presence there for these many years will prove effective now in the strength of the Faith of the Black people of Atlanta who must see a Church concerned for them not just symbolically through the presence of a particular group of sisters, but really in the whole Church present throughout the entire personnel and the various institutions of the diocese."[35] In the wake of the Civil Rights Movement, Fitzgerald realized that Black Catholic concerns could not simply be outsourced to a handful of missionary religious orders like the SBS, while white Catholics enjoyed the full resources of their local diocese or archdiocese. The Archdiocese of Atlanta had to make the SBS mission of Black uplift its own if it wanted to retain and grow its Black Catholic population.

Thomas Donnellan's response to Fitzgerald's announcement of withdrawal was an emotional acknowledgment of the historical and contemporary importance of the SBS's work and uncertainty about how the Archdiocese of Atlanta could adequately engage in Black ministry after decades of neglect. He admitted that the reasons Fitzgerald mentioned for leaving were valid but said that the need for them to stay was even more urgent than it had been a year prior. He stressed the centrality of Our Lady of Lourdes to the Catholic Church's outreach to the Black community in Atlanta:

> Recently, as part of a Seminar for Priests and Sisters working among Blacks, I walked the streets of a Black area about five miles from Our

Lady of Lourdes asking strangers (all Black) if they knew the Catholic Church, how they knew it, what it did for the Black community. Consistently, those who knew it had encountered the Church, or heard of it: first, through Our Lady of Lourdes School; second, through Saint Paul of the Cross; third, through the work of one or another priest. In response to what the Church did for the Black Community, the answer frequently was that they gave the children a good education.[36]

The tentative goodwill created through Catholic schools in Black neighborhoods was tempered by lingering resentment regarding the closing of Drexel High, a feeling that was exacerbated by rumors that St. Joseph's was slated to be closed because of its high rates of Black enrollment (St. Joseph's would close in 1976). If providing increased educational opportunities was what the Catholic Church was known for among Atlanta's Blacks, closing the flagship Black Catholic school and parish would do irreparable damage to the Church's reputation.

The distress that the Our Lady of Lourdes community felt when the sisters left was not unusual. Parishes of all sorts were losing their teaching sisters. But the relationship the SBS had with it and other Black communities set their withdrawals apart. For the members of Our Lady of Lourdes in particular and the Auburn Avenue community in general, the SBS were among the few white people who treated them as equals, who showed a genuine interest in their lives and community affairs. SBS visitations often meant going into areas of Black Atlanta that were unhealthy, dangerous, or otherwise considered undesirable for "respectable" white women. For example, a 1915 letter from Sr. Mary Carmelita to Katharine Drexel describes an incident in which she and Sr. Mary Thomas Aquinas checked on Adelaide Thomas, an elderly member of Our Lady of Lourdes who had been sick. Upon finding Thomas living in squalor due to her infirmity, the sisters cleaned her house, bought and cooked her food, and restarted her boiler. Thomas repaid the sisters with half a dozen eggs and a live hen. The SBS's support for the Civil Rights Movement was a natural outgrowth of the solidarity that the sisters had demonstrated with Atlanta's Black community since their physical arrival in 1913.[37]

In some cases, the SBS maintained a small presence consisting of one or two sisters in areas where they had once maintained larger missions.

This was the case in Atlanta, where Sister Loretta McCarthy, the last SBS principal of the Our Lady of Lourdes School, received permission to open a house of prayer in 1990 in the Old Fourth Ward. Houses of prayer were a post–Vatican II apostolate that the SBS had created. They performed intercessory prayers for the city in which they were embedded and engaged in hospitality, educational programs, and spiritual direction, especially for the poor and homeless. The SBS's Atlanta house of prayer was called Maisha House, because "Maisha" meant "life" in Swahili and had biblical, Eucharistic, and Afro-centric connotations. Although Maisha House was not formally affiliated with Our Lady of Lourdes, it had a close relationship with the parish from its inception; upon arriving in Atlanta, Sister Loretta spoke to the Our Lady of Lourdes congregation about the new ministry, and Our Lady of Lourdes's priest at the time, Fr. Henry Gracz, said Maisha House's inaugural Mass. Maisha House eventually closed in 2007, when Sister Loretta McCarthy left Atlanta upon being elected vice president of the SBS.[38]

After the departure of the SBS in 1974, Donnellan found another sister to act as principal of Our Lady of Lourdes School, Sister Margaret McAnoy, an Immaculate Heart sister who had taught for five years at St. Pius. Upon arriving at Our Lady of Lourdes, McAnoy eliminated grades six, seven, and eight. According to McAnoy, the rationale for eliminating the middle school grades was because "children at that age are more into sports and for that you need money. And we as a school did not have the money to do it, so I thought they would, I would concentrate on early elementary grades." Accordingly, a kindergarten, which had been discontinued in the 1950s, was added, so Our Lady of Lourdes School could focus on instilling and reinforcing basic literacy and numeracy skills in its students. McAnoy managed to get the school's enrollment up to 330 students, although by 1987 it had dipped again to 180. The school continued to receive substantial funding from the archdiocese, including money for scholarships, so it could continue to serve Atlanta's poor Black population.[39]

Although Donnellan feared that Our Lady of Lourdes School would close shortly after the departure of the SBS, it lasted for almost twenty-seven years afterward, closing on May 30, 2001. When the archdiocese finally ended its funding, both Our Lady of Lourdes School and the St. Anthony of Padua School were forced to close. Whereas St. Anthony accepted the closure of its school, the Our Lady of Lourdes community made an effort to raise the million dollars necessary to keep their school open. In addition to the fundraising campaign, the members of the parish held a number of meetings and protested at Archbishop Wilton Gregory's residence to convince the archdiocese to reconsider its decision. They were ultimately unsuccessful, and the Our Lady of Lourdes School became the Katharine Drexel Community Center after its closure. However, the determination of Black Catholics to retain their educational institutions stands in contrast to how the parish schools associated with the white in-town parishes withered away without significant protest. By the time of their closures, the Our Lady of Lourdes School and the St. Anthony of Padua School were the last of the pre-Vatican II parish schools left in the Archdiocese of Atlanta.[40]

6

Reviving Our Lady of Lourdes through Liturgical Renewal and Liturgical Justice

With the withdrawal of the SBS, a dwindling membership, and the precarious state of the community's finances, the story of Our Lady of Lourdes—both the parish and the school—should have ended in the early 1970s. This was the case for many Black Catholic institutions in the South, which were closed after the passage of the Civil Rights Act to facilitate desegregation, regardless of their viability or the feelings of the parishioners. The closure of Black Catholic schools and parishes coincided with the rise of Black Power, which led to a call for increased autonomy and representation behind the altar and in the hierarchy. The backlash the Archdiocese of Atlanta had received from the Black community after the closure of Drexel Catholic High was such that it was reluctant to unilaterally close Our Lady of Lourdes. Archbishop Thomas Donnellan felt compelled to keep the parish and school afloat, not only because of its centrality to Atlanta's Black Catholic identity but also out of a sense of obligation due to the failure of the Catholic Church to adequately minister to the city's Blacks.[1]

Even though the archdiocese allowed Our Lady of Lourdes to remain open, the parish was characterized by chronic financial problems and physical disrepair from the late 1960s until the 1980s. An archdiocesan inspection of Our Lady of Lourdes School on February 5, 1969, discovered that the heating system was in poor condition, the lower floor was infested with termites, and "the cement is falling out the windows." All of these problems needed to be resolved immediately at a cost of seventeen thousand dollars if the school was to stay open. However, Our Lady of Lourdes was too poor to pay for the repairs, necessitating the parish to request, and successfully receive, funding from the archdiocesan Board of Education. The physical state of the school was so bad at this point that the board asked the SBS if they thought it would be better for the school to close than to be repaired. In 1971, the SBS convent had to be demolished, once again at the expense of the archdiocese, because of a sinking foundation and outdated electrical wiring.[2]

Upon becoming pastor of Our Lady of Lourdes in 1979, Fr. Frank J. Giusta wrote a letter to Rev. Monsignor Jerry Hardy about the parish's worsening financial and maintenance problems. He thanked Hardy for providing funds to pay for a broken rectory wall as well as helping with paying to have the parish's water pipes fixed. Although the church building needed paint on its interior and exterior, Giusta said he could use volunteer labor to accomplish the job. The letter suggested that Our Lady of Lourdes's financial woes were due to sloppy bookkeeping, as Giusta found a number of unnecessary and unexplained expenses at the parish, including a water meter that had never been used, outstanding bills, and the presence of a savings account of unknown origin containing $595. Giusta ended the letter by stating that his goal was to make Our Lady of Lourdes a self-sustaining parish, but he was not optimistic about when or if this could be accomplished.[3]

At the end of 1979, Giusta submitted a report to Archbishop Donnellan and Rev. Monsignor Jerry Hardy in which he discussed the current state of Our Lady of Lourdes. Giusta began by stating that there were only "220 registered units" at Our Lady of Lourdes and that the vast majority of members who lived near the parish were senior citizens. The main reason why parishioners felt compelled to return to Our Lady of Lourdes was due to their "emotional attachment" to the church and the school, but because younger people lacked this fondness, there was no reason for them to choose Lourdes over a parish in their respective neighborhoods. Giusta was concerned about the future ramifications of the proliferation of civil rights monuments on Auburn Avenue for the future of Our Lady of Lourdes. He feared that Auburn Avenue would be "transformed into a living museum with necessary parking lots and other facilities," which would further displace the residents who remained in the neighborhood. He was pessimistic about the future of Our Lady of Lourdes, predicting that it would become "an empty church with a great past and a very privileged location." The report concluded by suggesting three possibilities for Our Lady of Lourdes: closing the parish, saving Our Lady of Lourdes by urging Atlanta's Black Catholics to join their "mother parish," or eliminating Our Lady of Lourdes's status as an ethnically based personal prelature and assign it normal territorial boundaries. Giusta seemed to tentatively support regularizing Our Lady of Lourdes's status and borders, while also stating that doing so would require more resources, especially pastoral, than the parish could afford.[4]

Believing that a larger congregation would help alleviate Our Lady of Lourdes's money problems, Giusta embarked upon an evangelization campaign to attract new members in October 1979. Even though Giusta's report to Hardy indicated his intention to target Blacks living in the Auburn Avenue area, an evangelization flyer that was produced for this endeavor emphasized that "Our Lady of Lourdes is no longer an all Black Catholic Church. We enjoy and welcome people of all races and economic backgrounds to our celebration of the good news of Jesus Christ." The flyer also emphasized the aspect of Catholicism in general and Our Lady of Lourdes in particular that would be most appealing to outsiders: the global nature of the Catholic Church, the welcoming atmosphere at Our Lady of Lourdes, the presence of a school, and the transformative properties of the Mass.[5]

It is unclear whether Giusta's evangelization efforts yielded significant long-term results; a lengthy 1987 profile of Our Lady of Lourdes's seventy-fifth anniversary in the *Georgia Bulletin* in 1987 suggests that the membership level remained static, as the stated number of parishioners was 220 units, the same number Giusta gave in his report to Monsignor Jerry Hardy in 1979. According to Fr. Joseph Cavallo, Our Lady of Lourdes's pastor at the time, the parish had finally become self-supporting, other than the subsidy the school received, but remained small in size and materially poor. "Lourdes is going to have to look and see what it is that is going to draw people," Cavallo was quoted as saying. Implied throughout the article was the sentiment that Our Lady of Lourdes was a poor but scrappy parish, rich in history and community but not much else. However, the article also highlights the devotion the members had to securing a future for Our Lady of Lourdes. For example, the renovation of the church's sanctuary was funded in part by parishioners who ran a concession booth at Atlanta–Fulton County Stadium, which allowed nonprofit groups to operate stands and keep 10 percent of what they earned.[6]

Although the situation at Our Lady of Lourdes was particularly dire during the 1970s and 1980s, all of the archdiocese's majority-Black parishes struggled to some extent during this period. The minutes of a meeting at the chancery with Fathers Giusta, John Adamski of St. Anthony, and Henry Gracz of Saints Peter and Paul in the increasingly Black suburb of Decatur stated that the pastors of majority-Black, inner-city parishes felt institutionally isolated from the rest of the archdiocese, which was largely white and suburban. These priests charged that white Catholics, both lay and ordained, were "not aware of, or perhaps interested in, these [Black] parishes and what is (or is not) going on in them." The pastors noted that wealthier parishes in northern Atlanta and its adjacent suburbs could embark on ambitious building projects, while their parishes could barely afford core personnel, such as secretaries and religious education teachers. They pointed out that even the south metro deanery at Sacred Heart was disinterested in what was happening at the Black parishes, and the *Georgia Bulletin*, the official newspaper of the archdiocese, seldom covered the activities held at Black parishes.

Perhaps most egregious from the perspective of growing the Black apostolate, the pastors claimed that the archdiocese continued to neglect Black talent and leadership by failing to appoint a priest to Atlanta University, by not hiring Black professionals to work at the archdiocesan offices, and by closing the Urban Affairs Office. The core problem was "the attitude of indifference from the larger segment of the Church of Atlanta which is white and middle class." The pastors suggested a variety of solutions, including increasing programing for the Black parishes, an affirmative action program to increase the number of Blacks working for the archdiocese, and adding a section in the *Georgia Bulletin* that would focus on urban events. Overall, the priests expressed their frustration not only that the physical survival of majority-Black parishes was in danger but that they suffered from institutional marginalization from the archdiocese itself.[7]

Despite its chronic budgetary problems and alienation from the rest of the archdiocese, Our Lady of Lourdes remained active in local outreach and social justice efforts during the 1970s and 1980s. Under the leadership of Mattie Smith, a Lourdes member since 1944, the parish social action committee involved itself in a plethora of issues that affected poor Blacks in the Auburn Avenue neighborhood. The group worked with the Homeless Union and hosted a consciousness raising group for the unhoused in the Our Lady of Lourdes cafeteria, where they could discuss the barriers preventing them from getting off the streets. Another project was Food for the Neighborhood, which distributed food parcels to the poor, including a number of older widows who were members of the parish. In 1987, the *Georgia Bulletin* reported that Our Lady of Lourdes was preparing to establish a free Sunday breakfast program in response to the number of indigent people coming to the parish in search of food.[8]

Our Lady of Lourdes was also active in local ecumenical activities pertaining to Black history, especially those related to Auburn Avenue's most famous son, Martin Luther King Jr. While the federally recognized Martin Luther King Jr. holiday was first celebrated in 1986, King's birthday had become an unofficial holiday in areas with substantial Black populations, including Atlanta, as early as 1969. Our Lady of Lourdes was the first Catholic school in the Archdiocese of Atlanta to close for King's birthday on January 14, 1971. The following year, the first pan-archdiocesan Martin Luther King Mass was held at Lourdes, "with representatives from all Catholic schools attending." Martin Luther King Sr. preached at the Mass, a notable change from when he dismissively referred to Our Lady of Lourdes School as "that white school."[9]

In 1977, the body of Martin Luther King Jr. had been moved from its original resting place at Southview Cemetery to a plot of land across the street from Our Lady of Lourdes that would later become the Martin Luther King Jr. Center for Non-Violent Social Change (i.e., the King Center). Coretta Scott King established the King Center in 1968 as a combination library, archives, memorial, and civil rights organization. She ran the King Center out of her basement before deciding to build a permanent location on Auburn Avenue.[10] As Coretta Scott King raised money to build the King Center complex, King Jr.'s body stayed in a temporary crypt surrounded by a white picket fence. The schoolchildren from Our Lady of Lourdes School used the area around the crypt as a makeshift playground until construction of the physical plant began. The gravesite attracted numerous visitors, including the occasional politician or head of state. According to Sr. Margaret McAnoy, a sister with Sisters of the Immaculate Heart of Mary who was principal of the school at this time, "Any time someone notable like a king, whoever came to the grave, our whole school, little school would walk across and be there during the ceremony. . . . I thought, 'These children would never see a king.' So it was great."[11]

A Sunday bulletin from January 4, 1976, implored the Our Lady of Lourdes community to respond to a special appeal from Martin Luther King Sr. for the parish to contribute five hundred dollars toward a permanent tomb for King Jr. at the space that would later become the King Center. "All of you are aware of the many changes taking place across the street at the gravesite of Dr. Martin Luther King, Jr. as construction proceeds for his permanent entombment. As one of the local churches in the area, we have received a special request from Martin Luther King, Sr. asking us to participate financially by contributing $500.00 so the permanent entombment may become a reality by January 15, 1976 . . . we will be taking up a special collection at Our Lady of Lourdes Church on January 11th in response to that request."[12] The $216 Our Lady of Lourdes contributed was far less than the $500 King Sr. requested, but it was only $49 short of the $265 that was collected for the Offertory for that week. Regardless, the bulletin for January 18, 1976, thanked parishioners for being so generous in contributing for a common vision for the Auburn Avenue community. The eagerness of the Our Lady of Lourdes congregation to contribute to King Jr.'s permanent tomb seems to belie Giusta's concerns about the potential negative effects that civil rights memorials might have on the Auburn Avenue community.[13]

The parish had, of course, always been connected to its Protestant neighbors and the larger Black community. An earlier bulletin from July 7, 1974, expressed condolences of the Our Lady of Lourdes community after a June 30 mass shooting at Ebenezer Baptist Church claimed the life of Alberta Williams King, mother of King Jr. and Deacon Edward Boykin. The bulletin reprinted the telegram that had been sent to King Sr. in the name of the entire congregation: "We extend our sympathy to you at this difficult time and sincerely deplore the senseless violence responsible for the death of Mrs. King and Deacon Boykin. They have been included in our prayers, as also we remember those who were wounded, and the misguided young man who caused this tragedy. Be strong in the Lord. The Congregation of Our Lady of Lourdes Catholic Church." The bulletin also indicated that two lay members, Phyllis Benjamin and Don Watson, had attended a memorial for Mrs. King on

July 2, while Fr. Bob Kinast had been present at the funeral at Southview Cemetery on July 3.[14]

The 1977 play put on by the students at Our Lady of Lourdes School, titled "Our Lady of Lourdes—A Pilgrim People," provides insight into how the parish community interpreted being Black and Catholic in Atlanta and how they were asserting their place in an evolving Auburn Avenue community. The play was a dramatic interpretation of the founding and history of Our Lady of Lourdes in honor of the sixty-fifth anniversary of the parish. The cast of characters included everyone from Katharine Drexel to the "angry citizens" who had objected to building Our Lady of Lourdes on Highland Avenue, Christine Bullock, Our Lady of Lourdes's first convert and the SBS's longtime housekeeper, and Martin Luther King Jr. Text at the bottom of the program read, "We ask everyone to join in singing, 'If We Could Share' at the end of the program and over at Martin Luther King's grave."

This program provides insight into how the Our Lady of Lourdes community interpreted its past and future during a period of contraction. Unlike Northern parishes that adhered to the "parish boundaries" model, where territorial parishes tended to be monoethnic and monoreligious, non-Blacks and non-Catholics were always a part of the Our Lady of Lourdes story. Whites acted as sisters, priests, patrons, and (beginning in the late 1960s) fellow parishioners, while non-Catholic Blacks in the wider Auburn Avenue community, such as Martin Luther King Jr., were neighbors and comrades in the fight for social justice. While white ethnics felt like their neighborhoods and parishes lost their sacred character when their monoethnic character was threatened by new Black migration patterns, Auburn Avenue remained sacred in the eyes of Black Catholics and Protestants, even as the neighborhood entered a period of economic and demographic decline.[15]

As the Martin Luther King Jr. Historical Site emerged on the properties adjacent to the church throughout the 1980s, Our Lady of Lourdes itself became a tourist attraction. The Martin Luther King Jr. Birth Home was located behind the church, while the King Center was across the street. This renewed visibility provided a stream of visitors who were curious about the presence of a Catholic parish in the Auburn Avenue neighborhood, but it also posed a problem for the archdiocese, which remained undecided about what to do with Our Lady of Lourdes. Closing a Black Catholic parish in such a high-traffic area would lead to negative publicity for the archdiocese at a time when it was still struggling to rectify its past mistakes vis-à-vis the Black community.[16]

These events illustrate the evolving relationship Our Lady of Lourdes had to the Auburn Avenue neighborhood in the post–Vatican II / post–Jim Crow era. Although Our Lady of Lourdes members had extensive dealings with the other religious institutions on Auburn Avenue because of family and community ties, the parish as an institution remained aloof from cooperating with other churches. The SBS annals describe the sisters interacting with white Catholics and the various denizens in Atlanta's Black community, but not with representatives from other churches in the area. This was not surprising in the pre–Vatican II era, given that ecumenical activity was condemned as giving tacit assent to the claims of "false churches." The fact that the SBS and the Society of African Missions (SAM) priests assigned to Our Lady of Lourdes were white may also have made them suspect in the eyes of Black religious leaders. However, a mutual interest in civil rights activity, combined with Vatican II's emphasis on building ties with "separated brethren," helped increase interactions between Our Lady of Lourdes and Auburn Avenue's Protestant churches. By the time Our Lady of Lourdes was involving itself in ecumenical activities in the 1970s, the parish was beginning to embrace its identity not just as a majority-Black parish, but specifically as a historically Black parish in the Auburn Avenue area and all of the storied history associated with that location.

Although the Auburn Avenue area had begun to show signs of deterioration by the 1970s, there were many Blacks who refused to give up on the once great neighborhood. A coterie of Black community leaders, including Coretta Scott King, established the Historic District Development Corporation (HDDC) in 1980 to help revitalize the Auburn Avenue community. The HDDC operates with three guiding principles: nondisplacement of existing residents, historic preservation, and economic diversity. In practical terms, this means balancing the desire to preserve Auburn Avenue's illustrious past with the need to make the area a living neighborhood for the people that reside there, including elderly and low-income residents who tend to be pushed out by economic development. Since its inception, the HDDC has restored or built 120 single family homes, 500 multifamily units, 275 affordable housing units of both types, and over 40,000 square feet of commercial space.

Despite the successes of the HDDC in reversing some of the blight that has affected the Auburn Avenue community since the 1970s, the development of commercial space in the area remains sparse in comparison to the building of residential units. The retail spaces that have emerged on Auburn Avenue tend to be the kind of trendy boutique stores that are often associated with gentrifying areas, but not those that would help long-term residents with their daily needs. Rapidly rising rents and property values threaten the ability of many Blacks to stay in the neighborhood. Still, it seems unlikely that Auburn Avenue's identity as a historic cauldron of Black culture will ever be completely subsumed by gentrification. Today, many of Auburn Avenue's buildings, both historical and more recent, sport colorful murals of civil rights figures and scenes of Black liberation, making a visual claim on the neighborhood's future.[17]

It is difficult to say how the changing demographics of the Old Fourth Ward and Auburn Avenue area have directly impacted membership at Our Lady of Lourdes. According to a parish-wide census conducted in 2019, Blacks still make up a majority of membership at 71 percent, but the white membership of Our Lady of Lourdes is 13 percent.[18] Marshall Thomas and Sandra Criddell, two of the Black Catholics interviewed for this work, asserted that gentrification and the subsequent influx of whites into Our Lady of Lourdes played a large role in revitalizing the parish.[19] However, the latest geodemographic data compiled by the Archdiocese of Atlanta in 2016 state that only 5 percent of Our Lady of Lourdes members live in the parish's zip code of 30312, while 83 percent come from zip codes listed as "other." Many of these "other" zip codes are not in the City of Atlanta but are located in outlying suburbs such as College Park, Mableton, and Fayetteville. These data suggest that gentrification may have spurred on improvements that lessened the worst of the Auburn Avenue area's blight, which made individuals from outside the Old Fourth Ward feel safe enough to visit locations like Our Lady of Lourdes.[20]

That the bulk of Our Lady of Lourdes's membership comes from outside of the immediate neighborhood is not unusual, especially since neighborhood and parish membership have largely been decoupled in the post–Vatican II era. This is illustrated by the fact that when the territorial boundaries of Our Lady of Lourdes were finally clarified in 1996, the matter had become a bureaucratic formality. During this process, Our Lady of Lourdes and St. Paul of the Cross became territorial parishes rather than the ethnic personal parishes they had been since their respective establishments. The boundaries of Sacred Heart, St. Anthony of Padua, and Saints Peter and Paul were also changed in response to the creation of permanent borders for Our Lady of Lourdes and St. Paul of the Cross. However, as Monsignor Edward J. Dillon said in a letter from August 14, 1996, "These changes will not really affect any of the parishes in question in practice—but they will enable us to bring their canonical status in line with all our other parishes." At this point, a significant portion of the members at all of the parishes in question were commuting from outside their boundaries, which made the boundaries themselves irrelevant from the practical standpoint of parish membership.[21]

The geodemographics for Atlanta's three other in-town pre–Vatican II parishes (Basilica of the Sacred Heart, Shrine of the Immaculate Conception, and St. Anthony of Padua) also indicate that the majority of their members originate from a multiplicity of zip codes outside of where the parish in question is physically located. Of these, St. Anthony of Padua has the smallest percentage of parishioners from "other" zip codes (64 percent), and the largest percentage of members coming from core zip codes near the parish itself (37 percent). However, the percentage of "other" zip codes is highest at Our Lady of Lourdes. This illustrates that while all of these parishes are attracting a significant percentage of their members from outside their respective boundaries and outside of the City of Atlanta itself, this trend is most evident at Our Lady of Lourdes.[22]

The appeal of Our Lady of Lourdes to those outside of the neighborhood stems from the way in which the parish reinvented itself by fully embracing inculturation to an extent not seen in Atlanta's other majority-Black parishes. This process started in the 1970s, when Our Lady of Lourdes embraced its unique identity as a historic Black Catholic parish located in the same neighborhood that nurtured Martin Luther King Jr. The second phase commenced in 1990, when newly hired choir director Melody Cole introduced jazz, gospel, and spirituals into the parish choir's repertoire. Although the use of Black music at Our Lady of Lourdes appears to have started in the early 1980s, it does not seem to have been widely used until the end of the decade when *Lead Me, Guide Me: The African American Catholic Hymnal* was published. *Lead Me, Guide Me* contained both spirituals and Gregorian chants, essentially putting both on equal footing within the liturgical setting for Black Catholics. It may have been the case that the issuing of *Lead Me, Guide Me* provided an official imprimatur on Black music in the Catholic liturgy that won over the more skeptical Lourdes parishioners. Regardless of the circumstances, under Cole's leadership, the choir at Our Lady of Lourdes helped to remake the parish's liturgy and the composition of the parish.[23]

The Black Catholic Movement and Liturgical Reform

This was the genesis of the "Lourdes Experience," which would distinguish it not just from the majority-white parishes in Atlanta, but also from other Black parishes such as St. Paul of the Cross and St. Anthony of Padua. A 1990 article in the *Atlanta Journal-Constitution* about Our Lady of Lourdes stated, "[The choir's] solos inspire applause, sometimes in the middle of songs. Their ballads move people to tears. Their gospel songs get folks clapping and tapping their feet." The spirit of Our Lady of Lourdes's liturgy was embodied by other aspects of parish life, especially in its social justice and community outreach ministries. These organizations had always been a key part of life at Our Lady of Lourdes, but the way in which the liturgy was conducted reinforced the link between the Gospel, the liturgy, and social action in the way envisioned by early twentieth-century Liturgical Movement pioneers like Dom Virgil Michel.[24]

The seeds of the Lourdes Experience were planted in the early 1970s with the emergence of the Black Catholic Movement, which promoted the application of Black Power concepts to liturgy, identity, and practice among Black Catholics.[25] Two weeks after the assassination of Martin Luther King Jr., the newly formed Black Clergy Caucus issued a statement that condemned racism in the religious and secular realms. It not only demanded that "Black people control their own affairs and make decisions for themselves" but also argued for an extension of Black leadership in the Church as a whole. The Black Clergy Caucus stated that the Catholic Church needed to reassess its views on Black militancy, especially given the institution's tacit approval of white supremacist violence. They declared that the time of Black nonviolence (defined as Blacks passively waiting for white concessions on racial issues) was over, declaring that "the appropriateness of responsible, positive militancy against racism is the only Christian attitude against this or any other kind of evil." Although the statement said that white priests generally lacked the psychological awareness to learn from Black Catholics, it also stated that "Black-thinking" white priests should be assigned to Black parishes if no Black priests were available. However, any white priest or sister working in the Black community needed to be aware that they were not going to receive the kind of automatic deference that they had once enjoyed from Black Catholics in the pre–Vatican II / pre–civil rights era.[26]

The National Black Sisters' Conference released a similar statement in 1969. Like the declaration issued by the Black Clergy Caucus, the National Black Sisters stated their outrage at continuing white supremacy at the institutional and individual levels. However, the National Black Sisters asserted that their religious vocation demanded that they speak out against the evil of racism because remaining silent would be a betrayal of their commitment to God. Their ultimate goal was nothing short of the "total liberation" of the Black community through communal action and empowerment. The declaration called for increased solidarity in the Black community, and it stated that the National Black Sisters' Conference would be doing so by participating in the Central Office for Black Catholicism (later the National Office for Black Catholics [NOBC]).[27]

Black Catholics also made progress in terms of representation in the hierarchy. The first Black bishop, Joseph Howze, was consecrated auxiliary bishop of Natchez-Jackson, Mississippi, and later became bishop of Biloxi, Mississippi, in 1977. By 1984, the number of Black bishops in the American Church had grown to ten, and they collectively issued a pastoral letter titled "What We Have Seen and Heard" that instructed Black Catholics that "the Black Catholic community in the American Church has come of age" and that they had an obligation to "reclaim our roots and to shoulder the responsibilities of being both Black and Catholic." The American bishops established the Secretariat for African

American Catholics in 1986 to address Black Catholic concerns at the episcopal level.[28]

The Archdiocese of Atlanta was one of the territories that experienced firsthand the leadership from this first cohort of Black bishops. Eugene Marino, a Black bishop from the Josephite order, was consecrated as archbishop of Atlanta on May 5, 1988. Marino was the U.S. Catholic Church's first Black archbishop, and his installation ceremony garnered international interest. The event was covered extensively on national news broadcasts as well as being given front-page coverage in publications such as the *New York Times*, *Washington Post*, and *Atlanta Constitution*. The superior generals of the women's religious orders that ministered to Blacks—the SBS, the Oblate Sisters of Providence, the Holy Family Sisters, and the Holy Ghost Sisters—had a place of prominence during the ceremony. An unprecedented crowd of forty-six hundred crammed into Atlanta's Civic Center to watch Marino's installation Mass, including civil rights figures such as Andrew Young and Coretta Scott King.[29]

As archbishop of Atlanta, Marino focused on "those weakest and most vulnerable members of the flock ... for those on the fringes, those most likely to stray, those most threatened by danger." To that end, he emphasized the need for greater understanding and compassion for the imprisoned, ethnic minorities, individuals with AIDS, and other groups that were often ignored in mainstream Catholic discourse. Marino was also heavily involved in ecumenical and civic activities in Metropolitan Atlanta; he was part of a clergy coalition against violence, publicly backed a desegregation proposal for DeKalb County that would involve transferring teachers, rather than students, urged Catholics in Gwinnett County to support the building of the county's first synagogue, and performed religious services at the Carter Presidential Center.[30]

However, Marino's tenure as archbishop ended abruptly when an illicit sexual relationship with a lay minister, Vicki R. Long, was exposed in 1990. He resigned from his post on July 10, 1990, stating that the Archdiocese of Atlanta "needs a shepherd who is physically, spiritually, and psychologically healthy."[31] Marino entered seclusion at a hospital to seek treatment for his personal demons and upon release spent the rest of his life counseling other priests who struggled with substance abuse and sexual misconduct.[32]

Despite the ignominious end to Marino's tenue as archbishop of Atlanta, he is still remembered fondly by many in Atlanta's Black Catholic community. On the event of the twentieth anniversary of Marino's consecration, Fr. Edward Branch, the chaplain at the Lyke House—Atlanta University Center, wrote the following recollection in the *Georgia Bulletin*: "We here in the Atlanta University Center remember and celebrate because it was [Marino] who proclaimed the construction of a Newman Center for the Atlanta University Center.... We cannot forget him because we experienced in his pastoral way the change in church and society that we now see taking place in our midst. The world church had come to Atlanta. Archbishop Marino's kindness and patience and self-giving will create of us all the brothers and sisters we must be to eliminate racism and classism in our day." To Black Catholics such as Fr. Branch, Marino represented the culmination of the hopes of the Civil Rights Movement and the Black Catholic Movement. Marino and his work made Black Catholics feel seen and appreciated in a way that the members of the white hierarchy could not.[33]

After Marino's resignation, Bishop James Patterson Lyke, a Black Franciscan friar and former auxiliary bishop of Cleveland, became the fourth archbishop of Atlanta, on June 24, 1991. He had initially arrived in Atlanta to be the apostolic administrator of the archdiocese in the wake of Marino's resignation. According to Fr. Henry Gracz, who was then the vicar for clergy and the archdiocese, Lyke had a "creative and visionary spirit much like that of Archbishop [Paul] Hallinan. He had a strong drive in him for the Church to be the best that Christ would want it to be, a church of justice, of good liturgical prayer and a church of involvement."[34] Lyke worked to increase the public profile of the Catholic Church in the South, empower the Church to be more of a "grassroots community," and further integrate the Archdiocese of Atlanta.[35] Lyke had an interest in fostering a Black Catholic liturgical tradition, playing a key role in the writing and dissemination of the *Lead Me, Guide Me* hymnal. Noting the rising numbers of Hispanic Catholics moving to the Archdiocese of Atlanta, Lyke built a Spanish-language mission serving the Chamblee and Doraville areas and required all seminarians to be able to speak Spanish.[36]

However, Lyke's tenure as archbishop was cut short when he died of inoperable cancer on December 27, 1992.[37] A traditional Black vigil was held for Lyke at the Cathedral of Christ the King, where the choirs from Our Lady of Lourdes, St. Anthony of Padua, and Saints Peter and Paul performed Black spirituals from the *Lead Me, Guide Me* hymnal.[38] Both the Lyke Center at the Atlanta University Center and the Archbishop Parish Lyke Center at St. Anthony of Padua are named after the late prelate.

Alongside this organizational action, the Black Catholic liturgical renaissance of the 1970s emerged as a natural outgrowth of the Black Arts Movement. According to Black theater scholar Larry Neal, the stated aim of the Black Arts Movement was to create art that "speaks directly to the needs and aspirations of Black America. In order to perform this task, the Black Arts Movement proposes a radical reordering of the western cultural aesthetic. It proposes a separate symbolism, mythology, critique, and iconology. The Black Arts and the Black Power concept both relate broadly to the Afro-American's desire for self-determination and nationhood."[39] Much like how Black Power demanded that Black people define themselves on their own terms, the Black Arts Movement stated that Black artists should depict the needs and aspirations of the Black community. The primary audience of the Black artist should be the Black community, without any regard to the opinions of white audiences. Black art should reflect a new Black aesthetic that consciously rejected Eurocentric standards of beauty since preexisting Western art forms were inherently anti-Black.

Although many Black Power proponents had an ambivalent attitude toward Christianity, the Black Arts Movement considered gospel music to be one of the most authentic, if not the most authentic, iterations of Black aesthetics. This is because "Gospel has distilled the aesthetic essence of the Black arts into a unified whole. It is a colorful kaleidoscope of Black oratory, poetry, drama and dance. One has only to experience a gospel 'happening' in its cultural setting to hear Black poetry in the colorful oratory of the Black gospel preacher, or to see the drama of an emotion-packed performance of a Black gospel choir interacting with its gospel audience, and the resulting shout of the holy dance. It is indeed a culmination of the Black aesthetic experience."[40] Unlike Black musical styles like jazz that were the products of syncretism between Western and African cultures, gospel contained almost no signs of European influence. Thus, for proponents of Black aesthetics like Pearl Williams-

Jones, the cultural conservatism of Black Protestant churches became an asset since the gospel music produced by these churches could be regarded as an accurate representation of the religious culture of the West African societies affected by slavery. The music found in Black churches in the South, particularly in impoverished rural areas, was believed to be the most authentic representation of gospel music, as they were physically and culturally isolated from outside influences.[41]

The extent to which Black Catholics engaged with the more secular aspects of the Black Arts Movement is unclear. However, Black Catholic intellectuals such as Brother Joseph Davis, Sister Thea Bowman, and Sister Martin de Porres Grey were clearly influenced by the idea of a Black religious sensibility that transcended not only sectarian boundaries but also regional and national borders. According to these scholars and activists, Black Catholic life needed to be informed and embodied according to this Black religious tradition, while still being rooted in the norms of the Roman Rite.[42]

The influence of the Black Arts Movement on Black Catholic aesthetics is evident in the numerous artistic works created during the 1970s. Foremost among these are the compositions of Fr. Clarence J. Rivers, a priest in the Diocese of Cincinnati who is generally considered the Father of Black Catholic liturgy. Rivers first came to prominence as a composer and liturgist in 1963 when he unveiled his *American Mass Program*, which embedded a Black aesthetic in the context of the Roman Rite. He was the first director of the NOBC's Department for Culture and Worship, and under his leadership, this division sponsored workshops, lectures, conferences, and publications that advanced an inculturated approach to Black Catholic liturgical expression. The work of the conferences was particularly important since their purpose was to "educate and 'liberate' Black Catholics to reclaim the fullness of their religious and ritual heritage, and to train ministers for the tasks of leadership." These conferences also provided a forum for newer composers, such as Grayson Brown, Robert Ray, and Ronald Harbor, to collaborate and test out new compositions.[43]

Rivers's ultimate goal as a liturgist was not simply to incorporate Black elements within the rubrics of the Roman Rite but to make Catholic worship *effective* for Black Catholic communities via the liturgy. He defined "effective worship" as a ritual that created an atmosphere of transcendent experience, addressed the material and psychological circumstances of the participants, and was enjoyable, leading up to the metanoia experience (i.e., constant renewal of the heart that led to the creation of committed disciples). A liturgical event that was merely "valid" according to canon law but was otherwise characterized by spiritually dead music and preaching could hardly be considered effective. Rivers believed that Catholic worship for Blacks needed to speak to their collective and individual conditions by appealing to their whole selves, both to their Black roots and to the heritage of Latin Christendom.[44]

The culmination of the Black liturgical renaissance was the publication of *Lead Me, Guide Me: The African American Catholic Hymnal* in 1987. The National Black Clergy Caucus authorized the creation of a Catholic hymnal that reflected the cultural heritage of Blacks in 1983. The Black Hymnal Committee was a cross-section of Black Catholics from different walks of life, such as clergy, composers, musicians, officials from the National Office for Black Catholics (NOBC), and a representative from the Knights and Ladies of Peter Claver (a Black corollary to the Knights of Columbus). The finished hymnal contained not just gospel and spiritual songs but also notations for Gregorian chant, hymns in Latin and English, and civil rights–era freedom songs. The cover design of the hymnal was a visual representation of the dual heritage of Black Catholics, containing the Chi-Ro and a stylized M for the Virgin Mary on a kente cloth background. James P. Lyke, the auxiliary bishop of Cleveland, and William Norvel, the president of the National Black Catholic Clergy Caucus, wrote the preface, which they signed and dated on "April 4, 1987, The Anniversary of the Deaths of Saint Benedict the Black and Reverend Dr. Martin Luther King, Jr." *Lead Me, Guide Me* quickly became not only the default hymnal in majority-Black parishes across the United States but also the primary means of achieving inculturation in said parishes.[45]

Despite the achievements of the Black Catholic Movement in terms of increasing representation and institutional strength, many Black Catholics still felt devalued and disempowered within a Eurocentric and white-dominated Church. This led to serious discussion about whether Black Catholics should petition for a separate rite within the Catholic Church. The idea was not without precedent, as the bishops of the Democratic Republic of the Congo petitioned the Vatican in 1969 for permission to create a rite that would be more culturally relevant to the Catholics of that nation. While the bishops waited for the Vatican's response, they convened a committee to research and design an experimental liturgy for their country. The bishops finally received definitive approval for what is now referred to as the Zaire Usage on April 30, 1988, despite the fact that the Vatican was clamping down on liturgical experimentation at that time.

According to Nathan David Chase, the rubrics of the Zaire Usage are inspired by three sources: the post–Vatican II Roman Missal, the priest as traditional Congolese chief within the context of the sanctuary, and the concept of the African assembly that empowers the congregation. The order of the Zaire Use liturgy is slightly different than that of the Roman Rite; the penitential rite comes after the homily, and the spirits of the ancestors are invoked, along with the intercession of the saints. An announcer, whose role is to introduce and provide commentary on the different aspects of the Mass, is an official position in the Zaire Use. The most controversial addition to the Zaire Use is liturgical dance, a practice that is considered an aberration at best among many white Catholics in Europe and the Americas. The Zaire Use is technically not a rite in and of itself but rather a specific, local expression of the Roman Rite, and it is approved for use only within the borders of the Democratic Republic of Congo. However, the fact that the Vatican allowed the Zaire Use to exist in the first place suggested that a similar arrangement could be allowed for Blacks in the United States.[46]

The question of whether Black Catholics should continue to inculturate the preexisting Roman Rite or seek greater autonomy came to a head in 1989, when Fr. George Stallings Jr., a Black priest in the Archdiocese of Washington, D.C., announced his intention to establish an independent Black Catholic congregation as a way to force the hierarchy into approving an African American Rite. Stallings had been a rising star in the American Church; while he was pastor of St. Teresa of Avila Catholic Church in Washington, D.C., he raised membership from two hundred to two thousand, and he was director of evangelism for the archdiocese until he embarked on his schismatic activities. Despite this success, Stallings claimed that he felt devalued by the hierarchy in a 1989 article. In *Ebony* magazine, he wrote, "As a successful Black priest, I recognized I could write my own ticket, but I never felt at peace. . . . No matter what

I wanted to do, I always had to get the stamp of the White establishment. I realized the church is a White racist institution controlled by a preponderantly Euro-American White male hierarchy that for a century had decided the fate of Black people in the Catholic Church. My Blackness could no longer tolerate it."[47] He said the first Mass for his new congregation, Imani Temple, on July 2, 1989, in the auditorium of Howard University. The following day, Cardinal James Hickey of Washington, D.C., suspended Stallings for his "destructive" and "disobedient" actions, but he did not excommunicate him at that time. Stallings formally announced his intention to leave the Catholic Church to establish the African American Catholic Congregation while giving a speech at DePaul University in Chicago on February 1, 1990.[48]

Although fears that there would be a mass exodus of Black Catholics into the African American Catholic Congregation proved to be unfounded, most agreed with Stallings's assertions about pervasive racism and the devaluation of Black culture within the Catholic Church. The Stallings affair did have the desired effect of starting discussion in the hierarchy about whether an African American Rite was necessary. On July 26, 1989, several weeks after Stallings's first Mass at Imani Temple, the American Church's Black bishops announced their intention to commission a research committee about a possible African American Rite. In August, the National Black Clergy Caucus, the National Black Sisters' Conference, and the National Black Catholic Seminarians Conference held a joint event with Stallings in attendance to advocate for the creation of an African American Rite and to support Stallings's claims of racism in the Church. The NOBC also studied the feasibility of an African American Rite in a three-day workshop in August 1989, but the group's board of directors did not directly endorse a separate Black rite, and ultimately an African American Rite was not adopted. D. Reginald Whitt writes that according to an opinion poll commissioned by the National Black Catholic Congress in January 1995, 75 percent of those surveyed opposed the creation of an African American Rite, but almost two-thirds supported more inculturation in the Roman Rite.[49]

It is unclear how the parishioners of Our Lady of Lourdes and the other Black parishes in the Archdiocese of Atlanta felt about the controversies raised by the Black Catholic Movement or the Stallings affair. During the late 1960s, members of the Black Catholic Movement in Chicago shocked white sensibilities with Black Unity Masses infused with fiery Black nationalist rhetoric, whereas the parishioners at Our Lady of Lourdes were arguing about the propriety of guitars and Folk Masses. Perhaps the dynamics of Chicago's de facto segregation, Black Power, and an urban area where white Catholics formed a plurality of the population created a situation where a significant number of Black Catholics favored open rebellion against the white hierarchy, at least when it came to cultural expression in the liturgy. In Atlanta, pan-African and Black nationalist concepts would not have been unknown to Black Catholics during this time, given the popularity of such ideas on the Atlanta University Center campus and in the West End neighborhood, where the now majority-Black St. Anthony's was located.

But those ideas seem not to have been the animating influences in the post–civil rights and post–Vatican II life of Our Lady of Lourdes. Rather, during these two decades, the parish was redefining its identity (and working to ensure its material survival) by emphasizing its association with Auburn Avenue and Martin Luther King Jr. Our Lady of Lourdes understood that it had a unique history and patrimony, but it had yet to fully comprehend how this heritage could be expressed in its liturgy. Once the parish fully committed to an inculturated approach to liturgy in 1990, it was able to create an environment that was reflective of its roots as a Southern, Black, and Catholic religious institution.

The Lourdes Experience and Social Justice

A significant part of the Lourdes Experience consists of the history found in the surrounding neighborhood and the parish itself. When one visits the parish today, one is greeted by a historical marker from the Georgia Historical Society outside the church building. It recounts a brief history of the parish, including the role of the SBS in the Civil Rights Movement.[50] This descriptor roots Our Lady of Lourdes in the larger tradition of Black liberation and protest found on Auburn Avenue, topics that are not usually associated with the Catholic Church. The exterior of the church is similarly "uncatholic." While it is red brick that matches the former Our Lady of Lourdes School (now the Katharine Drexel Community Center), the design is reminiscent of many small Southern Protestant churches—a squat, rectilinear building with a steeple and a gently sloping roof. Elsewhere on the grounds of the church is a "prayer trail," a modern interpretation of the pre–Vatican II Mary Garden that contains a statue of the Virgin Mary, green space, and areas for contemplation.

The building, which was finished in 1960, is relatively small, given that the parish now consists of 710 families. On the day that I visited, the sanctuary was tightly packed during Masses, which created a homey atmosphere. The interior of the sanctuary is typical of the simplicity characteristic of many parishes that have undergone extensive post–Vatican II renovations. The roof consists of timbered wood with rafters that taper down to eye level. The space is brightly lit with both natural and artificial light, including overhead hanging lamps, mini spotlights in the ceiling, and windows containing white and blue glass. A large crucifix adorns the wall containing the tabernacle and is flanked by two banners whose colors and themes change with the liturgical year. The Mary and St. Joseph sides of the sanctuary that were marked by side altars during the pre–Vatican II era have been replaced by wall statues. The altar is slightly raised on a platform that is two steps high, and it is centered so that it is underneath the crucifix. A statue of St. Martin de Porres is positioned next to the Mary statue, with an Our Lady of Guadalupe votive candle altar opposite it. Plaques of the Stations of the Cross line the walls, with the figures depicted within it having African features.

Mass at Our Lady of Lourdes employs a number of instruments, some traditional to the Roman Rite (piano and organ) and others that are more commonly associated with gospel and jazz (drums, tambourines, and saxophone). Because of its historically small membership levels, Our Lady of Lourdes never had enough space to justify the building of a choir loft, and the parish's choir is located to the right of the main altar, under the St. Joseph statue. Choir members wear kente cloth choir robes as a visual reminder of the parish's racial and cultural background. The choirmaster stands in front of the choir and the instrumentalists to direct both the audience and the singers.

Mass was led by Fr. Jeffrey Ott, who became Our Lady of Lourdes's first Black priest in June 2009 upon the retirement of longtime pastor Fr. John Adamski. Like many of Our Lady of Lourdes's parishioners, Ott was a product of the network of educational institutions and parishes established by the Sisters of the Blessed Sacrament, having attended SBS parochial schools in New Orleans as a child before attending Xavier University of Louisiana for college. While attending Xavier, two SBS suggested to Ott that he might have a vocation to the priesthood. This led him to becoming a Dominican friar, eventually becoming the chaplain at Xavier before being sent to Our Lady of Lourdes. Ott's appointment to Our Lady of Lourdes represented the start of a new era in the parish's history, in which the leadership of the parish was reflective of the demographic makeup of the membership.[51]

The Lourdes Experience is also distinctive for the way in which all parts of the ordinary and the proper have been infused with a Black cultural idiom. This tone is set during the entrance, as the congregation claps and sings along with numerous musical refrains even after the Mass participants have taken their places in the sanctuary. Repeated refrains are unremarkable in Black Protestant churches but are foreign to the streamlined way the Roman Rite tends to be practiced in white Catholic parishes. Unsurprisingly, longer music leads to longer Mass times; Mass at Our Lady of Lourdes typically lasts between an hour and forty minutes and two hours, whereas Mass at the neighboring Basilica of the Sacred Heart is generally forty-five minutes to an hour. However, the spirit of the music and the congregation ensures that everyone who is present is active and engaged in the liturgical actions.

Other parts of the Mass show similar degrees of inculturation. The penitential rite is sung in a call-and-response style presided over by the choirmaster, as is the responsorial. The parts of the Mass that are supposed to invoke feelings of joy and praise, such as the Gloria and the Agnus Dei, are sung in an exuberant style that mixes elements of gospel and jazz. When the priest gives the homily, he does so directly in front of the congregation, using a Black preaching style. On some Sundays (but not the one I observed), the Mass contains liturgical dancing. The giving of the sign of peace is a lengthy exercise in hospitality involving hugs, handshakes, and friendly small talk.

If one takes for granted that the liturgy can and should be enjoyable, as Clarence J. Rivers asserted, then it should not be surprising why Mass at Our Lady of Lourdes and other majority-Black parishes lasts twice as long as Mass at majority-white parishes. However, many conservative white Catholics frown on a sensual approach to the liturgy, whether in terms of lively music or having physical contact with other parishioners. They view such things as "liturgical abuses" that are an affront to God and the dignity of the Mass. Rivers, on the other hand, argued that Western Christianity, whether in its Protestant or Catholic forms, suffers from a pervasive "puritanism" that deems anything too emotional, sensual, or enjoyable to be sinful. Rivers stated that the root cause of this negative response to the sensual is an "ocular-based cultural orientation" that regards that which can be seen as more intellectual, while those things that can be perceived by touch or other bodily senses are considered to be morally base and "fallen." This tendency to value the ocular over other modes of perception began with Plato and Aristotle and would eventually culminate in the belief, shared by Catholic theologians and secularists alike, that emotion was the enemy of reason, logic, and objectivity. The logic of the ocular-based society also extended to music, with melodic music being favored over rhythmic music because the latter breaks the continuity of the musical line. Since Western liturgical traditions arose in a cultural atmosphere with a bias toward the ocular and the melodic, the rhythmic music that tends to be characteristic of African cultures is condemned as being dangerously worldly and sensual, and thus unfit for the church sanctuary. Consequently, when white Christians observe their Black coreligionists engaged in worship that is livelier than what is found in their own churches, they interpret it as "doing Christianity wrong."[52]

Members of the parish are aware that many aspects of the Lourdes Experience, especially the aesthetics and the emotion, tend to be viewed negatively by some white Catholics. Our Lady of Lourdes member Sandra Criddell counters this view, saying,

> [Visitors are attracted to] our music, our style of preaching, I guess you could say our hospitality, because the majority of people come to Lourdes say that we were so warm and welcome.... I've been to [the Cathedral of Christ the King], and people there don't even look at you, they don't speak to you, they just come in, they go to Mass, and they go. And that's it.... When we pray the Our Father, the thing is to, at Lourdes, is to hold hands and give the sign of peace, we shake hands. But, at one point, the archbishop had sent out a letter, saying that you, that we were not required to do that, and if we did not want to, if you give somebody the sign

of peace, I don't know how you're going to give someone a sign of peace and you don't touch them. But he sent out a letter saying you did not have to do that if you did not want to, and my assumption is that it came, you know, the majority of the Catholics in the city of Atlanta are white, but it came from them. But you know, the Black churches I've visited still doing it. Why, I would say that, and, and you can tell the difference when you go to white Catholic churches and Black Catholic churches. The, the hospitality, you know, Black folks going to speak to you, even if they don't even know you. At the sign, the sign of peace, they're going to shake your hand and give you a hug. Not at the white Catholic churches, I have to say. They will turn around and look at you, and some of them will shake your hand, some of them won't.[53]

Ms. Criddell's statement suggests that the emotionally detached Mass experience that many white Catholics equate with "reverence" and "piety" comes off as cold and alien from a Black Catholic perspective. The very fact that the Lourdes Experience is so different from the atmosphere found at other parishes appears to be precisely what attracts members from so many zip codes across Atlanta.

For Rivers, the sacramentality that infused Catholic theology and practice meant that the liturgy could not be a purely spiritual affair, disconnected from the realities of being a human being that existed in a particular place and time.[54] The sacramentality of particular places and times is also expressed in a parish's engagement with the needs of its community. Certain parts of the Mass at Our Lady of Lourdes make clear the interplay between liturgical inculturation and social justice. The Prayers of the Faithful, for example, are conducted in an interactive manner. The priest begins with prayers that reflect the general concerns of the community, at the local, national, and global levels. On the Sunday I observed, these prayers included calls for an end to the death penalty, homelessness, and human trafficking. Such prayers might be considered too political or otherwise controversial in another parish, but these petitions are a natural extension of "Beloved Community" philosophy at Our Lady of Lourdes. Once the priest has finished, the individual members of the congregation are free to shout out their own prayer requests to the community. Like most aspects of liturgy at Our Lady of Lourdes, the interactive and often political nature of the Prayers

Figure 6.1. Sanctuary of Our Lady of Lourdes, 2021. Courtesy of Chris Aluka Berry.

of the Faithful lengthens the running time of Mass. But building a real community requires just this sort of immersion in each other's lives.

Social justice and liturgical renewal lead this parish to express hospitality in a number of ways. Visitors to Our Lady of Lourdes are asked to identify themselves and are given miniature loaves of bread prior to the Benediction. Attached to the bread bag is a tag with contact information about the parish. The giving of complimentary bread to visitors represents the giving and receiving of material bread, in addition to the sacred bread of the Eucharist. It also symbolizes that all people who arrive at Our Lady of Lourdes are part of the "work of the people" (i.e., the liturgy) as well as their "Beloved Community." Liturgical action (i.e., the Eucharist) and social action (ordinary bread) have a symbiotic relationship, with one empowering the individual congregants to perform the other.

The extent to which the Lourdes Experience differs from the way the liturgy operates at St. Anthony and St. Paul of the Cross is a matter of degree. As mentioned previously, the entirety of the ordinary and the propers at Our Lady of Lourdes is inculturated according to a Black aesthetic, whereas at St. Paul of the Cross liturgical inculturation extends only to using spirituals and Black hymns in the Roman Rite. At St. Anthony, some parts of the ordinary and propers are expressed in a Black idiom, but not to the same extent as at Our Lady of Lourdes. Other practices found at Our Lady of Lourdes, such as positioning the choir and the instrumentalists next to the altar, would not work at St. Anthony's and St. Paul of the Cross because of the practical limitations of their pre–Vatican II architecture. However, all three parishes have incorporated Afrocentric artwork into their respective sanctuary designs and exhibit a demonstrativeness during Mass that is generally absent in white parishes.

Our Lady of Lourdes's approach to liturgy is not objectively better than those of other majority-Black parishes in Atlanta; each has incorporated inculturated practices in its own way. What Black Catholics have achieved in these parishes is the ability to bring their "whole selves" to the liturgy and to have themselves and their cultural backgrounds respected by the wider Church. The combination of liturgy, social justice, and community that has emerged at Our Lady of Lourdes has been a magnet strong enough to draw both Black and white Atlantans from throughout the region to the historic district in which they are located.[55]

Conclusion

In his 1920 book *Europe and the Faith*, Anglo-French Catholic author Hilaire Belloc famously proclaimed, "The Church is Europe: and Europe is The Church," indicating not only that the Catholic perspective on European history was the only valid perspective on the subject, but also that the European Catholic had a special understanding of and relationship to the Church. While nonwhites and non-Catholics should and must be incorporated into the Church, if only for "civilizing" purposes, they could only aspire to being background characters in the ongoing story of European Catholic Christendom. Belloc's belief in the interchangeability of Catholic history and Western European history was factually incorrect even when Belloc first uttered it in 1920, but it sums up a belief that persists into the present day that the Catholic Church is inextricably bound up in the European story to such an extent that it excludes and belittles those with cultural and racial roots outside the Continent.[1]

Today, the numerical strength of global Catholicism has shifted from Western Europe to Latin America, and the Catholic populations in Africa and Asia are also increasing. According to a Pew Research survey from 2013, the most recent year for which data are available, six out of ten of the countries with the largest numbers of Catholics—Brazil, Mexico, the Philippines, the United States, Colombia, and the Democratic Republic of Congo—are outside of Europe. The report estimates that even in 1910, ten years before *Europe and the Faith* was published, Brazil's Catholic population was the third largest in the world, surpassed only by France and Italy.[2]

The demographics of the Catholic Church in the United States have also become more reflective of the diversity found in the global Church. According to statistics from the websites of the U.S. Conference of Catholic Bishops and the Pew Research Center, non-Hispanic whites still constitute the largest ethnic group in the American Church at 59 percent, but Hispanic Catholics now account for 34 percent of the overall Catholic population in the United States. Other nonwhite ethnic groups have also become more visible in post–Vatican II American Catholicism; as of 2010, the last year for which data are available, there were roughly three million Asian American Catholics and half a million Native American Catholics in the United States.[3]

Similarly, Metropolitan Atlanta's Catholic population has greatly expanded since the pre–Vatican II period, mostly due to an influx of non-Southern Catholics in the post–civil rights era. The area covered by the Archdiocese of Atlanta is still majority-Protestant, but the percentage of Catholics within this territory has risen to 14 percent. As of this writing, the Archdiocese of Atlanta consists of 104 parishes and missions serving 1.2 million Catholics. The racial and ethnic composition of Atlanta's Catholic population also goes beyond the strict Black-white binary of the past. Although the Archdiocese of Atlanta does not appear to keep data on its ethnic or racial demographics, the increase it has experienced in terms of its racial and ethnic diversity can be ascertained by the fact that Mass is currently offered in fourteen languages: English, Spanish, French, Portuguese, Polish, Latin, Indonesian, Chinese, Vietnamese, Korean, Haitian, Creole, Igbo, and Croatian. The Chancery now includes an Office of Intercultural and Ethnic Diversity to better address the needs of the disparate Catholic communities that reside in the archdiocese.[4]

As the changing demographics of the Catholic Church at the global, national, and local levels illustrate, Catholicism has spread and indigenized far outside of the post-Counter-Reformation European heartland. Thus, an alternative way to interpret the post–Vatican II "liturgical wars" is as a struggle over the implications of what it means to be a "catholic" (i.e., universal) church that purports to have the ability to represent all peoples in all times, despite the fact that its rituals and iconography originated in specific cultural and temporal contexts. Although pre-councilar popes such as Benedict XV insisted that being Catholic did not entail replacing the "native culture" with that of European culture, the subsequent controversies over the music and visual aesthetics of the Mass demonstrate the practical difficulty of parsing out which aspects of Tridentine Catholic liturgical practice were universal and which ones were culturally based. Once Catholic missionaries from Europe traveled outside of Eurasia and began successfully making converts in Latin America, Africa, and East Asia, it was inevitable that the missionized subjects would reframe Catholicism in terms that were relevant to their respective cultures, even if these new practices diverged widely from Belgian, French, or Italian Catholicism. If the Church is *not* Europe, nor Europe the Church, as Belloc claimed, then Catholicism is free to become truly Catholic, as at home in the Congo or the Auburn Avenue neighborhood as it is in Italy or France.[5]

Possibilities for Future Research

The story of Our Lady of Lourdes demonstrates the need to situate American Catholic history in specific cultural contexts. Although the Catholic Church asserted that it was the "True Church" all people were obliged to join, the hierarchy in the United States showed little interest in evangelizing Blacks, especially those in the South. The hierarchy, whether the Italian nobles who staffed the Holy See or the Irish Americans who composed most of the prelates in the United States, lacked the conceptual tools to understand how racism, whether at the individual or institutional level, negatively impacted the "Negro apostolate." When Our Lady of Lourdes was established in 1912, anti-Blackness was justified as the Southern way of life and Catholicism was considered potentially subversive to the racial order. As a "colored mission" operating in the Jim Crow South, Our Lady of Lourdes was isolated from other Catholics and Catholic institutions in Atlanta. In the neighborhood, Our Lady of Lourdes was surrounded by Protestant churches and its parishioners had ties to Black Protestantism, in terms of both cultural background and familial ties. Our Lady of Lourdes had a transient congregation during its early history, as many of the converts made during the early twentieth century migrated to Northern cities during the Great Migration. The convergence of Vatican II and the Civil Rights Movement gave the Our Lady of Lourdes community new avenues for political, cultural, and liturgical expression. Our Lady of Lourdes survived with the threat of being shuttered for almost twenty-five years until it experienced an influx of new members through liturgical renewal and an embrace of its unique heritage. The history of Our Lady of Lourdes is a story of Black resilience and creativity, in spite of almost a century of institutional abandonment and indifference.

This research advances our knowledge about the Catholic Church in the United States by illustrating the ways in which Southern Black Catholicism differs from the iterations of the faith found in the North. It suggests that Black Catholic involvement in the Civil Rights Movement may have been more extensive than previously believed, at least among laypeople. Research also illustrates the close ties between Black Catholics and Black Protestants in the Jim Crow / pre–Vatican II period and how those relationships influenced later ideas about inculturation at Our Lady of Lourdes. Finally, this volume has provided an example of how successful liturgical inculturation can be effective in transforming declining parishes. However, Atlanta's longtime reputation, real or imagined, for racial and political moderation means that the experiences of Black Catholics in other parts of the Deep South may be significantly different from those of Our Lady of Lourdes's parishioners.

The idea that pre-councilar Catholicism in the United States possessed a singular moral, liturgical, theological, and devotional unity that was shattered by the relativism and pluralism inspired by the Council ignores the diversity of "actually existing Catholicism" during the pre–Vatican II period. The formation of a seemingly monolithic white Catholic identity in the postwar era belies the serious conflicts that existed between different groups of white ethnic Catholics at the religious, political, cultural, and devotional levels. As Robert Orsi related in *The Madonna of 115th Street: Faith and Community in Italian Harlem, 1880–1950*, the Irish looked down upon the Italian *feste* as pagan, ostentatiously foreign, and a waste of resources that should have gone toward building parishes and schools. They considered Italian devotional practices to be "doing Catholicism wrong."[6] Similarly, the experiences of Our Lady of Lourdes parishioners detailed in this volume are not only distinct from those of white ethnic Catholics in the urban North (regardless of the ethnic community in question) but also very different from those of the Black Catholics in Chicago detailed in Matthew Cressler's *Authentically Black and Truly Catholic: The Rise of Black Catholicism in the Great Migration*. If there was no normative way for white ethnics to be Catholic in the pre–Vatican II era, the same is true for Black Catholics.[7]

Our Lady of Lourdes also contradicts the assumption that post–Vatican II American Catholicism has been uniformly characterized by contraction, in terms of both the vitality of Catholic institutions and the numbers of practicing Catholics. Until the 1990s, Our Lady of Lourdes had a precarious existence as a small and often overlooked Black mission in an overwhelmingly white Archdiocese. It was not until the parish transitioned from an explicitly Eurocentric manner of "doing church" to one that reflected its own unique cultural and historical patrimony that Our Lady of Lourdes was able to truly thrive. Although part of this growth resulted from an increase in the number of white Catholics in the Old Fourth Ward / Auburn Avenue area, the fact that Our Lady of Lourdes's white members would choose to attend a majority-Black parish, rather than Sacred Heart or the Shrine of the Immaculate Conception, indicates that they perceive that Lourdes possesses certain qualities and opportunities for spiritual growth that these majority-white downtown parishes lack.

Discussions about the effects and interpretation of Vatican II tend to assume that the effects of Vatican II were uniformly negative across the many iterations of global Catholicism. However, a recent quantitative study by Darren W. Davis and Donald B. Pope-Davis indicates that Black Catholics exhibit high levels of religious engagement and faithfulness, especially in comparison to white Catholics. Davis and Pope-Davis discovered that Black Catholic interviewees who attended majority-Black parishes such as Our Lady of Lourdes had levels of religiosity that were akin to those of Black Baptists, the most religiously engaged demographic in the United States. Their data suggest that these majority-Black parishes have the freedom to model their parish life using the broader Black religious tradition, which includes a high level of religious commitment. The Black Catholics who attended multiracial but predominantly white parishes were still more religiously engaged than white Catholics, though not to the same degree as Black Protestants or Black Catholics with memberships at majority-Black Catholic religious institutions. Davis and Pope-Davis's research suggests that Vatican II has not negatively impacted Black Catholic engagement or faithfulness in the Church.[8]

Unlike their white coreligionists, there does not appear to be significant disagreement about the meaning of Vatican II or whether it was a positive development among Black Catholics. This is largely because Black Catholics saw the council as an opportunity to implement the same spirit of social change within the Church that the Civil Rights

Movement was accomplishing in secular society. The reforms of Vatican II created new opportunities to refashion and reinterpret Catholicism in ways that were more meaningful to Black Catholics, whether it meant creating inculturated Masses or contributing a Black aesthetical sense to a multiracial parish. In comparison, conservative white Catholics interpreted these same changes as a full-frontal attack on the moral, theological, and liturgical unity that they believed had characterized pre-councilar Catholic identity. For whatever reason, the issues that have compromised and challenged the faith of many white Catholics do not seem to have had the same effect on Black Catholics.[9]

Possibilities for Future Research on Black Catholics in the United States

In the years since Vatican II, American political culture has shifted significantly, moving many white Catholics into the Republican Party. While there are many reasons for this shift, future studies could profitably examine the role of liturgical preferences. There is some indication that conflicts about the liturgy or the meaning of Vatican II among whites are indicators of views on political and social issues. In contrast, the findings of this research suggest that this may not be the case for Black Catholics. All of the Black Catholics interviewed for this project believed that Vatican II was a positive development in the history of the Church and had little nostalgia for pre–Vatican II Catholicism.

Likewise, even those few who were nostalgic for the Latin Mass remained politically identified with the Democratic Party and expressed concerns about the corrosive effects of anti-Black racism in American society. Two of the interviewees stated that they preferred the Latin Mass, but neither believed that it was objectively better than Mass in the vernacular. Valencia White reported that she missed the Latin Mass because of its ability to transcend modern racial, ethnic, and language barriers. Accordingly, she chose her current parish, St. John the Evangelist in Hapeville, Georgia, because it is a multiracial parish that reflects the diversity of the global Church. She is not opposed to inculturated Masses like those found at Our Lady of Lourdes, but she does not want a Mass that she feels is indistinguishable from a "Black Baptist church." Andrew Hill indicated that he preferred the Latin Mass for aesthetic reasons, while also expressing concern that conservative prelates, such as Pope Emeritus Benedict XVI, are trying to reverse the reforms of Vatican II. Both White and Hill identify politically with the Democratic Party, and they expressed their concerns about the corrosive effects of anti-Black racism in American society. These responses suggest that the link between liturgical preferences and political beliefs may not be as clear-cut among Black Catholics as among their white coreligionists.[10]

Another subject that would benefit from future study is the question of how a sacramental worldview manifests differently among Black and white Catholics. As McGreevy's *Parish Boundaries* relates, white ethnic Catholics in the urban North experienced their parish-dominated neighborhoods as having a sacred quality. However, they saw the sacredness of their neighborhoods as contingent on retaining a certain fortress-like quality. When non-Catholics and members of other ethnic groups, especially Blacks, moved in it became profaned beyond repair. In comparison, Blacks, regardless of religion, appear to regard a neighborhood of significance as sacred, even if its character has fundamentally changed over the decades due to urban decay, gentrification, or demographic change, as the example of the Auburn Avenue community indicates. The Auburn Avenue community is regarded as a sacred place, not just because of its connection to Martin Luther King Jr. but because the area once embodied, and has the potential to do so again, a counterpublic space that encourages communal Black flourishing. The fact that the current-day Auburn Avenue area is a hodgepodge of Black poverty and homelessness juxtaposed with white gentrification does not take away from the area's sacral character but is merely a clarion call to continue the work of restoring and protecting the neighborhood. Unlike the monoethnic neighborhoods described in *Parish Boundaries*, the presence of gentrifying whites in the Auburn Avenue community does not alter its sacred status; rather, whites are simply irrelevant or tangential to what makes Auburn Avenue special, even if their gentrifying activities pose an existential threat for the poor Black people who remain in the area. More research needs to be done on how the forced concentration of Black populations caused by segregation, of the both Jim Crow and de facto varieties, led to the inadvertent creation of shared sacred geography among Blacks of varying religious orientations.[11]

The history of Our Lady of Lourdes is part of a larger story, not just about the intersection of race and Catholicism in the South, but also about how the Church's purportedly universal pronouncements are interpreted at the local level. Although Catholic theology and ecclesiology have placed a great deal of emphasis on the supposed uniformity of Catholic faith and practice, especially after the early nineteenth-century process of Romanization and the declaration of papal infallibility after Vatican I, there has always been variation in how particular communities express their respective understandings of Catholicism. The pre–Vatican II history and culture of Our Lady of Lourdes was a reflection of a multiplicity of political and religious events and discourses: the pervasive reality of Jim Crow, the Catholic Church's institutional neglect of Black concerns, a Southern religious culture that was characterized by an overabundance of church options, frustrated Black political ambitions, and conversations about freedom that were separate from the manner in which whites understood these topics. The difficulties and successes that Our Lady of Lourdes has experienced over the decades cannot be explained without an understanding of the city and the neighborhood in which it was built.

ACKNOWLEDGMENTS

This book is a result of my long-term interest in the history and sociology of the Black Catholic population in the United States and an outgrowth of my research in religious studies at Boston University. I am extremely grateful to numerous individuals and institutions that have supported me as I worked to complete this book. I am especially indebted to Dr. Nancy Ammerman, my academic advisor at Boston University, whose advice and mentorship proved invaluable. In addition, Dr. Matthew Cressler, Dr. Theodore Hickman-Maynard, and Dr. Anthony Petro provided thoughtful feedback that allowed me to refine my research for this book.

This volume builds upon preexisting literature, but primary sources and oral histories were crucial to the completion of my research. The Archives of the Sisters of the Blessed Sacrament, located at the Catholic Historical Research Center of the Archdiocese of Philadelphia, was an invaluable aid. The annals and letters produced by the Sisters of the Blessed Sacrament assigned to Our Lady of Lourdes from 1912 to 1974 provide a timeline for every major event that occurred during their tenure at the parish. Most of the documents pertaining to the internal working of the Catholic Church in Atlanta were obtained from the Office of Archives and Records of the Archdiocese of Atlanta. A special thank-you is extended to Geoffrey Hetherington, the Archdiocese of Atlanta's archivist and records analyst, who provided me with many requested materials and offered guidance on how to obtain additional documents. The Auburn Avenue Research Library in Atlanta contained a treasure trove of data related to the Drexel Catholic High School controversy of the late 1960s, and archivists with the Roman Catholic Diocese of Savannah graciously provided me with unprocessed correspondence between Bishop Benjamin Keiley and Cardinal James Gibbons that is cited in chapter 1. I am also grateful for assistance from the archival staff with the Catholic University of America in Washington, D.C. Catholic University's Paul J. Hallinan Vatican II Collection provided me with invaluable information about how the Second Vatican Council was implemented in Atlanta. Last, the African American and the Roman Catholic Church Collection located at the Xavier University of Louisiana Archives and Special Collections provided me with invaluable articles from the *Georgia Bulletin* about Archbishops Eugene Marino and James P. Lyke.

This project could not have come to fruition without the assistance of oral histories secured from individuals associated with the churches discussed in this book. I am deeply indebted to the following persons who graciously answered my many questions and provided additional insight: Nellie Adams, PhD, Ruth Clark, Sandra Criddell, Gwendolyn Elmore, Andrew Hill, Deion Hutchinson, Georgia Hutchinson, Leona James, Margaret Jones, Howard King, Kenneth Laster, Richard Marion, Anita Martin, Sister Mary Margaret McAnoy, Lucille Neely, Cassandra Peters-Johnson, PhD, William Petty, Miriam Redding, Willie Louise Robinson, Marshall Thomas, Fanyette West, Anita Whatley, Paulyne Morgan White, Valencia White, and Juanita Wilson.

A very special thank-you is extended to the University of Notre Dame's Cushwa Center for the Study of American Catholicism. I was the first recipient of the Cyprian Davis, O.S.B. Prize. Funds received with this award were used to support research-related expenses needed to complete this volume. I also want to express my gratitude to Chris Aluka Berry for providing me with the photograph of Our Lady of Lourdes Catholic Church and to Carl Chasten of the City of Atlanta's planning department for creating a map of the Auburn Avenue / Old Fourth area.

Jennifer Hammer, my editor with New York University Press, provided superb guidance throughout the process of writing this book. I am immensely grateful for her assistance. I am also appreciative of the entire New York University Press team that brought this project to a successful conclusion.

Finally, a special and heartfelt thank-you is extended to my family—my mother, father, and brother—who provided encouragement, emotional support, and intellectual banter during the dissertation and book writing process.

NOTES

INTRODUCTION

1 Shannen Dee Williams has provided much-needed attention to the role of Black nuns, but the racial bridging of the Sisters of the Blessed Sacrament (SBS) has received less attention. See, for example, Shannen Dee Williams, "Forgotten Habits, Lost Vocations: Black Nuns, Contested Memories, and the 19th Century Struggle to Desegregate U.S. Catholic Religious Life," *Journal of African American History* 101, no. 3 (2016): 231–60.
2 Sisters of the Blessed Sacrament, "Annals of Our Lady of Lourdes Convent, January 1962–August 1973," Archives of the Sisters of the Blessed Sacrament, H40 B2, GA: Atlanta Our Lady of Lourdes, 1913–1974, box 1, folder 5, Catholic Historical Research Center of the Archdiocese of Philadelphia, Philadelphia.
3 Francis E. Hyland, March 26, 1950, Archives of the Sisters of the Blessed Sacrament, H40 B2, GA: Atlanta Our Lady of Lourdes, 1913–1974, box 1, folder 4, Catholic Historical Research Center.
4 Andrew S. Moore, *The South's Tolerable Alien: Roman Catholics in Alabama and Georgia, 1945–1970* (Baton Rouge: Louisiana State University Press, 2007), 3–5.
5 Lawrence E. Lucas, *Black Priest / White Church: Catholics and Racism* (Trenton, NJ: Africa World Press, 1992), 11–15; E. Franklin Frazier, *Black Bourgeoisie* (New York: Free Press, 1997), 89–90, 113–15; Andrew Hill, interview by Leah Mickens, digital recording, April 24, 2019.
6 Sr. Mary Aquinas to Katherine Drexel, n.d., Archives of the Sisters of the Blessed Sacrament, H40 B2, GA: Atlanta Our Lady of Lourdes, 1913–1974, box 1, folder 7, Catholic Historical Research Center.
7 Andrew S. Moore, "Black and Catholic in Atlanta: Challenge and Hope," in *Catholics in the Vatican II Era: Local Histories of a Global Event*, ed. Karen Sprows Cummings, Timothy Matovina, and Robert A. Orsi (New York: Cambridge University Press, 2018), 136–38.
8 Massimo Faggioli, "The Liturgical Reform from 1963 until Today . . . and Beyond," *Toronto Journal of Theology* 32, no. 2 (2016): 201–2.
9 Matthew J. Cressler, *Authentically Black and Truly Catholic: The Rise of Black Catholicism in the Great Migration* (New York: New York University Press, 2017), 138–44.
10 Russell A. Kazal, "The Interwar Origins of the White Ethnic: Race, Residence, and German Philadelphia, 1917–1939," *Journal of American Ethnic History* 23, no. 4 (2004): 79–81, 118.

11 Will Herberg, *Protestant, Catholic, Jew: An Essay in American Religious Sociology* (Chicago: University of Chicago Press, 1983), 137–61, 158.
12 Jay P. Dolan, *The American Catholic Experience: A History from Colonial Times to the Present* (Garden City, NY: Doubleday, 1985); Colleen McDannell, *The Spirit of Vatican II: A History of Catholic Reform in America* (New York: Basic Books, 2011).
13 John T. McGreevy, *Parish Boundaries: The Catholic Encounter with Race in the Twentieth-Century Urban North* (Chicago: University of Chicago Press, 1996), 7–13, 29–38.
14 Gerald H. Gamm, *Urban Exodus: Why the Jews Left Boston and the Catholics Stayed* (Cambridge, MA: Harvard University Press, 1999), 17–27, 239.
15 Lucas, *Black Priest / White Church*, 1–41, 225–70; Cyprian Davis, *The History of Black Catholics in the United States* (1970; repr., New York: Crossroad, 1995).
16 Lucas, *Black Priest / White Church*, 97–100; Herberg, *Protestant, Catholic, Jew*, 158.
17 Cressler, *Authentically Black and Truly Catholic*, 1–11.
18 Sr. Mary Anita to Mother Mary Elizabeth Fitzgerald, April 21, 1973, Archives of the Sisters of the Blessed Sacrament, H40 B2, GA: Atlanta Our Lady of Lourdes, 1913–1974, box 1, folder 11, Catholic Historical Research Center.
19 Mark Newman, *Desegregating Dixie: The Catholic Church in the South and Desegregation, 1945–1992* (Jackson: University Press of Mississippi, 2018).
20 Moore, *South's Tolerable Alien*.
21 Moore, "Black and Catholic in Atlanta," 135–56.
22 Michael J. Pfeifer, *The Making of American Catholicism: Regional Culture and the Catholic Experience* (New York: New York University Press, 2021), 46–60.
23 Pfeifer, *Making of American Catholicism*, 3–5, 17–30.

1. RACE AND THE CATHOLIC CHURCH, IN THEORY AND PRACTICE
 1 Mark Newman, *Desegregating Dixie: The Catholic Church and Desegregation, 1945–1992* (Jackson: University Press of Mississippi, 2018), 3–16.
 2 Pope Pius V and the Roman Catholic Church, *The Catechism of the Council of Trent*, trans. John A. McHugh and Charles J. Callan (Charlotte, NC: TAN Books, 1982); Louis LaRavoire Morrow, *My Catholic Faith: A Catechism in Pictures* (Kansas City, MO: Sarto House, 2005), 140–41.
 3 Albert J. Raboteau, *Slave Religion: The "Invisible Institution" in the Antebellum South* (New York: Oxford University Press, 1980), 98–103; Katharine Gerbner, *Christian Slavery: Conversion and Race in the Protestant Atlantic World* (Philadelphia: University of Pennsylvania Press, 2018), 14, 19–20; Maura Jane Farrelly, "American Slavery, American Freedom, American Catholicism," *Early American Studies* 10, no. 1 (2012): 90–92.
 4 Randall M. Miller, "The Failed Mission: The Catholic Church and Black Catholics in the Old South," in *Catholics in the Old South*, ed. Randall M. Miller and Jon L. Wakelyn (Macon, GA: Mercer University Press, 1999), 40, 152–54, 158; Jay P. Dolan, *Catholic Revivalism: The American Experience, 1830–1900* (Notre Dame,

IN: University of Notre Dame Press, 1978), 3–10; Stephen J. Ochs, *Desegregating the Altar: The Josephites and the Struggle for Black Priests, 1871–1960* (Baton Rouge: Louisiana State University Press, 1993), 15–16.

5   William Henry Elder, "Letter of William Henry Elder, Bishop of Natchez, to the Society for the Propagation of the Faith, in Which He Describes His Ministry to Slaves, 1858," in *"Stamped with the Image of God": African Americans as God's Image in Black*, ed. Cyprian Davis and Jamie Phelps (Maryknoll, NY: Orbis Books, 2003), 32–33.
6   Joseph T. Leonard, *Theology and Race Relations* (Milwaukee, WI: Bruce, 1963), 222–25.
7   Randall M. Miller, "A Church in Cultural Captivity: Some Speculations on Catholic Identity in the Old South," in Miller and Wakelyn, *Catholics in the Old South*, 10–11, 15–17; Newman, *Desegregating Dixie*, 3–5; Dennis C. Rousey, "Catholics in the Old South: Their Population, Institutional Development, and Relations with Protestants," *U.S. Catholic Historian* 24, no. 4 (2006): 19–20.
8   Miller, "Failed Mission," 155; Rousey, "Catholics in the Old South," 10.
9   James J. Thompson, "Southern Baptists and Anti-Catholicism in the 1920's," *Mississippi Quarterly* 32, no. 4 (1979): 617–21.
10 Richard Nelson, "The Cultural Contradictions of Populism: Tom Watson's Tragic Vision of Power, Politics, and History," *Georgia Historical Quarterly* 72, no. 1 (1988): 1, 27–28.
11 Philip N. Racine, "The Ku Klux Klan, Anti-Catholicism, and Atlanta's Board of Education, 1916–1927," *Georgia Historical Quarterly* 57, no. 1 (1973): 67–71.
12 Jay Rubin, "Black Nativism: The European Immigrant in Negro Thought, 1830–1890," *Phylon* 39, no. 3 (1978): 193–201; Ochs, *Desegregating the Altar*, 16–17.
13 Andrew S. Moore, "Black and Catholic in Atlanta: Challenge and Hope," in *Catholics in the Vatican II Era: Local Histories of a Global Event*, ed. Karen Sprows Cummings, Timothy Matovina, and Robert A. Orsi (New York: Cambridge University Press, 2018), 135–36.
14 A. J. Laube, "Catholic Mission Work among the Negroes of Georgia," *Bulletin of the Catholic Laymen's Association of Georgia*, January 1, 1921.
15 John T. McGreevy, *Parish Boundaries: The Catholic Encounter with Race in the Twentieth-Century Urban North* (Chicago: University of Chicago Press, 1996), 13–15.
16 Sr. Patricia Lynch, *Sharing the Bread in Service: Sisters of the Blessed Sacrament, 1891–1991*, vol. 1 (Bensalem, PA: Sisters of the Blessed Sacrament, 1998), 35–80, 220–26, 277–79; Cyprian Davis, *The History of Black Catholics in the United States* (New York: Crossroad, 1990), 135–36; Newman, *Desegregating Dixie*, 8.
17 Matthew J. Cressler, *Authentically Black and Truly Catholic: The Rise of Black Catholicism in the Great Migration* (New York: New York University Press, 2017), 3–6; Shannen Dee Williams, "'You Could Do the Irish Jig, But Anything African Was Taboo': Black Nuns, Contested Memories, and the 20th Century Struggle to Desegregate U.S. Catholic Religious Life," *Journal of African American History* 102, no. 2 (2017): 133–36.

18 Newman, *Desegregating Dixie*, 9.
19 Charles E. Curran, "Catholic Social Teaching," *Good Society* 10, no. 1 (2001): 1–2; Joe Holland, *Modern Catholic Social Teaching: The Popes Confront the Industrial Age, 1740–1958* (New York: Paulist Press, 2003), 3–5; Pope Leo XIII, "Rerum Novarum" (Vatican, May 15, 1891), www.vatican.va.
20 Holland, *Modern Catholic Social Teaching*, 119–22.
21 James W. Silver, *Mississippi: The Closed Society* (New York: Harcourt, Brace & World, 1966), 28–40, 83–106; Carolyn Renée Dupont, *Mississippi Praying: Southern White Evangelicals and the Civil Rights Movement, 1945–1975* (New York: New York University Press, 2013), 8–10, 26–28.
22 Franklin M. Garrett, *Atlanta and Environs: A Chronicle of Its People and Events, 1820s–1870s*, vol. 1. *Atlanta and Environs* (Athens: University of Georgia Press, 1969), 240.
23 John Hanley, *The Archdiocese of Atlanta: A History* (Strasbourg, France: Editions Du Signe, 2006), 27.
24 "Atlanta Roman Catholic Records, Sacramental Records of the Enslaved," n.d., Sacramental Records Collection, 1846–1971, Office of Archives and Records, Roman Catholic Archdiocese of Atlanta.
25 Hanley, *Archdiocese of Atlanta*, 27.
26 Hanley, *Archdiocese of Atlanta*, 36–37.
27 Carleen Thomas, interview by Office of Black Catholic Ministry, Archdiocese of Atlanta, VHS cassette, May 25, 1994, Atlanta Interfaith Broadcasters oral history interviews, Auburn Avenue Research Library, Atlanta.
28 Sisters of the Blessed Sacrament, "Annals of Our Lady of Lourdes Convent, January 1962–August 1973," Archives of the Sisters of the Blessed Sacrament, H40 B2, GA: Atlanta Our Lady of Lourdes, 1913–1974, box 1, folder 5, Catholic Historical Research Center.
29 Andrew Hill, interview by Leah Mickens, digital recording, April 24, 2019; Sandra L. Criddell et al., interview by Leah Mickens, digital recording, April 16, 2019.
30 Benjamin Keiley to James Gibbons, December 7, 1920, Unprocessed Executive Records—Right Rev. Benjamin J. Keiley, CBS Correspondence—Ecclesiastical Hierarchy, Folder: James Cardinal Gibbons, Archives and Records Department of the Catholic Diocese of Savannah.
31 "Father Ignatius Lissner, S.M.A., Founder of Colored Missions in Georgia, Dies in New Jersey," *Bulletin of the Catholic Laymen's Association of Georgia*, August 21, 1948, 28.
32 Benjamin Keiley to James Gibbons, February 26, 1920, Unprocessed Executive Records—Right Rev. Benjamin J. Keiley, CBS Correspondence—Ecclesiastical Hierarchy, Folder: James Cardinal Gibbons, Archives and Records Department of the Catholic Diocese of Savannah.

2. ATLANTA'S RELIGIOUS AND POLITICAL ECOLOGY AND THE ESTABLISHMENT OF OUR LADY OF LOURDES

1. "Society of African Missions Nearly Thirty Years in Georgia," *Bulletin of the Catholic Laymen's Association of Georgia*, January 31, 1936, 9; Sr. Patricia Lynch, *Sharing the Bread in Service: Sisters of the Blessed Sacrament, 1891–1991*, vol. 1 (Bensalem, PA: Sisters of the Blessed Sacrament, 1998), 183–85.
2. Our Lady of Lourdes, "A Journey of Faith, Spirituality and Social Justice: A History of Our Lady of Lourdes Catholic Church, Atlanta, Georgia, 1912–2012," 2012, Our Lady of Lourdes Parish Collection, 1921–2011, Office of Archives and Records, Roman Catholic Archdiocese of Atlanta; Lynch, *Sharing the Bread in Service*, 1:185–88.
3. Sr. Mary Aquinas to Katherine Drexel, 1913, Archives of the Sisters of the Blessed Sacrament, H40 B2, GA: Atlanta Our Lady of Lourdes, 1913–1974, box 1, folder 7, Catholic Historical Research Center; Sisters of the Blessed Sacrament, "Annals, 1912–1934," 1934 1912, Archives of the Sisters of the Blessed Sacrament, H40 B2, GA: Atlanta Our Lady of Lourdes, 1913–1974, box 1, folder 1, Catholic Historical Research Center.
4. Sr. Mary Aquinas to Katherine Drexel, February 11, 1914, Archives of the Sisters of the Blessed Sacrament, H40 B2, GA: Atlanta Our Lady of Lourdes, 1913–1974, box 1, folder 7, Catholic Historical Research Center.
5. Sisters of the Blessed Sacrament, "Annals, Our Lady of Lourdes, Atlanta, Ga, 1912–1934," 1934 1912, Archives of the Sisters of the Blessed Sacrament, H40 B2, GA: Atlanta Our Lady of Lourdes, 1913–1974, box 1, folder 1, Catholic Historical Research Center.
6. Clifford M. Kuhn, Harlon E. Joye, and E. Bernard West, *Living Atlanta: An Oral History of the City, 1914–1948* (Athens: University of Georgia Press, 2005), 138.
7. Jay Winston Driskell Jr., *Schooling Jim Crow: The Fight for Atlanta's Booker T. Washington High School and the Roots of Black Protest Politics* (Charlottesville: University of Virginia Press, 2014), 140–41.
8. Our Lady of Lourdes, "A Journey of Faith, Spirituality and Social Justice."
9. Driskell, *Schooling Jim Crow*, 67–70.
10. Sr. Mary Aquinas to Katherine Drexel, n.d., Archives of the Sisters of the Blessed Sacrament, H40 B2, GA: Atlanta Our Lady of Lourdes, 1913–1974, box 1, folder 7, Catholic Historical Research Center.
11. Alton Hornsby Jr., *Black Power in Dixie: A Political History of African Americans in Atlanta* (Gainesville: University of Florida Press, 2009), 32–36.
12. Hornsby, *Black Power in Dixie*, 48.
13. Hornsby, *Black Power in Dixie*, 47–50.
14. Driskell, *Schooling Jim Crow*, 85–90.
15. John Temple Graves, "For Information of the Outside World," *Atlanta Georgian*, September 24, 1906, 6; "The Atlanta Riots," *North Georgia Citizen*, September 27, 1906, 4; "Race Riot in Atlanta: Mob Attacks Negroes in Revenge for Many Assaults on White Women," *Banks County Journal*, September 27, 1906, 1.

16. Kuhn, Joye, and West, *Living Atlanta*, 99–108; Joshua F. J. Inwood, "Constructing African American Urban Space in Atlanta, Georgia," *Geographical Review* 101, no. 2 (2011): 148–50; Nancy Fraser, "Rethinking the Public Sphere: A Contribution to the Critique of Actually Existing Democracy," *Social Text*, no. 25/26 (1990): 67–70.
17. Kuhn, Joye, and West, *Living Atlanta*, 252; Evelyn Brooks Higginbotham, *Righteous Discontent: The Women's Movement in the Black Baptist Church, 1880–1920* (Cambridge, MA: Harvard University Press, 1994), 7–13.
18. Wheat Street Baptist Church, *Forty-Fifth Pastoral Anniversary, Rev. William Holmes Borders, 1937–1982* (Atlanta: Josten's Yearbook Company, 1982), 8–9.
19. James W. English, *Handyman of the Lord: The Life and Ministry of the Reverend William Holmes Borders* (New York: Meredith Press, 1967), 54–56.
20. Anita Martin, interview by Leah Mickens, digital recording, April 2, 2019.
21. Gwendolyn Elmore, interview by Leah Mickens, digital recording, April 22, 2019.
22. Nellie Adams et al., interview by Leah Mickens, digital recording, April 3, 2019.
23. English, *Handyman of the Lord*, 63–65.
24. Wheat Street Baptist Church, *Forty-Fifth Pastoral Anniversary*, 9.
25. Lewis Baldwin, *The Voice of Conscience: The Church in the Mind of Martin Luther King, Jr.* (New York: Oxford University Press, 2010), 22–28.
26. Kuhn, Joye, and West, *Living Atlanta*, 97–98.
27. Kuhn, Joye, and West, *Living Atlanta*, 252.
28. L. H. Whelchel, *Sherman's March and the Emergence of the Independent Black Church Movement: From Atlanta to the Sea to Emancipation* (New York: Palgrave Macmillan, 2014), 26–27.
29. Big Bethel AME Church, "History of Big Bethel" (2019), www.bigbethelame.org.
30. Baldwin, *Voice of Conscience*, 31.
31. Willie Taylor Robinson and Lucille Neely, interview by Leah Mickens, digital recording, April 2, 2019.
32. Sandra L. Criddell et al., interview by Leah Mickens, digital recording, April 16, 2019.
33. Louis LaRavoire Morrow, *My Catholic Faith: A Catechism in Pictures* (1954; repr., Kansas City, MO: Sarto House, 2005), 193.
34. Pope Pius IX, "Nostis et Nobiscum" (Papal Encyclicals Online, December 8, 1849), www.papalencyclicals.net; Pope Gregory XVI, "Mirari Vos" (Papal Encyclicals Online, August 15, 1832), www.papalencyclicals.net; Pope Pius IX, "The Syllabus of Errors" (Papal Encyclicals Online, December 8, 1864), www.papalencyclicals.net.
35. Pope Pius V and the Roman Catholic Church, *The Catechism of the Council of Trent*, trans. John A. McHugh and Charles J. Callan (Charlotte, NC: TAN Books, 1982), 99.
36. John T. McGreevy, *Parish Boundaries: The Catholic Encounter with Race in the Twentieth-Century Urban North* (Chicago: University of Chicago Press, 1996), 20–25.
37. Andrew Hill, interview by Leah Mickens, digital recording, April 24, 2019.
38. Anita Whatley, interview by Leah Mickens, digital recording, April 17, 2019.
39. Cassandra Peters-Johnson, interview by Leah Mickens, digital recording, April 28, 2019.

40 McGreevy, *Parish Boundaries*, 30–32.
41 Elmore interview.
42 Kuhn, Joye, and West, *Living Atlanta*, 285.
43 Pope Gregory XVI, "Summo Iugiter Studio" (Papal Encyclicals Online, May 27, 1832), www.papalencyclicals.net; Morrow, *My Catholic Faith*, 348–49.
44 Whatley interview.
45 Sisters of the Blessed Sacrament, "Annals, August 1922 to June 1929," 1929, Archives of the Sisters of the Blessed Sacrament, H40 B2, GA: Atlanta Our Lady of Lourdes, 1913–1974, box 1, folder 2, Catholic Historical Research Center.
46 Kuhn, Joye, and West, *Living Atlanta*, 243–44; "Medical Mission Sisters Are Taking Over Colored Mission, Clinic in Atlanta," *Bulletin of the Catholic Laymen's Association of Georgia*, October 28, 1944, 1; "Christianity in Action Found in Atlanta at Catholic Colored Clinic Conducted by Medical Mission Sisters," *Bulletin of the Catholic Laymen's Association of Georgia*, February 25, 1950, 22.
47 "The Catholic Colored Mission of Atlanta," n.d., Catholic Colored Clinic, folder 1, Office of Archives and Records, Roman Catholic Archdiocese of Atlanta; Gerald O'Hara to F. Garesche, May 6, 1942, Catholic Colored Clinic, folder 1, Office of Archives and Records, Roman Catholic Archdiocese of Atlanta; F. Garesche to Gerald O'Hara, April 17, 1942, Catholic Colored Clinic, folder 1, Office of Archives and Records, Roman Catholic Archdiocese of Atlanta.
48 Sr. Mary Clare to Joseph E. Moylan, January 30, 1947, Catholic Colored Clinic, folder 1, Office of Archives and Records, Roman Catholic Archdiocese of Atlanta; Joseph Moylan to Sr. Mary Clare, February 10, 1947, Catholic Colored Clinic, folder 1, Office of Archives and Records, Roman Catholic Archdiocese of Atlanta.
49 "Passionist Provincial Names Rev. Emmanuel Traynor C.P. to Head New Atlanta Mission," *The Bulletin*, January 22, 1955, 1.
50 "History of the Cathedral of Christ the King," *Bulletin of the Catholic Laymen's Association of Georgia*, December 8, 1956, 3; "Proclamation of Diocese of Savannah-Atlanta," *Bulletin of the Catholic Laymen's Association of Georgia*, April 30, 1937, 3; Mark Newman, *Desegregating Dixie: The Catholic Church and Desegregation, 1945–1992* (Jackson: University Press of Mississippi, 2018), 20.

3. OUR LADY OF LOURDES, THE CIVIL RIGHTS MOVEMENT, AND SCHOOL DESEGREGATION

1 Mary E. McGann and Eva Marie Lumas, "The Emergence of African American Catholic Worship," in *Let It Shine! The Emergence of African American Catholic Worship*, ed. Mary E. McGann (New York: Fordham University Press, 2008), 3–8; Mary Jo Weaver, "Introduction: Who Are the Conservative Catholics?," in *Being Right: Conservative Catholics in America*, ed. Mary Jo Weaver and R. Scott Appleby (Bloomington: Indiana University Press, 1995, 1–14), 1–3.
2 Moore, *The South's Tolerable Alien: Roman Catholics in Alabama and Georgia, 1945–1970* (Baton Rouge: Louisiana State University Press, 2007), 103–12; George Coleman, "Drexel's Death Shows You Still Just Can't See Us," *Georgia Bulletin*,

March 30, 1967; Andrew S. Moore, "Black and Catholic in Atlanta: Challenge and Hope," in *Catholics in the Vatican II Era: Local Histories of a Global Event*, ed. Karen Sprows Cummings, Timothy Matovina, and Robert A. Orsi (New York: Cambridge University Press, 2018), 142–44.

3 Aldon D. Morris, *The Origins of the Civil Rights Movement: Black Communities Organizing for Change* (New York: Free Press, 1984), xii.

4 Willie Taylor Robinson and Lucille Neely, interview by Leah Mickens, digital recording, April 2, 2019.

5 Julian Bond, "SNCC: What We Did," *Monthly Review* 52, no. 5 (2000): 14–16; Gwendolyn Elmore, interview by Leah Mickens, digital recording, April 22, 2019; Alysha Conner, "Legacy of the Atlanta Student Movement," *Atlanta Voice*, February 22, 2019, www.theatlantavoice.com.

6 Marshall Thomas, interview by Leah Mickens, digital recording, April 19, 2019.

7 Tomiko Brown-Nagin, *Courage to Dissent: Atlanta and the Long History of the Civil Rights Movement* (New York: Oxford University Press, 2011), 143.

8 Conner, "Legacy of the Atlanta Student Movement."

9 Mark Newman, *Desegregating Dixie: The Catholic Church and Desegregation, 1945–1992* (Jackson: University Press of Mississippi, 2018), 181; L. G. Allain et al. to Francis E. Hyland, December 11, 1960, Archbishops' Office Subject Files and Correspondence, Office of Archives and Records, Roman Catholic Archdiocese of Atlanta.

10 Sisters of the Blessed Sacrament, "Annals of Our Lady of Lourdes Convent, January 1962–August 1973," Archives of the Sisters of the Blessed Sacrament, H40 B2, GA: Atlanta Our Lady of Lourdes, 1913–1974, box 1, folder 5, Catholic Historical Research Center; Newman, *Desegregating Dixie*, 111; Sr. Patricia Lynch, *Sharing the Bread in Service: Sisters of the Blessed Sacrament, 1891–1991*, vol. 2 (Bensalem, PA: Sisters of the Blessed Sacrament, 1998), 116.

11 Pope John XXIII, "Pacem et Terris" (Vatican, April 11, 1963), www.vatican.va.

12 "Students, Teachers March, Hundreds Join in Protest," *The Tattler*, March 19, 1965, 1, Drexel High School Alumni Collection, box 2, folder 5, Auburn Avenue Research Library, Atlanta; Sisters of the Blessed Sacrament, "Annals of Our Lady of Lourdes Convent, January 1962–August 1973"; Lynch, *Sharing the Bread in Service*, 2:116.

13 Gary M. Pomerantz, *Where Peachtree Meets Sweet Auburn: A Saga of Race and Family* (New York: Penguin, 1996), 359–61.

14 Lynch, *Sharing the Bread in Service*, 2:17.

15 Sharlene Sinegal Decuir, "'Nothing Is to Be Feared': Norman C. Francis, Civil Rights Activism, and the Black Catholic Movement," *Journal of African American History* 101, no. 3 (2016): 312–15, 321–22; Newman, *Desegregating Dixie*, 173, 181.

16 Lynch, *Sharing the Bread in Service*, 2:37–51.

17 Sisters of the Blessed Sacrament, "Annals 1950–1961, Our Lady of Lourdes Convent," 1950–1961, Archives of the Sisters of the Blessed Sacrament, H40 B2, GA: Atlanta Our Lady of Lourdes, 1913–1974, box 1, folder 4, Catholic Historical Research Center.

18   "Third Diocesan School Opens: Drexel High Located in North West Atlanta," *Georgia Bulletin*, December 9, 1961, 1, Drexel High School Alumni Collection, box 2, folder 1, Auburn Avenue Research Library, Atlanta.
19   Daniel J. O'Connor, "Arguments for the Consolidation of St. Joseph High School and Drexel Catholic High School," April 1, 1967, 1, Drexel High School Alumni Collection, box 2, folder 12, Auburn Avenue Research Library, Atlanta.
20   "Third Diocesan School Opens: Drexel High Located in North West Atlanta," *Georgia Bulletin*, December 9, 1961, Drexel High School Alumni Collection, box 2, folder 1, Auburn Avenue Research Library, Atlanta; "New Diocesan High School to Open in Fall: New School Plant for North West Atlanta," *Georgia Bulletin*, July 22, 1961, Drexel High School Alumni Collection, box 2, folder 1, Auburn Avenue Research Library, Atlanta.
21   R. Ray McCain, "Reactions to the United States Supreme Court Segregation Decision of 1954," *Georgia Historical Quarterly* 52, no. 4 (1968): 371.
22   Elizabeth Egan Henry and Katherine Hankins, "Halting White Flight: Parent Activism and the (Re)Shaping of Atlanta's 'Circuits of Schooling,' 1973–2009," *Journal of Urban History* 38, no. 3 (2012): 534.
23   Archbishops and Bishops of the United States, "Discrimination and Christian Conscience," in *Pastoral Letters of the American Hierarchy, 1792–1970*, ed. Hugh J. Nolan (Huntington, IN: Our Sunday Visitor, 1971), 506–10; Andrew S. Moore, "Practicing What We Preach: White Catholics and the Civil Rights Movement in Atlanta," *Georgia Historical Quarterly* 89, no. 3 (2005): 334–35, 341–42.
24   "Bishop Hyland Would Deplore Closing Georgia Public Schools over Racial Segregation Issue," *The Bulletin*, December 26, 1959, Diocese of Savannah edition, 8.
25   Charlayne Hunter-Gault, *In My Place* (New York: Vintage, 1993), 116–17; Harold H. Martin, *Atlanta and Environs: A Chronicle of Its People and Events, 1940s–1970s*, vol. 3. *Atlanta and Environs* (Athens: University of Georgia Press, 1987), 321, 326–27; "Charlayne Hunter: 'Madonna Is Permanent Fixture of My Room,'" *The Bulletin*, January 21, 1961, Diocese of Savannah edition, 1; Sisters of the Blessed Sacrament, "Annals 1950–1961, Our Lady of Lourdes Convent," 1950–1961, Archives of the Sisters of the Blessed Sacrament, H40 B2, GA: Atlanta Our Lady of Lourdes, 1913–1974, box 1, folder 4, Catholic Historical Research Center.
26   Newman, *Desegregating Dixie*, 154.
27   Francis J. Hyland to Michael McKeever and Dennis Walsh, April 10, 1961, box 036/6, folder 49, Office of Archives and Records, Roman Catholic Archdiocese of Atlanta; Allain et al. to Hyland, December 11, 1960.
28   "Our Lady of Lourdes Solemn Dedication," February 12, 1961, Our Lady of Lourdes Parish Collection, 1921–2011, Office of Archives and Records, Roman Catholic Archdiocese of Atlanta.
29   Francis E. Hyland, "Sermon of the Most Rev. Francis E. Hyland, D.D.J.C.D., Bishop of Atlanta, on the Occasion of the Dedication of the Church of Our Lady of Lourdes," February 12, 1961, Our Lady of Lourdes Parish Collection, 1921–2011, Office of Archives and Records, Roman Catholic Archdiocese of Atlanta.

30 Newman, *Desegregating Dixie*, 61.
31 "Atlanta Named Archdiocese: Holy See Creates New Province in the South," *The Bulletin*, March 3, 1962, Diocese of Savannah edition, 1; "Apostolic Delegate Installs Archbishop Paul J. Hallinan: Metropolitan of New Province of Atlanta," *The Bulletin*, March 31, 1962, Diocese of Savannah edition, 1; Moore, "Practicing What We Preach," 344; Sisters of the Blessed Sacrament, "Annals of Our Lady of Lourdes Convent, January 1962–August 1973."
32 John T. McGreevy, *Parish Boundaries: The Catholic Encounter with Race in the Twentieth-Century Urban North* (Chicago: University of Chicago Press, 1996), 43–44.
33 Paul J. Hallinan, "Archbishop's Letter," in *A Syllabus on Racial Justice for Use in the Catholic Schools, Grades 7–12, of the Archdiocese of Atlanta under the Direction of the Most Reverend Paul J. Hallinan, Archbishop of Atlanta* (Atlanta: Archbishop's Office, n.d.), i–ii.
34 Sisters of the Blessed Sacrament, "Annals of Our Lady of Lourdes Convent, January 1962–August 1973."
35 "Drexelite Tells of Selma March," *Georgia Bulletin*, April 15, 1965, Drexel High School Alumni Collection, box 2, folder 1, Auburn Avenue Research Library, Atlanta; "Exchange Visit: Pi-Hi Journalists Guests at Drexel," *Georgia Bulletin*, n.d., Drexel High School Alumni Collection, box 2, folder 1, Auburn Avenue Research Library, Atlanta.
36 Anita Whatley, interview by Leah Mickens, digital recording, April 17, 2019.
37 Newman, *Desegregating Dixie*, 148.
38 Daniel J. O'Connor to Paul J. Hallinan, February 21, 1967, Drexel High School Alumni Collection, box 2, folder 14, Auburn Avenue Research Library, Atlanta.
39 "The Drexel Story . . . Reflections of a 17 Year Old," August 5, 1995, Drexel High School Alumni Collection, box 2, folder 11, Auburn Avenue Research Library, Atlanta.
40 Julia Lyles and Rubye D. Neal, "Report of Meeting: Drexel Catholic High School Home and School Association Committee with the Most Reverend Paul J. Hallinan, Archbishop of Atlanta, Saturday, March 25, 1967," n.d., Drexel High School Alumni Collection, box 2, folder 16, Auburn Avenue Research Library, Atlanta; "Arguments on Closing of Drexel Aired at Education Board Meeting," *Georgia Bulletin*, April 6, 1967, 1–2, Drexel High School Alumni Collection, box 2, folder 9, Auburn Avenue Research Library, Atlanta.
41 Lynch, *Sharing the Bread in Service*, 2:101; Moore, "Black and Catholic in Atlanta," 142–43.
42 Andrew Hill, interview by Leah Mickens, digital recording, April 24, 2019.
43 George Coleman, "Drexel's Death Shows You Still Just Can't See Us," *Georgia Bulletin*, March 30, 1967; Lyles and Neal, "Report of Meeting."
44 "Drexel Story"; Lyles and Neal, "Report of Meeting."

45 Hill interview; Henry and Hankins, "Halting White Flight," 535; Kevin M. Kruse, *White Flight: Atlanta and the Making of Modern Conservatism* (Princeton, N.J.: Princeton University Press, 2007).
46 Whatley interview.
47 "Drexel Story."
48 O'Connor to Hallinan, February 21, 1967; Newman, *Desegregating Dixie*, 39–40.
49 Henry and Hankins, "Halting White Flight," 535–36.
50 Moore, "Black and Catholic in Atlanta," 140–42.
51 James F. Scherer, "Down-Town Parish Meeting Notes," January 11, 1967, Our Lady of Lourdes Parish, 1921–2011, Office of Archives and Records, Roman Catholic Archdiocese of Atlanta.
52 "Meeting Notes," January 26, 1967, OLL Correspondence, Our Lady of Lourdes Parish, 1921–2011, Office of Archives and Records, Roman Catholic Archdiocese of Atlanta.
53 "Meeting Notes"; Scherer, "Down-Town Parish Meeting Notes."
54 William R. Headley, "A Study of Attitudes Concerning Desegregation of Catholic Parishes among Northeast Atlanta's White and Negro Catholics," June 1970, Our Lady of Lourdes Parish, 1921–2011, Office of Archives and Records, Roman Catholic Archdiocese of Atlanta.

4. LITURGICAL RENEWAL AND THE SECOND VATICAN COUNCIL IN ATLANTA

1 Sisters of the Blessed Sacrament, "Annals of Our Lady of Lourdes Convent, January 1962–August 1973," Archives of the Sisters of the Blessed Sacrament, H40 B2, GA: Atlanta Our Lady of Lourdes, 1913–1974, box 1, folder 5, Catholic Historical Research Center; Pope John XXIII, "Text of Papal Bull Convoking Second Vatican Council" (The Press Department, National Catholic Welfare Conference, December 25, 1961), Paul J. Hallinan—Vatican Council II Collection, box 1, folder 3, American Catholic History Research Center and University Archives, Catholic University of America, Washington, DC.
2 Rita Ferrone, *Liturgy: Sacrosanctum Concilium* (New York: Paulist Press, 2007), 60–63.
3 William D. Dinges, "'We Are What You Were': Roman Catholic Traditionalism in America," in *Being Right: Conservative Catholics in America*, ed. Mary Jo Weaver and R. Scott Appleby (Bloomington: Indiana University Press, 1995), 243; Ferrone, *Liturgy*, 57–60.
4 Mary E. McGann and Eva Marie Lumas, "The Emergence of African American Catholic Worship," in *Let It Shine! The Emergence of African American Catholic Worship*, ed. Mary E. McGann (New York: Fordham University Press, 2008), 5–7.
5 Sandra L. Criddell et al., interview by Leah Mickens, digital recording, April 16, 2019; Anita Whatley, interview by Leah Mickens, digital recording, April 17, 2019; Andrew Hill, interview by Leah Mickens, digital recording, April 24, 2019.

6 Louis LaRavoire Morrow, *My Catholic Faith: A Catechism in Pictures* (Kansas City, MO: Sarto House, 2005), 384–85; Ann Taves, *The Household of Faith: Roman Catholic Devotions in Mid-Nineteenth Century America* (Notre Dame, IN: University of Notre Dame Press, 1986), 22–24; Herbert Thurston, "Popular Devotions," in *The Catholic Encyclopedia* (New York: Robert Appleton, 1911), www.newadvent.org; Jay P. Dolan, *The American Catholic Experience: A History from Colonial Times to the Present* (Garden City, NY: Doubleday, 1985), 212.

7 James F. White, *Roman Catholic Worship: Trent to Today* (Collegeville, MN: Liturgical Press, 2003), 11–15; Louis Bouyer, *Liturgical Piety* (Notre Dame, IN: University of Notre Dame Press, 1955), 3.

8 Taves, *Household of Faith*, 93; Carl Watkins, "'Folklore' and 'Popular Religion' in Britain during the Middle Ages," *Folklore* 115, no. 2 (2004): 145–46.

9 Taves, *Household of Faith*, 89–96, 114–18; Joe Holland, *Modern Catholic Social Teaching: The Popes Confront the Industrial Age, 1740–1958* (New York: Paulist Press, 2003), 54–57.

10 Taves, *Household of Faith*, 102–12; Dolan, *American Catholic Experience*, 219–20, 224.

11 Taves, *Household of Faith*, 4, 8–10; Rachel Bean, "The Art and Advertising of Benziger Brothers' Church Goods Manufacture, New York, 1879–1937," *Studies in the Decorative Arts* 11, no. 2 (2004): 80–81, 83; Dolan, *American Catholic Experience*, 219, 243–44, 247.

12 Taves, *Household of Faith*, 21, 27; Dolan, *American Catholic Experience*, 219–20, 230–31.

13 *My Pocket Prayerbook: A Manual of Prayers and Devotional Exercises* (New York: C. Wildermann, 1922), 83–118; Joseph F. Stedman, *My Sunday Missal Explained* (Brooklyn, NY: Confraternity of the Blessed Blood, 1942), 35–66; Taves, *Household of Faith*, 42–43; Ernest Benjamin Koenker, *The Liturgical Renaissance in the Roman Catholic Church* (Chicago: University of Chicago Press, 1966), 63–64.

14 Koenker, *Liturgical Renaissance*, 61–63.

15 Roland Millare, "The Spirit of the Liturgical Movement: A Benedictine Renewal of Culture," *Logos* 17, no. 4 (2014): 132–33; Koenker, *Liturgical Renaissance*, 10–11; Ferrone, *Liturgy*, 5–6.

16 Robert A. Skeris, "Sarto, the 'Conservative Reformer'—100 Years of the 'Motu Proprio' of Pope St. Pius X," *Sacred Music* 130, no. 4 (2003): 5–6; Pope Pius X, "Tra Le Sollecitudini, Instruction on Sacred Music" (Adoremus: Society for the Renewal of the Sacred Liturgy, November 22, 1903), https://adoremus.org; Ferrone, *Liturgy*, 8; Koenker, *Liturgical Renaissance*, 11–12.

17 Koenker, *Liturgical Renaissance*, 12–17; Catherine Vincie, "The RCIA and the Liturgical Movement," *Liturgy* 31, no. 2 (2016): 4.

18 "II.-1. The Missal for the Laity," *Dublin Review*, 1846, 259–60; Koenker, *Liturgical Renaissance*, 47.

19 Koenker, *Liturgical Renaissance*, 47–48, 50, 198.

20 Pope Pius XII, "Mediator Dei" (Vatican, November 20, 1947), www.vatican.va.

21 James Baldovin, "The Roots of Reform: Context and Background for Vatican II," *The Hymn* 64, no. 4 (2013): 9.
22 Koenker, *Liturgical Renaissance*, 49; Pope Leo XIII, "Supremi Apostolatus Officio" (Vatican, September 1, 1883), www.vatican.va; R. Kevin Seasoltz, *A Sense of the Sacred: Theological Foundations of Christian Architecture and Art* (New York: Bloomsbury Academic, 2005), 232.
23 Katharine E. Harmon, "'That Word "Liturgy" Is So Unfortunate': Learning the Mystical Body and Practicing Catholic Action in the U.S. Liturgical Movement (c. 1926–1955)," *American Catholic Studies* 127, no. 1 (2016): 26–27; Baldovin, "Roots of Reform," 9.
24 Virgil George Michel, "The Liturgy and Modern Thought," *Orate Fratres* 13, no. 5 (March 19, 1939): 210–11; Edward Day Stewart, "Christianity and Communism," *Orate Fratres* 9, no. 7 (May 18, 1935): 308–10.
25 Harmon, "'That Word "Liturgy" Is So Unfortunate,'" 42.
26 Dorothy Day, "Liturgy and Sociology," *Catholic Worker*, December 1935, www.catholicworker.org.
27 Dorothy Day, "To Christ—To the Land," *Catholic Worker*, January 1936, www.catholicworker.org.
28 Koenker, *Liturgical Renaissance*, 48.
29 Ferrone, *Liturgy*, 13–15.
30 Thomas J. Shelley, *Paul J. Hallinan: First Archbishop of Atlanta* (Wilmington, DE: Michael Glazier, 1989), 165–66; Melissa J. Wilde, *Vatican II: A Sociological Analysis of Religious Change* (Princeton, NJ: Princeton University Press, 2007), 29–56.
31 Shelley, *Paul J. Hallinan*, 62–65.
32 Thomas J. Shelley, "Slouching toward the Center: Cardinal Francis Spellman, Archbishop Paul J. Hallinan and American Catholicism in the 1960s," *U.S. Catholic Historian* 17, no. 4 (1999): 35.
33 Colleen McDannell, *The Spirit of Vatican II: A History of Catholic Reform in America* (New York: Basic Books, 2011), 66–67; Thomas J. Shelley, "'Sacrosanctum Concilium': Archbishop Paul J. Hallinan and the Constitution on the Sacred Liturgy," *U.S. Catholic Historian* 30, no. 2 (2012): 39.
34 Ferrone, *Liturgy*, 16–17; Shelley, "'Sacrosanctum Concilium,'" 40–41; L. McReavy, "Analysis of the Debate 'De Liturgia' to the End of Chapter I," 1962, and L. McReavy, "Analysis of Main Point of Controversy in Chapter II, De Liturgia," 1962, both in Paul J. Hallinan Vatican II Collection, box 1, folder 10, American Catholic History Research Center and University Archives, Catholic University of America, Washington, DC.
35 Paul J. Hallinan, "Translation of Speech by Paul J. Hallinan (Atlanta) on October 31, 1962 (First Session of Vatican II) on: The Liturgy: Intelligible, Public and Ecumenical," October 31, 1962, and Paul J. Hallinan, "In Capite II: De Sactrosancte Eucharistiae Mysterio," October 31, 1962, both in The Paul J. Hallinan—Vatican Council II Collection, box 1, folder 8, American Catholic History Research Center and University Archives, Catholic University of America, Washington, DC.

36. Paul J. Hallinan, "On Liturgy: Address by Most Rev. Paul J. Hallinan, Archbishop of Atlanta, Georgia, Made at the Press Conference in Rome on October 31, 1962" (Divine Word News Service, October 31, 1962), Paul J. Hallinan Vatican II Collection, box 1, folder 8, American Catholic History Research Center and University Archives, Catholic University of America, Washington, DC.
37. Andrew S. Moore, "Black and Catholic in Atlanta: Challenge and Hope," in *Catholics in the Vatican II Era: Local Histories of a Global Event*, ed. Karen Sprows Cummings, Timothy Matovina, and Robert A. Orsi (New York: Cambridge University Press, 2018), 137.
38. Shelley, "'Sacrosanctum Concilium,'" 54; Ferrone, *Liturgy*, 60.
39. Sisters of the Blessed Sacrament, "Annals of Our Lady of Lourdes Convent, January 1962–August 1973."
40. Moore, "Black and Catholic in Atlanta," 151; Criddell et al. interview.
41. Second Vatican Council, "Constitution on the Sacred Liturgy: Sacrosanctum Consilium, Solemnly Promulgated by His Holiness Pope Paul VI" (Vatican, December 4, 1963), www.vatican.va.
42. Koenker, *Liturgical Renaissance*, 159–62; Ferrone, *Liturgy*, 1, 14, 97.
43. Joseph L. Bernardin to John J. Mulroy, February 13, 1968, Archdiocese Commission for Liturgy, 1959–1984, Archdiocesan Liturgical Commission, Office of Archives and Records, Roman Catholic Archdiocese of Atlanta.
44. "Lourdes on the Move since Vatican II," n.d., Archives of the Sisters of the Blessed Sacrament, H40 B2, GA: Atlanta Our Lady of Lourdes, 1913–1974, box 2, folder 21, Catholic Historical Research Center.
45. "Liturgy and Creativity in Atlanta," *SBS News and Views*, January 1972, Archives of the Sisters of the Blessed Sacrament, H40 B2, GA: Atlanta Our Lady of Lourdes, 1913–1974, box 2, folder 21, Catholic Historical Research Center.
46. Ferrone, *Liturgy*, 33, 44.
47. Matthew Fox, *The Pope's War: Why Ratzinger's Secret Crusade Has Imperiled the Church and How It Can Be Saved* (New York: Sterling Ethos, 2011), 42–43.
48. Moore, "Black and Catholic in Atlanta," 145–46.

5. THE WITHDRAWAL OF THE SISTERS OF THE BLESSED SACRAMENT FROM OUR LADY OF LOURDES

1. Sr. Patricia Lynch, *Sharing the Bread in Service: Sisters of the Blessed Sacrament, 1891–1991*, vol. 1 (Bensalem, PA: Sisters of the Blessed Sacrament, 1998), 184.
2. Timothy Walch, *Parish School: A History of American Catholic Parochial Education from Colonial Times to the Present* (Arlington, VA: National Catholic Educational Association, 2016), 83; Michael P. Caruso, *When the Sisters Said Farewell: The Transition of Leadership in Catholic Elementary Schools* (Lanham, MD: Rowman & Littlefield, 2012), 10–14.
3. Caruso, *When the Sisters Said Farewell*, 30–31; Walch, *Parish School*, 81–83.
4. Walch, *Parish School*, 82–83.
5. Caruso, *When the Sisters Said Farewell*, 8, 51–53.

6   Walch, *Parish School*, 124–26.
7   Lynch, *Sharing the Bread in Service*, 1:191.
8   Sr. M. Regina, "Pray Ye the Lord of the Harvest," 1928, Archives of the Sisters of the Blessed Sacrament, H40 B2, GA: Atlanta Our Lady of Lourdes, 1913–1974, box 1, folder 9, Catholic Historical Research Center.
9   Our Lady of Lourdes, "A Journey of Faith, Spirituality and Social Justice: A History of Our Lady of Lourdes Catholic Church, Atlanta, Georgia, 1912–2012," 2012, 23–24, Our Lady of Lourdes Parish Collection, 1921–2011, Office of Archives and Records, Roman Catholic Archdiocese of Atlanta; Sisters of the Blessed Sacrament, "Annals of Our Lady of Lourdes Convent, January 1962–August 1973," Archives of the Sisters of the Blessed Sacrament, H40 B2, GA: Atlanta Our Lady of Lourdes, 1913–1974, box 1, folder 5, Catholic Historical Research Center; Lynch, *Sharing the Bread in Service*, 1:395.
10 "Drexel Catholic High School Reunion Celebration: 1961–1967," December 27, 1995, Drexel High School Alumni Collection, box 2, folder 18, Auburn Avenue Research Library, Atlanta; St. Pius X Catholic High School, "History" (n.d.), www.spx.org; Daniel J. O'Connor, "Arguments for the Consolidation of St. Joseph High School and Drexel Catholic High School," April 1, 1967, 9–11, Drexel High School Alumni Collection, box 2, folder 12, Auburn Avenue Research Library, Atlanta.
11 Walch, *Parish School*, 126–29.
12 O'Connor, "Arguments for the Consolidation," 7–8; John Hanley, *The Archdiocese of Atlanta: A History* (Strasbourg, France: Editions Du Signe, 2006), 31, 34.
13 Daniel J. O'Connor to Noel C. Burtenshaw, January 10, 1969, Drexel High School Alumni Collection, box 2, folder 15, Auburn Avenue Research Library, Atlanta; Joseph L. Bernadin to Sam McQuaid, April 17, 1967, Drexel High School Alumni Collection, box 2, folder 12, Auburn Avenue Research Library, Atlanta.
14 Patricia Wittberg, *The Rise and Fall of Catholic Religious Orders: A Social Movement Perspective* (Albany: State University of New York Press, 1994), 210–11.
15 Wittberg, *Rise and Fall of Catholic Religious Orders*, 211–12; Carol K. Coburn, "Ahead of Its Time . . . or Right on Time? The Role of the Sister Formation Conference for American Women Religious," *American Catholic Studies* 126, no. 3 (2015): 29–30.
16 Lynch, *Sharing the Bread in Service*, 2:151–52; Caruso, *When the Sisters Said Farewell*, 24.
17 Lynch, *Sharing the Bread in Service*, 2:146–47.
18 Lynch, *Sharing the Bread in Service*, 2:153–54, 156.
19 Lynch, *Sharing the Bread in Service*, 2:157–58.
20 Sisters of the Blessed Sacrament, "Annals of Our Lady of Lourdes Convent, January 1962–August 1973."
21 Lynch, *Sharing the Bread in Service*, 2:162–63.
22 Lynch, *Sharing the Bread in Service*, 2:158–59.
23 Helen Rose Fuchs Ebaugh, *Becoming an Ex: The Process of Role Exit* (Chicago: University of Chicago Press, 1988), 102, 115–37.

24 Wittberg, *Rise and Fall of Catholic Religious Orders*, 209–10.
25 Andrew S. Moore, "Black and Catholic in Atlanta: Challenge and Hope," in *Catholics in the Vatican II Era: Local Histories of a Global Event*, ed. Karen Sprows Cummings, Timothy Matovina, and Robert A. Orsi (New York: Cambridge University Press, 2018), 144.
26 Walch, *Parish School*, 126–27.
27 Sisters of the Blessed Sacrament, "Annals August 1934–June 1950," 1950 1934, Archives of the Sisters of the Blessed Sacrament, H40 B2, GA: Atlanta Our Lady of Lourdes, 1913–1974, box 1, folder 3, Catholic Historical Research Center; Sr. M. Judith, "Observations Concerning Our Lady of Lourdes School," n.d., Archives of the Sisters of the Blessed Sacrament, H40 B2, GA: Atlanta Our Lady of Lourdes, 1913–1974, box 1, folder 11, Catholic Historical Research Center; Walch, *Parish School*, 89–91, 130; Jay P. Dolan, *The American Catholic Experience: A History from Colonial Times to the Present* (Garden City, NY: Doubleday, 1985), 288–89.
28 Sr. Loretta McCarthy to Mother Mary Elizabeth Fitzgerald, May 7, 1973, Archives of the Sisters of the Blessed Sacrament, H40 B2, GA: Atlanta Our Lady of Lourdes, 1913–1974, box 1, folder 11, Catholic Historical Research Center.
29 Sr. Maureen Immaculate to Mother Mary Elizabeth Fitzgerald, May 6, 1973, Archives of the Sisters of the Blessed Sacrament, H40 B2, GA: Atlanta Our Lady of Lourdes, 1913–1974, box 1, folder 11, Catholic Historical Research Center.
30 Sr. M. Judith, "Observations Concerning Our Lady of Lourdes School."
31 McCarthy to Fitzgerald, May 7, 1973.
32 Sr. M. Patrick Thomas Lynch to Mother Mary Elizabeth Fitzgerald, May 2, 1973, Archives of the Sisters of the Blessed Sacrament, H40 B2, GA: Atlanta Our Lady of Lourdes, 1913–1974, box 1, folder 11, Catholic Historical Research Center.
33 Sr. Carole Eden to Mother Mary Elizabeth Fitzgerald, n.d., Archives of the Sisters of the Blessed Sacrament, H40 B2, GA: Atlanta Our Lady of Lourdes, 1913–1974, box 1, folder 11, Catholic Historical Research Center.
34 Thomas Donnellan to Mother Mary Elizabeth Fitzgerald, February 9, 1972, Archives of the Sisters of the Blessed Sacrament, H40 B2, GA: Atlanta Our Lady of Lourdes, 1913–1974, box 1, folder 11, Catholic Historical Research Center.
35 Mother Mary Elizabeth Fitzgerald to Thomas Donnellan, October 12, 1973, Archives of the Sisters of the Blessed Sacrament, H40 B2, GA: Atlanta Our Lady of Lourdes, 1913–1974, box 1, folder 11, Catholic Historical Research Center.
36 Thomas Donnellan to Mother Mary Elizabeth Fitzgerald, October 24, 1973, Archives of the Sisters of the Blessed Sacrament, H40 B2, GA: Atlanta Our Lady of Lourdes, 1913–1974, box 1, folder 11, Catholic Historical Research Center.
37 Sisters of the Blessed Sacrament, "Annals, Our Lady of Lourdes, Atlanta, Ga, 1912–1934."; Sr. M. Carmelita to Katherine Drexel, 1915, Archives of the Sisters of the Blessed Sacrament, H40 B2, GA: Atlanta Our Lady of Lourdes, 1913–1974, box 1, folder 7, Catholic Historical Research Center; Sisters of the Blessed Sacrament, "Annals of Our Lady of Lourdes Convent, January 1962–August 1973."

38 Lynch, *Sharing the Bread in Service*, 2:282–83; "Claver House Taking Root after Maisha House Closes," *Georgia Bulletin*, January 11, 2007.
39 Sr. Margaret Mary McAnoy, interview by Leah Mickens, digital recording, June 14, 2019; Rita McInerney, "Our Lady of Lourdes—75 Years: Parish Reflects Black Catholic History," *Georgia Bulletin*, November 3, 1987, Our Lady of Lourdes Parish Collection, 1921–2011, Office of Archives and Records, Roman Catholic Archdiocese of Atlanta.
40 S. A. Reid, "Lourdes Backers Hoping for 'Miracle'; $50,000 Raised so Far, with $1 Million Needed by July 15," *Atlanta Constitution*, May 17, 2000, Home Edition, sec. City Life Atlanta; Sandra L. Criddell to Leah Mickens, "Assistance in Answering a Few More Questions about Our Lady of Lourdes," June 16, 2020.

6. REVIVING OUR LADY OF LOURDES THROUGH LITURGICAL RENEWAL AND LITURGICAL JUSTICE

1 Mark Newman, *Desegregating Dixie: The Catholic Church and Desegregation, 1945–1992* (Jackson: University Press of Mississippi, 2018), 197–98.
2 Sisters of the Blessed Sacrament, "Annals of Our Lady of Lourdes Convent, January 1962–August 1973," 1973, Archives of the Sisters of the Blessed Sacrament, H40 B2, GA: Atlanta Our Lady of Lourdes, 1913–1974, box 1, folder 5, Catholic Historical Research Center.
3 Frank J. Giusta to Jerry Hardy, May 28, 1979, Our Lady of Lourdes Parish, 1921–2011, Office of Archives and Records, Roman Catholic Archdiocese of Atlanta.
4 Frank J. Giusta, "Size and Composition of the Congregation," December 5, 1979, Our Lady of Lourdes Parish, 1921–2011, Office of Archives and Records, Roman Catholic Archdiocese of Atlanta.
5 Giusta, "Size and Composition of the Congregation"; Our Lady of Lourdes Catholic Church, "We Care! Come Share . . . ," n.d., Our Lady of Lourdes Parish, 1921–2011, Office of Archives and Records, Roman Catholic Archdiocese of Atlanta.
6 Rita McInerney, "Our Lady of Lourdes—75 Years: Parish Reflects Black Catholic History," *Georgia Bulletin*, November 3, 1987, Our Lady of Lourdes Parish Collection, 1921–2011, Office of Archives and Records, Roman Catholic Archdiocese of Atlanta.
7 "Minutes of Meeting with Fathers Adamski, Giusta, and Gracz," September 23, 1980, Our Lady of Lourdes Parish, 1921–2011, Office of Archives and Records, Roman Catholic Archdiocese of Atlanta.
8 McInerney, "Our Lady of Lourdes."
9 Our Lady of Lourdes, "A Journey of Faith, Spirituality and Social Justice: A History of Our Lady of Lourdes Catholic Church, Atlanta, Georgia, 1912–2012," 2012, 30, Our Lady of Lourdes Parish Collection, 1921–2011, Office of Archives and Records, Roman Catholic Archdiocese of Atlanta.
10 Jacqueline Trescott, "The New Coretta Scott King: Emerging from the Legacy; Assuming the Burden; Beyond the Legacy; The Widow Has Assumed Her Husband's Burden—and More," *Washington Post*, January 15, 1978, final ed., sec. Style, N1.

11 Sr. Margaret Mary McAnoy, interview by Leah Mickens, digital recording, June 14, 2019.
12 "Our Lady of Lourdes Church Sunday Bulletin," January 4, 1976, Our Lady of Lourdes Parish Collection, 1921–2011, box 4, folder 7, Office of Archives and Records, Roman Catholic Archdiocese of Atlanta.
13 "Our Lady of Lourdes Church Sunday Bulletin," January 18, 1976, Our Lady of Lourdes Parish Collection, 1921–2011, box 4, folder 7, Office of Archives and Records, Roman Catholic Archdiocese of Atlanta.
14 "Our Lady of Lourdes Church Sunday Bulletin," July 7, 1974, Our Lady of Lourdes Parish Collection, 1921–2011, box 4, folder 6, Office of Archives and Records, Roman Catholic Archdiocese of Atlanta.
15 Our Lady of Lourdes Church and School Community, "Our Lady of Lourdes Anniversary Pageant: 'Our Lady of Lourdes—A Pilgrim People 1912–1977,'" 1977, Archives of the Sisters of the Blessed Sacrament, H40 B2, GA: Atlanta Our Lady of Lourdes, 1913–1974, box 2, folder 21, Catholic Historical Research Center.
16 Andrew S. Moore, "Black and Catholic in Atlanta: Challenge and Hope," in *Catholics in the Vatican II Era: Local Histories of a Global Event*, ed. Karen Sprows Cummings, Timothy Matovina, and Robert A. Orsi (New York: Cambridge University Press, 2018), 148–49.
17 Jennifer F. Giarratano and David J. Sjoquist, "Auburn Avenue," *Economic Development Journal* 17, no. 2 (2018): 11.
18 Lourdes Build Group, "Our Lady of Lourdes Catholic Church: This Is Who We Are . . ." (Our Lady of Lourdes, November 22, 2019), http://lourdesatlanta.org.
19 Sandra L. Criddell to Leah Mickens, "Assistance in Answering a Few More Questions about Our Lady of Lourdes," June 16, 2020; Marshall Thomas, telephone interview by Leah Mickens, June 12, 2020.
20 Archdiocese of Atlanta, "Our Lady of Lourdes Geo-Demographic Summary" (August 12, 2016), https://archatl.com.
21 Edward J. Dillon to Stephen T. Churchwell, August 14, 1996, Our Lady of Lourdes Parish Collection, 1921–2011, Office of Archives and Records, Roman Catholic Archdiocese of Atlanta.
22 Archdiocese of Atlanta, "Sacred Heart of Jesus, Atlanta: Geo-Demographic Summary" (August 12, 2016), https://archatl.com; Archdiocese of Atlanta, "Shrine of the Immaculate Conception Geo-Demographic Summary" (August 11, 2016), https://archatl.com; Archdiocese of Atlanta, "Saint Anthony of Padua, Atlanta Geo-Demographic Summary" (August 12, 2016), https://archatl.com.
23 Patti Puckett, "A Joyful Noise: Choir's Reputation Is Built on Sounds from Church Classics to Jazz, Reggae Beats," *Atlanta Journal-Constitution*, December 1, 1994, sec. City Life / Your Community, N/09.
24 Puckett, "Joyful Noise"; Our Lady of Lourdes, "A Journey of Faith, Spirituality and Social Justice."
25 Matthew J. Cressler, "Black Power, Vatican II, and the Emergence of Black Catholic Liturgies," *U.S. Catholic Historian* 32, no. 4 (2014): 113–14.

26 The Black Clergy Caucus, "A Statement of the Black Clergy Caucus, 1968," in *"Stamped with the Image of God": African Americans as God's Image in Black*, ed. Cyprian Davis and Jamie T. Phelps (Maryknoll, NY: Orbis Books, 2003), 111–14.
27 National Black Sisters' Conference, "The Survival of Soul: National Black Sisters' Conference Position Paper, 1969," in Davis and Phelps, *"Stamped with the Image of God,"* 114–16.
28 Cyprian Davis, "God of Our Weary Years: Black Catholics in American Catholic History," in *Taking Down Our Harps: Black Catholics in the United States*, ed. Diana L. Hayes and Cyprian Davis (Maryknoll, NY: Orbis Books, 1998), 40; Joseph L. Howze et al., "'What We Have Seen and Heard': A Pastoral Letter on Evangelization from the Black Bishops of the United States" (United States Conference of Catholic Bishops, September 9, 1984), www.usccb.org.
29 Robert E. McCall, "America's First Black Catholic Archbishop," *Josephite Harvest*, Summer 1988, Xavier University of Louisiana Archives and Special Collections, African Americans and the Roman Catholic Collection, box 12, folder 2, 1, 5–6.
30 Paula Day, "Two Years Long Enough for Archbishop to Win Hearts," *Georgia Bulletin*, July 19, 1990, Xavier University of Louisiana Archives and Special Collections, African Americans and the Roman Catholic Collection, box 12, folder 3.
31 "Archbishop Marino Resigns; Administrator Named," *Georgia Bulletin*, July 19, 1990, Xavier University of Louisiana Archives and Special Collections, African Americans and the Roman Catholic Collection, box 12, folder 3.
32 Douglas Martin, "Eugene Marino, Black Archbishop, Dies at 66," *New York Times*, November 16, 2000, www.nytimes.com.
33 Edward Branch, "We Still Remember," *Georgia Bulletin*, May 1, 2008, https://georgiabulletin.org.
34 Paula Day, "Georgians Reflect on Archbishop's Spirit, Vision," *Georgia Bulletin*, January 7, 1993, 8, Xavier University of Louisiana Archives and Special Collections, African Americans and the Roman Catholic Collection, box 6, folder 7.
35 Thea Jarvis, "Compassion, Humility Were Marks of Leadership," *Georgia Bulletin*, January 7, 1993, 11, Xavier University of Louisiana Archives and Special Collections, African Americans and the Roman Catholic Collection, box 6, folder 7.
36 Day, "Georgians Reflect on Archbishop's Spirit, Vision," 8.
37 Gretchen Keiser, "Archbishop James Lyke, OFM—1939–1992," *Georgia Bulletin*, January 7, 1993, 1, Xavier University of Louisiana Archives and Special Collections, African Americans and the Roman Catholic Collection, box 6, folder 7.
38 Thea Jarvis, "Friends Share Memories at 'Home-Going Vigil'" *Georgia Bulletin*, January 7, 1993, 10, Xavier University of Louisiana Archives and Special Collections, African Americans and the Roman Catholic Collection, box 6, folder 7.
39 Larry Neal, "The Black Arts Movement" (National Humanities Center Resource Toolbox, 1968), http://nationalhumanitiescenter.org.
40 Pearl Williams-Jones, "Afro-American Gospel Music: A Crystallization of the Black Aesthetic," *Ethnomusicology* 19, no. 3 (1975): 346.
41 Williams-Jones, "Afro-American Gospel Music," 375–76.

42 Cressler, "Black Power, Vatican II, and the Emergence of Black Catholic Liturgies," 114–16.
43 Mary E. McGann and Eva Marie Lumas, "The Emergence of African American Catholic Worship," in *Let It Shine! The Emergence of African American Catholic Worship*, ed. Mary E. McGann (New York: Fordham University Press, 2008), 9–10.
44 Mary E. McGann, "Clarence R.J. Rivers' Vision of Effective African American Worship," in McGann, *Let It Shine!*, 57–58.
45 M. Shawn Copeland, "'The African American Catholic Hymnal' and the African American Spiritual," *U.S. Catholic Historian* 19, no. 2 (2001): 67–68; Wendelin J. Watson, "Lead Me, Guide Me: The African American Catholic Hymnal," *Black Sacred Music* 3, no. 1 (1989): 69–70.
46 Mark Pattison, "Approval for Zairian Rite Was a Long Time Coming, Says Congolese Cardinal," *Catholic Philly*, August 10, 2016, https://catholicphilly.com; Nathan Peter Chase, "A History and Analysis of the Missel Romain Pour Les Dioceses Du Zaire," *Obsculta* 6, no. 1 (2013): 31–33.
47 Laura B. Randolph, "What's behind the Black Rebellion in the Catholic Church? A Charismatic Priest and His Imani Temple Spark Debate," *Ebony* 45, no. 1 (November 1989): 160.
48 Arthur Jones, "Rowe's Leaving Is a Way to 'Stop Colluding,'" *National Catholic Reporter*, April 25, 1997, 12; "Stallings Starts Own Church," *Michigan Citizen*, February 17, 1990, 12.
49 Marjorie Hyler, "Prelates to Study Need for African American Rite; Panel of Black Catholics to Determine if Consensus Exists in Wake of Stallings's Schism," *Washington Post*, July 26, 1989, final ed., A16; Marjorie Hyler, "National Lay Group for Black Catholics Backs Separate African American Rite," *Washington Post*, August 6, 1989, A17; D. Reginald Whitt, "Varietates Legitimae and an African-American Liturgical Tradition," in Hayes and Davis, *Taking Down Our Harps*, 270.
50 "Our Lady of Lourdes Catholic Church: Atlanta's First African-American Catholic Church" (Georgia Historical Society, September 16, 2014), https://georgiahistory.com.
51 Michael Alexander, "New Lourdes Pastor Feels 'Prepared' to Lead There," *Georgia Bulletin*, October 28, 2010.
52 Clarence-Rufus J. Rivers, "The Oral African Tradition versus the Ocular Western Tradition: The Spirit in Worship," in Hayes and Davis, *Taking Down Our Harps*, 234–44; McGann, "Clarence R.J. Rivers' Vision," 57, 68–69.
53 Sandra L. Criddell et al., interview by Leah Mickens, digital recording, April 16, 2019.
54 Rivers, "Oral African Tradition," 234–36.
55 Kim R. Harris, "Sister Thea Bowman: Liturgical Justice through Black Sacred Song," *U.S. Catholic Historian* 35, no. 1 (2017): 99–101.

CONCLUSION

1 Bryan N. Massingale, *Racial Justice and the Catholic Church* (Maryknoll, NY: Orbis Books, 2014), 80; Hilaire Belloc, *Europe and the Faith* (1920), www.gutenberg.

org; Pope Leo XIII, "Orientalium Dignitas" (Papal Encyclicals Online, November 30, 1894), www.papalencyclicals.net.
2   Pew Research Center, "The Global Catholic Population" (February 13, 2013), www.pewforum.org.
3   Michael Lipka, "A Closer Look at Catholic America" (Pew Research Center, September 14, 2015), www.pewresearch.org.
4   Archdiocese of Atlanta, "We Are the Church" (2018), https://archatl.com; "Parishes with a Strong Black Catholic Presence" (United States Conference of Catholic Bishops, 2020), www.usccb.org.
5   Pope Benedict XV, "Maximum Illud" (Vatican, November 30, 1919), www.vatican.va.
6   Robert Orsi, *The Madonna of 115th Street: Faith and Community in Italian Harlem, 1880–1950* (New Haven, CT: Yale University Press, 2002), 55–58.
7   Matthew J. Cressler, *Authentically Black and Truly Catholic: The Rise of Black Catholicism in the Great Migration* (New York: New York University Press, 2017).
8   Darren W. Davis and Donald B. Pope-Davis, *Perseverance in the Parish? Religious Attitudes from a Black Catholic Perspective* (New York: Cambridge University Press, 2017), 143–46.
9   Mary E. McGann and Eva Marie Lumas, "The Emergence of African American Catholic Worship," in *Let It Shine! The Emergence of African American Catholic Worship*, ed. Mary E. McGann (New York: Fordham University Press, 2008), 5–7; Mary Jo Weaver, "Introduction: Who Are the Conservative Catholics?," in *Being Right: Conservative Catholics in America*, ed. Mary Jo Weaver and R. Scott Appleby (Bloomington: Indiana University Press, 1995, 1–14), 2–6.
10 Andrew Hill, interview by Leah Mickens, digital recording, April 24, 2019; Valencia White, interview by Leah Mickens, digital recording, March 16, 2019.
11 Priscilla McCutcheon, "Food, Faith, and the Everyday Struggle for Black Urban Community," *Social and Cultural Geography* 16, no. 4 (2015): 399–403; John T. McGreevy, *Parish Boundaries: The Catholic Encounter with Race in the Twentieth-Century Urban North* (Chicago: University of Chicago Press, 1996), 3–5.

INDEX

Page numbers in italics indicate Photos

Abernathy, Ralph David (Reverend), 2
accreditation, 77, 79, 125–26
"active participation" of lay people, 17, 91, 94–96, 99–100
activism, 6–7, 11, 44, 47–48, 61–63. *See also* protests
Adams, Nellie, 45–46
aesthetics, 106, 148–49, 158–59, 162, 166–67
Africa, 19, 36, 161, 162–63
African American Catholic Congregation, 152
African American Rite, 10, 150–51
The American Catholic Experience (Dolan), 8
American Catholicism, 7–14, 18–19, 104–5, 118, 161–65; Vatican II affecting, 60, 96–97, 101. *See also* Catholic schools
American Mass Program (Rivers), 149
Americans with Disabilities Act, U.S., 44–45
Antebellum period, 8, 20, 22–23, 31, 42
anti-Blackness/anti-Negro, 2, 26, 33, 148, 163; in Atlanta, 25, 42–43; racism as, 19–20, 166–67
anti-Catholicism, 2, 4, 22–28, 58, 93, 113–14, 118
Aquinas, Mary Thomas (Sister), 5, 36–37, 38, 131; as Our Lady of Lourdes School principal, 4, 41
Archdiocese of Atlanta, 1–2, 12, 14–15, 32, 87, 108, 130, 162; Black bishops for, 145–46; demographics, 141–43; desegregation by, 17, 60, 68
arrests, 46, 62, 66
assassination of King, Martin Luther, Jr., 65, 144–45
Atlanta, Georgia, 1–2, 5, 29–31, 40, 46, 61, 153; anti-Catholicism in, 22–28; Board of Education, 25, 39, 69–70; Catholic population in, 3–4, 31–32, 59, 162. *See also* Archdiocese of Atlanta; Black Atlantans; neighborhoods, Atlanta; *specific churches*
Atlanta Daily World (newspaper), 44
Atlanta Fire of 1917, 36
Atlanta Journal-Constitution, 144
Atlanta Race Riot of 1906, 9, 42–43
Atlanta Student Movement, 61–63
Atlanta University Center (AUC), 32, 39, 57, 61–63, 147–48
Auburn Avenue, 1–4, 41–43, 141–42, 165, 167; churches on, 44–59, *50*; declining state of, 17–18, 82–83, 126–27; demographic changes to, 111–12, 125, 127. *See also specific Churches*
AUC. *See* Atlanta University Center
Authentically Black and Truly Catholic (Cressler), 11, 164

baptisms, 19–21, 38
Baptists, Black, 1, 23, 44–46, 51, 53, 165, 166. *See also specific churches*
Barry, John (Father), 31

193

Belloc, Hilaire, 161, 163
Benedict XV (Pope), 162
Benedict XVI (Pope), 166–67
Benjamin, Phyllis, 139–40
Bernard, Mary, 75
Bernardin, Joseph (Bishop), 84, 109–10, 119
Big Bethel African Methodist Episcopal AME Church (Big Bethel), 3, 7, 45–46, 48–49, 50, 54
bishops, American, 13, 22, 33, 104–6, 145–46
Black: aesthetics, 148–49, 158–59, 166; businesses, 42–43, 48, 57–58, 63; Catholic high schools, 60, 67, 77–82; children, 40–41; doctors, 56–57; men, 38–39, 41, 42–43; middle class, 7, 43, 83, 125; ministry, 28, 130–31; music, 144, 148–49; priests, 1–2, 5, 24–25; professionals, 43–44, 57–58, 137; sharecroppers, 40–41, 66. See also evangelization of Blacks; Southern Blacks
Black Arts Movement, 148–49
Black Atlantans, 26, 37–38, 43, 49–51, 70–71; on closing Drexel Catholic High School, 78–82, 85–87, 128–34
Black Catholic Movement, 144–53, 164
Black Catholics, 3, 7, 10, 15, 18, 32, 165–66; Black Protestants and, 15, 52–54, 58, 164; in Chicago, 6, 11–12, 164; Civil Rights Movement and, 17, 60–67; high school for, 60, 67, 77–82; Lissner increasing population of, 33–34; SBS interfacing with, 5, 37, 128–33; Vatican II and, 13, 60; white Catholics and, 85–86, 165; as "whitewashed," 4, 11
Black Clergy Caucus, 144–45, 150, 152
Black communities, 1, 4, 11, 12, 25, 44, 139; Civil Rights Movement and, 60–61; King, Martin Luther, Sr., addressing, 47–48; SBS and, 15, 27–28, 64–65, 85, 116–17
Black Franciscan sisters, 35

Black Power, 6, 11, 134, 144, 148, 153
Black Priest / White Church (Lucas), 10–11
Black Protestants, 9, 18, 39, 47, 61, 148–49, 161, 163; Black Catholics and, 15, 52–54, 58, 164
Black-white racial binary, 4, 9, 14, 162
Board of Education, Atlanta, 25, 39, 69–70
Bond, Julian, 61–62
Booker T. Washington High School, 66–67
books, prayer, 93–94, 97
Borders, William Holmes (Reverend), 44–45
Bouyer, Louis, 91
boycotts, 41, 46–48, 61, 123
Boykin, Edward, 139
Branch, Edward (Father), 147
Brown v. Board of Education, 68, 78–79
budgets, 62, 116–17, 137
Bulletin of the Catholic Laymen's Association of Georgia, 26–27, 34, 57
Burtenshaw, Noel C. (Reverend), 119
Bussard, Paul (Reverend), 97
Butler Street Bottoms (neighborhood), 42
Buttermilk Bottoms (neighborhood), 42

Calhoun, William (Father), 1–2, 6, 108
capitalism, 24, 99
Cathedral of Christ the King, 1–2, 3, 58–59, 72, 74
Catholic Church of Atlanta, 31
Catholic Colored Clinic, 56–57
"Catholic ghettos," Northern, 3–4, 60
Catholicism. *See specific topics*
Catholic Medical Mission Board of New York, 56
Catholic schools, 3, 113–24, 126–33, 138; consolidation of, 78, 117–18, 125; desegregation and, 63, 68, 70–76, 103; Protestants attending, 52–53. *See also specific schools*
Catholics in the Vatican II Era (Moore, A.), 13

Catholic social teachings (CST), 2, 14, 19, 28–34, 58, 69, 100, 123
Catholic Worker Movement, 100–101
Cavallo, Joseph (Father), 136
celibacy, 24
Central Presbyterian Church, 3
Chandler, Essie, 32
Chase, Nathan David, 151
Chicago, Illinois, 6, 11–12, 153, 164
children, Black, 40–41
churches, Auburn Avenue, 44–59, 50. *See also specific topics*
Church of Christ the King. *See* Cathedral of Christ the King
civil rights, 27–28, 46, 64, 67
Civil Rights Act, U.S., 134
Civil Rights Movement, 2, 4, 13, 15–16, 30, 131–32, 147; Black Catholics and, 17, 60–67 ; Borders involved in, 45–46; Vatican II and, 5–7, 28, 89, 163, 165–66
Civil War, 8, 22–28, 42, 49, 58
Clark College, 47
closure, 60, 68–69, 126; of Drexel Catholic High School, 17, 77–82, 85–87, 119, 128–34; and Our Lady of Lourdes Church, 14, 84–85, 87
Co-Cathedral of Cathedral of King. *See* Cathedral of Christ the King
Cole, Melody, 143–44
"colored mission," Our Lady of Lourdes Catholic Church as a, 9, 32–34, 126, 163
"colored schools," 77–78, 80–81
Communion, 21, 38, 74, 91–92, 98
communism, 52, 99
communities, 4, 29–31, 99. *See also* Black communities
Confederacy, 23, 30, 41
Confession, 55, 90
conservatism, 13, 60, 89, 96, 148–49, 166–67
consolidation of Catholic schools, 78, 117–18, 125

Constitution on the Sacred Liturgy (*Sacrosanctum Concilium*), 88–89, 102–7, 108–9
converts/conversions, Catholic, 21–22, 27, 37–38, 54–55, 70; Our Lady of Lourdes Church, 12, 140, 163
coreligionists, 9, 19; white, 10, 18, 21 27, 58, 165, 167
Corley, George, 32
correspondences/letters, 3, 21–22, 56–57, 63, 68–71, 131; by Aquinas, 5, 41; by Bernardin, 109–10, 119; by Giusta, 135; by Hallinan, 106; by Keiley, 33–34; by McCarthy, 126–28; SBS, 14–15, 129
costs, 77–78, 114, 117, 119–21, 126, 134–35
Council of Trent (1570), 6
counter-public spaces, 44, 167
Counter-Reformation, 52, 91–93, 109, 162
Crawford Long Hospital, 56
Creole people, 13–14
Cressler, Matthew, 11–12, 164
Criddell, Sandra, 51, 108, 142, 156–57
Crogan, Leo, 75
CST. *See* Catholic social teachings

dance, liturgical, 151, 155
David (Mother), 64, 121–22
Davis, Cyprian, 10
Davis, Darren W., 165
Davis Street School, 25
Day, Dorothy, 100
deaths, 34, 40–41, 43, 46, 139, 147–48, 150; of Hallinan, 107; of Williams, A., 47
decline/declining state: of Auburn Avenue, 17–18, 82–83, 126–27; in teaching sisters, 113–15, 117, 124–25, 131
Decree on the Renewal of Religious Life (*Perfectae Caritatis*), Vatican II, 121
Deep South, 21, 57, 61, 64, 74, 123, 164
de facto, 60; segregation, 8–10, 79, 153, 167
DeGive Construction Company, 72
de jure segregation, 23

Democratic Republic of Congo, 150–51, 161
Democrats, 166–67
demographics, 109, 111–12, 125, 127, 142–43, 155, 161–62
Desegregating Dixie (Newman, M.), 12
desegregation, 46, 60, 78–83, 85–87, 103; Hallinan on, 17, 63, 70, 74–75, 88; of public and parochial schools, 17, 67–77, 125–26
Detroit, Michigan, 12
devotions/devotionalism, 89, 95–97, 99–100, 102–3; popular, 17, 90, 91–92, 102; rosary as, 55, 90, 91–92, 93, 94, 98, 101, 116
Diekmann, Godfrey (Father), 103
Dillon, Edward J. (Monsignor), 143
Diocese of Atlanta, 58, 68, 74
Diocese of Savannah, 15, 32–34, 35, 57–59
direct action, 63, 100–101
discrimination, racial, 64, 68–69
"Discrimination and Christian Conscience" (letter), 68–69
Dolan, Jay P., 8
donations. *See* funding
Donnellan, Thomas (Archbishop), 129–33, 134–35
Doonan, Terrance, 31
Drexel, Katharine, 1, 5, 35–38, 41, 55, 67, 121–23, 140; Hyland on, 72–73; SBS founded by, 27–28
Drexel Catholic High School, 15, 62, 67, 76–82, 85–87, *86*, 117–19
Drexel Home School Association, 81
Driskell, Jay Winston, Jr., 39, 40
Dublin Review (magazine), 97
Duggan, Gregory (Father), 31
Dyer (Mrs.), *112*
D'Youville Academy, 67, 76

Ebenezer Baptist Church, 26, 45, *50*, 139; King, Martin Luther, Jr. at, 3, 7, 46; King, Martin Luther, Sr. at, 47–48

Ebony (magazine), 151–52
Eden, Carole (Sister), 129
Elder, William Henry (Bishop), 21–22
elementary schools, 115–16, 127, 132
Elmore, Gwendolyn, 45, 53–54
emancipation/emancipated slaves, 20–21, 23, 42, 48–49
Emancipation Proclamation, U.S., 53–54
English (language), 66, 108
enrollment, student, 80, 122; Our Lady of Lourdes School, 36–38, 41, 112–13, 117–18, 127–33
enslaved persons. *See* slavery/enslaved people
Equal Rights League, 46
ethnicity, 7–14. *See also specific ethnicities*
Eucharist. *See* Communion
Eurocentrism, 3, 89, 106, 148, 150, 165
Europe, Continental, 19, 74–75, 161
Europe and the Faith (Belloc), 161
European immigrants, 1, 3, 7–8, 14, 21–26
evangelization of Blacks, 1–2, 19–22, 26–27, 136; CST on, 28–29; in the South, 33–34, 163

fascism, 99
fears, 23–25, 34
federal government, U.S., 64, 67–68
Ferrone, Rita, 102
fertility of Black women, 40–41
First Congregational Church, 54
Fitzgerald, Mary Elizabeth (Mother), 124, 126–27, 129–30
folk Masses, 108, 153
Fox, Matthew, 110–11
France, 95, 104, 161, 163
Frazier, E. Franklin, 4
Freedom Riders, 65–66
Freeman, Dale (Father), 84–85
French liturgy, 95
French Revolution, 95
Friendship Baptist Church, 44

funding, Our Lady of Lourdes Church, 27, 35–37, 72, 134–39; by white Catholics, 9, 33, 56–57, 126
funding/fundraising, 38–39, 47, 56–57, 77–78, 81, 127–33

Gamm, Gerald, 9–10
Gate City Colored School, 49
General Chapter, SBS, 121, 123–24
gentrification, 142, 167
Georgia, 2–3, 31, 35, 39–41. *See also specific cities*
Georgia Bulletin (newspaper), 15, 76, 77, 106, 136–38, 147
Georgia Historical Society, 153
Georgian (newspaper), 46
Georgia Railroad, 31
Germany, 96, 98, 104
Gföllner, Johannes Maria (Bishop), 98
Gibbons, James (Cardinal), 15, 33–34
Gilded Age, 24
Giusta, Frank J. (Father), 135–37, 139
global Catholicism, 92, 161–62, 165, 166
Gracz, Henry (Father), 132, 137, 147
Grady Memorial Hospital, 56
Great Depression, U.S., 46
Great Migration, U.S., 11, 28, 40–41, 163
Greensboro, North Carolina, 61–62
Gregorian chants, 95–96, 101, 109, 144, 150
Gregory, Wilton (Archbishop), 133
Gregory XV (Pope), 93
Griffin, Janis, 26, 108
Griffin, Marvin, 33, 68
Guéranger, Dom Prosper, 95
guitars, 108–11, 153

Hallinan, Paul (Archbishop), 6, 13, 15, 78–82, 147; on desegregation, 17, 63, 70, 74–75, 88; *Sacrosanctum Concilium* and, 102–7
Hapeville, Georgia, 166
Hardy, Jerry (Reverend), 135–36
Harmon, Katherine, 99–100

Harris, Joel Chandler, 32
Hart, Phoebe, 47
HDDC. *See* Historic District Development Corporation
Headley, William (Reverend), 85–87
health care, Jim Crow era, 55–57
Herberg, Will, 8, 11
Hickey, James (Cardinal), 152
hierarchy, Catholic, 10–11, 16, 28–29, 70–71, 98–99
high schools, 66, 70, 118–19, 128; Black Catholic, 60, 67, 77–82. *See also specific schools*
Hill, Andrew, 52, 80, 166–67
Hispanic Catholics, 8, 147, 161–62
Historic District Development Corporation (HDDC), 141–42
The History of Black Catholics in the United States (Davis, C.), 10
Holmes, Hamilton, 70
Holy Family Hospital, 56–58
homelessness, 132, 137–38, 157, 167
Hornsby, Alton, Jr., 42
Horton (Father), 5
House of Representatives, U.S., 24
Howard University, 108, 152
"How to Understand Changes in the Liturgy" (Hallinan), 106
Howze, Joseph (Bishop), 145
human rights, 69, 73
Hunter, Charlayne, 70
Hurricane Katrina, 14
Hutchinson, Deion, 51
Hyland, Francis (Bishop), 3, 59, 63, 66; on desegregation, 17, 68–74; Drexel Catholic High School founded by, 67, 72–73

identity, 11–12, 21, 30, 61, 84, 99, 134, 143–44; pre-councilar Catholic, 164, 166; white ethnic Catholic, 8, 164
illiteracy, 10, 97–98
Imelda, Mary (Sister), 36

Immaculate Conception Church, 3, 31–33, 55, 83, 165
Immaculate Conception School, 119
immigrants, European, 1, 3, 7–8, 14, 21–26
inculturation, liturgical, 6, 17–18, 157, 158–59, 164, 166
individualism, 104–5
infant mortality, Black, 40–41
integration, 24, 42, 67–70, 77–82
intermarriage, 54
International Congress of Major Superiors (1952), 120
interracialism, 6, 64–65, 74, 76, 100
interwar period, 74–75, 99
Irish Catholics, 8–9, 24, 25, 31, 163, 164
Italian Catholics, 9, 24, 163, 164

Jewish people, 9–10, 24
Jim Crow era/laws, 41–44, 46, 60, 67–68, 141, 168; Black Catholics and, 15, 18; health care in, 55–57; Our Lady of Lourdes Catholic Church during, 4, 32–33; SBS and, 1, 27–28; segregation, 14, 32, 167; in the South, 9, 30, 71–72, 163
John XXIII (Pope), 88, 101
journalism, yellow, 42–43

Katharine Drexel Community Center, 133, 153–54
Keiley, Benjamin (Bishop), 15, 26, 30, 32–35, 40
Kemp, Matthew (Father), 1, 6, 110, 129
Kinast, Bob (Father), 139–40
King, Alberta Williams, 139–40
King, Coretta Scott, 138, 141, 146
King, Lonnie, 61–62
King, Martin Luther, Jr. (Reverend), 2, 64, 65, 129, 138–40, 143–44; at Ebenezer Baptist Church, 3, 7, 46–47
King, Martin Luther, Sr. (Reverend), 26, 47, 139
Koenker, Ernest, 101
Ku Klux Klan, 25

Laach, Maria (Mary Laach Abbey), 96
labor, 25–26, 29, 100–101, 114, 124
de Lai, Gaetano (Cardinal), 33
languages, 147, 162; translation and, 94, 96–97; vernacular, 96, 97–98, 101–4, 109, 166
Latin (language), 1, 101–3; masses, 108, 166–67; TLM in, 6, 23, 88–89, 93, 105, 107–8, 162
Latin America, 161, 162–63
Latin Christendom, 75, 150
"law-and-order," 63, 69–72
lay people/laity, 10, 60–67, 89–103; "active participation" of, 17, 91, 94–96, 99–100; missals, 96–98, 101, 108; teachers as, 78, 115–17, 119, 122
Lead Me, Guide Me (1987), 144, 147–48, 150
The Leaflet Missal (Bussard), 97
legislatures, state, 20–21, 39–41
Leo XIII (Pope), 29, 98
letters. *See* correspondences/letters
liberals/liberalism, 13, 52, 74, 89, 92–93. *See also* progressive/progressivism
life expectancy, Black, 40–41
Lissner, Ignatius (Father), 33–34, 35–36, 113
literacy, 92–93, 95, 132
Liturgical Commission, Vatican II, 102–4, 106
Liturgical Movement, 6, 89–102, 105–7, 109–11
liturgical reform: Black Catholic Movement and, 144–53; Hallinan advocating for, 6, 13, 88; Vatican II and, 17, 88–89, 94, 119–25
liturgical renewal, 18, 88–89, 107–11, 119–25, 163
"liturgical wars," 89–90, 162
liturgy/liturgical practice, 90–102, 149–50; inculturated, 6, 17–18, 157, 158–59, 164; Tridentine, 6, 23, 88–89, 93, 105, 107–8, 162

local devotions, 91–92
Long, Vicki R., 146
Lost Cause, cult of the, 4, 30
Louise Marie (Sister), *73*
Love, Law, Liberation Movement, 46
Lucas, Lawrence (Father), 4, 10–11
Lucy (Sister), *112*
Lyke, James P. (Archbishop), 15, 147, 150
Lynch, Patricia (Sister), 124, 128
lynchings, 46

MacDonough (Father), 108
The Madonna of 115th Street (Orsi), 164
Maisha House, SBS, 132
majority-Black parishes, 14, 136–37, 141, 143, 150, 155, 159, 165
majority-white parishes, 48, 87, 111, 144, 155, 165
The Making of American Catholicism (Pfeifer), 13
March on Washington, 64, 65
Marino, Eugene (Archbishop), 15, 146–47
Marist College High School, 67
Marist Fathers, 31–32
Martin, Anita, 45
Martin Luther King Jr. Center for Non-Violent Social Change, 138–39, 140–41
Mary Carmelita (Sister), 36, 126, 131
Mary Clare (Sister), 56–57
mass: media, 88, 93; protests, 61–62
Masses, 21, 31, 55, 103–4, 106, *107*, 154–59, 162, 166–67; lay disengagement from, 89–102; segregation of, 32–33, 48, 55; TLM, 6, 23, 88–89, 93, 105, 107–8, 162
Maureen Immaculate (Sister), 127
Maurin, Peter, 100
McAnoy, Margaret (Sister), 132, 138–39
McCarthy, Loretta (Sister), 126–28, 132
McClendon Hospital, 58
McCullough, Michael, 31
McDonough, Thomas J., 63, 70
McGreevy, John T., 9–11, 29–30, 74, 167
McIntyre, James Francis (Cardinal), 104–5

McKeever (Father), 66, 72, *107*, 107–8, 125
McManus, Frederick (Father), 102–3
McMullin, Mary J., 70
Mediator Dei (Pius XII), 97–98
Medical Mission Sisters, 56–57
membership for Our Lady of Lourdes Church, 1, 15–16, 40, 49–51, 58, 111–12, 136, 142–43; contraction in, 17–18, 125–35; white flight affecting, 82–87
Methodist Episcopal Church South, 49
Metropolitan See, 74
Michel, Dom Virgil, 96, 99–100, 144
middle class, 7, 43, 83, 125, 137
migration, Black, 30, 76, 82–87, 140. *See also* Great Migration, U.S.
Mildred, Mary (Sister), 36
Miller, Randall, 14, 21
minority status of Catholics, 3–4, 12–13, 14, 23, 54, 102–3, 105
The Missal for the Laity (Derby Press), 97
Missal of Paul VI, 88–89, 108
missals, lay, 96–98, 101, 108
missions/missionaries, 19, 22; in Atlanta, 162; Black, 35, 57; European, 162–63; among slaves, 20–21. *See also* Sisters of the Blessed Sacrament
Mitchell, Margaret, 30
M. Judith (Sister), 127
mobility, upward, 83, 125, 129
monoethnic: neighborhoods, 8–9, 52, 140, 167; parishes, 8–9, 52, 140
Moore, Andrew, 12–13, 26
Moore, Joey, 88
Morehouse College, 61–62
Morris, Aldon, 61, 108
Morris Brown College, 32, 45, 49
"Mother Church," Our Lady of Lourdes Church as a, 3, 7
Motherhouse, SBS, 27, 36, 114–15, 117, 121, 123
mother superior, 123–24
Moylan, Joseph (Monsignor), 56–57
M. Regina (Sister), 116

Mulroy, John J. (Father), 109
multiracial parishes, 165–66
music, 108, 144, 148–49, 154–56, 162;
    sacred, 101–2, 109
My Catholic Faith (textbook), 51–52
My Pocket Prayerbook (1922), 94
Mystical Body of Christ, 74–75, 99
My Sunday Missal (Stedman), 97

National Association for the Advancement of Colored People (NAACP), 27–28, 39, 44, 46–47, 63
National Black Sisters' Conference, 145, 152
National Catholic Education Association (1952), 120
nationalism, 74–75, 100
National Office for Black Catholics (NOBC), 145, 149–50, 152
Native Americans, 1, 27, 123, 162
nativism, 23–24, 26, 53
Neal, Larry, 148
"Negro apostolate," 1, 28, 66, 78, 163
"the Negro Question," 1, 5, 28–34
neighborhoods, Atlanta, 10, 35, 42, 43, 81–87; monoethnic, 8–9, 52, 140, 167; sacred status of, 8–9, 29–30, 167. *See also specific neighborhoods*
neo-Thomism, 29–30
Newman, John Henry, 103
Newman, Mark, 12
Newman Clubs, 70, 102–3, 104
New Orleans, Louisiana, 13–14, 65–66
NOBC. *See* National Office for Black Catholics
non-Catholics, 20, 36, 54–55, 127, 140, 161, 167
nonviolent protests, 62–64, 123
the North, 6, 9–11, 25, 27, 40; "Catholic ghettos" in, 3–4, 60
the North, white ethnic Catholics in, 3, 8, 22, 29–30, 40, 53–54, 164, 167
North Carolina A&T University, 61–62

O'Boyle, Patrick (Archbishop), 64
O'Connor, Daniel J., 119
Old Fourth Ward, 7, 16–17, 50, 132, 142, 165, 170. *See also* Auburn Avenue
"On Racial Harmony" (letter), 64
oral histories, 14–16, 47
Orate Frates (magazine), 96, 99
ordination of Black priests, 1–2
organ, 108–9, 122, 154
Orsi, Robert, 164
"otherness," Catholic, 4, 12–13
Ott, Jeffrey (Father), 154–55
Our Lady of Lourdes Catholic Church, 11, 35, 37, 50, 55, 73, 107, 158, 168; architecture of, 36, 39, 72, 134–35, 153–54; Black Catholic Movement and, 152–53; Civil Rights Movement and, 17, 60–67; as a "colored mission," 9, 32–34, 126, 163; converts/conversions at, 12, 143, 163; during Jim Crow era, 4, 32–33; liturgical renewal at, 107–11; as a "Mother Church," 3, 7; post-Vatican II, 13, 164–65; protesting by, 5–6; SAM operating, 33; SBS at, 14–15, 36–37, 110; white Catholics funding, 9, 33; white flight affecting, 82–87; as a white parish, 13–14. *See also* membership for Our Lady of Lourdes Church
Our Lady of Lourdes Catholic School, 26, 38, 55, 62, 135–40; desegregation of, 75–77; enrollment at, 36–38, 41, 112–13, 117–18, 127–33; principals of, 5, 41, 127, 132, 138; SBS withdrawal from, 17–18, 111–13, 124–34; tuition for, 39, 83, 125, 127–28, 130
Our Lady of Lourdes Mission and Clinic, 55–56
Our Lady of Sorrows, SBS mission, 116
Our Lady of the Assumption Mission, 66

Pacem et Terris (John XXIII), 64, 88, 101
Pamiés, Ignio Anglés, 101–2

Parish Boundaries (McGreevy), 8–9, 53, 167
"parish boundaries" model, 9, 30, 140
parishes, 7, 19, 31, 82–83; monoethnic, 8–9, 52, 140; territorial, 10, 31, 84–87, 140, 143. *See also* white parishes; *specific parishes*
parish school model, 113–14, 118, 124–27, 133
Parker, John A., 46
parochial schools, Atlanta, 27, 154–55; desegregation of, 17, 67–77, 125–26. *See also* Catholic schools; *specific schools*
Passionists, 57
paternalism, 5, 19–20, 27–28, 73; white, 9, 30, 57
patronage. *See* funding
Paul VI (Pope), 106–7
Perfectae Caritatis (Decree on the Renewal of Religious Life), Vatican II, 121
Peters-Johnson, Cassandra, 52–53
Pfeifer, Michael J., 13, 14
Phillips, Ruth (Sister), 65
Pierce, Joe, 61
Pittsburgh (neighborhood), 42
Pius IX (Pope), 93
Pius X (Pope), 95–98, 119–20
Pius XII (Pope), 58–59, 97–98, 119–20
plantations, slave, 19–22, 31
Plessy v. Ferguson, 42
Pontifical Institute of Sacred Music, 101–2
Poor Peoples' Campaign, 65
Pope-Davis, Donald B., 165
popes/papacy, 74, 92–93, 120. *See also specific popes*
popular devotions, 17, 90, 91–92, 102
populism, 24–25
post–Civil War, 22, 23–24, 30
post–Counter-Reformation Europe, 92, 162
post–Jim Crow era, 60, 141
post–Vatican II era, 109–11, 113, 161–62; American Catholicism, 18, 164–65
postwar era, 12, 58, 103, 115–16, 164

poverty, 40–41, 100, 113, 118, 120–21, 137–38, 167
power, 7–8, 92
prayers, 90, 98, 100–102, 157; books of, 93–94, 97
pre–Vatican II era, 2, 15–16, 20, 27, 51–52, 55, 89–102; Atlanta, 29–31, 142–43; Catholic schools in, 126–27; on segregation, 71–72; white ethnic Catholics in, 8, 162. *See also* Jim Crow era/laws
principals of Our Lady of Lourdes Catholic School, 5, 15, 41, 127, 132, 138
printing/print culture, 93
private hospitals, 56
private schools, 39, 67, 114
privatization of public schools, 68
progressive/progressivism, 1, 12, 96, 103–5
Protestant, Catholic, Jew (Herberg), 8
Protestants/Protestantism, 2, 6, 15–17, 20, 27, 33, 92, 100, 105; in Atlanta, 3, 161, 163; Catholics and, 4, 28–29; in public schools, 113–14; Southern, 9, 22–23; white, 4, 8, 23–26, 58, 63–64, 67–68. *See also* Black Protestantism; *specific churches*
protests, 5–6, 29, 41, 46, 47, 61–63, 153; nonviolent, 62–64, 123
public hospitals, 56
public schools, Atlanta, 25, 27, 38–39, 41, 47, 49–51; anti-Catholicism of, 113–14, 118; desegregation of, 17, 67–77, 125–26; parochial students compared to, 115–16

race, 6–7, 16; American Catholics and, 7–14; Vatican on, 19–20
racial binary, Black-white, 4, 9, 14, 162
racial discrimination, 64, 68–69
racial justice, 71, 74–75
racism, 8, 10–11, 16, 60, 74, 128, 144–45; anti-Black, 19–20, 166–67; of the Catholic Church, 151–52, 163; Catholic Church opposing, 4, 13, 69–70; violence and, 9, 40

rape, 23–24, 42–43
Rapier (Father), 36
Reconstruction era, 28, 30, 41
Regina Mundi Institution, 120
regionalism, 12–14, 22–23, 66–67, 92, 118–19, 149. *See also* the North; the South
religious renewal, 89, 115, 119–25
Republicans, 166
Rerum Novarum (Leo XIII), 29
residential segregation, 41–42
resignations, 33, 73–74, 146–47
Reynolds, Ignatius (Bishop), 31
rights, 6, 8, 25–26; civil, 27–28, 46, 64, 67; human, 69, 73
Riordan, Julia, 25
Rivers, Clarence J. (Father), 149–50, 155–56, 157
Robinson, Willie Taylor, 50–51
Roman devotions, 92–93
Romanization of Catholicism, 92, 95, 168
Roman Rite, 92, 95, 101–2, 106, 109, 149–52, 154–55, 158–59
Rome, Italy, 88, 92, 103–5, 120
rosary, 55, 90, 91–92, 93, 94, 98, 101, 116
Ryan, Abram (Father), 30
Ryan, Patrick John (Archbishop), 36

sacred: music, 101–2, 109; status of neighborhoods, 8–9, 29–30, 167
Sacred Heart Catholic Church, 5, 31–33, 35, 83, 85–87, 143, 165; Our Lady of Lourdes Church supported by, 36–37, 72
Sacred Heart Catholic School, 119, 126
Sacrosanctum Concilium (Constitution on the Sacred Liturgy), 88–89, 102–7, 108–9
Saints Peter and Paul Church, 31–32, 143
SAM. *See* Society of African Missions
SBS. *See* Sisters of the Blessed Sacrament
Scriptures, 6, 92, 105, 123
Second Vatican Council. *See* Vatican II
Secretariat for African American Catholics, 145–46

secular: activities, 44, 49–50; society, 60, 104–5, 149, 165–66
segregation, 2, 12, 18, 23, 27–28, 52–54, 65–66; Atlanta Student Movement opposing, 61–63; Catholic Church opposing, 4, 69–71; de facto, 8–9, 79, 153, 167; Jim Crow era, 14, 32, 167; of Masses, 32–33, 48, 55; residential, 41–42
sharecroppers, Black, 40–41, 66
Sheila (Sister), 112
Shelley, Thomas J., 103
Shrine of the Immaculate Conception. *See* Immaculate Conception Church; Immaculate Conception School
singing, 95–96, 102, 109–10
Sister Formation Conference, 121
sisters, 9, 11, 35. *See also* teaching sisters
Sisters of Charity, 116
Sisters of the Blessed Sacrament (SBS), 5, 40, 58, 112, 116–17, 119–25; Civil Rights Movement and, 17, 60–67, 131–32, 153; Drexel founding, 27–28, 35; Motherhouse, 27, 36, 114–15, 117, 121, 123; at Our Lady of Lourdes Church, 1, 36–37, 110, 141; withdrawal from Our Lady of Lourdes Church, 17–18, 111–12, 124–34
Sisters of the Immaculate Heart of Mary, 116
sister-teacher. *See* teaching sisters
slave masters, 20–22
slavery/enslaved people, U.S., 10, 16, 31, 48–49, 148–49; emancipation and, 20–21, 23, 42; evangelization and, 19–22; white ethnic Catholics on, 8, 23
Smith, Mattie, 137
SNCC. *See* Student Nonviolent Coordinating Committee
socialism, 52, 92–93
social justice, 153–59
Social Security Act, U.S., 122
social services, Black churches, 44, 46–47, 55–56, 137–38

Society for the Propagation of the Faith, 21–22
Society of African Missions (SAM), 33, 35–36, 40, 57, 83, 113, 141. *See also* specific missions
Society of St. Joseph of the Sacred Heart, 28
Society of the Divine Word, 28
soteriology, 16, 20, 28
the South, 3–6, 12–13, 18, 60, 168; anti-Catholicism in, 22–28; Deep, 21, 57, 61, 64, 74, 123, 164; Jim Crow laws in, 9, 30, 71–72, 163; Protestantism of, 9, 22–23
Southeastern Regional Interracial Commission, 65
Southern Blacks, 26–27, 40, 64; Catholics, 3, 11–12, 153, 164
The South's Tolerable Aliens (Moore, A.), 12
Spalding, Jack Johnson, 35–36
Special Chapter, SBS, 121–24
Spellman, Francis (Cardinal), 104, 115–16
Spelman College, 65
The Spirit of Vatican II (McDannell), 8
Stallings, George, Jr., 151–52
St. Anthony of Padua Catholic Church, 32–33, 83, 125, 143, 158–59
St. Anthony of Padua Catholic School, 76, 132–33
Stations of the Cross, 90, 91–92, 154
Stedman, Joseph (Reverend), 97
St. John the Evangelist, 166
St. Joseph Catholic High School, 67, 76, 78–80, 117–19, 128, 131
St. Paul of the Cross Catholic Church, 4–6, 57–58, 63, 71, 83, 125, 158–59
St. Paul of the Cross Catholic School, 58, 68, 76
St. Pius X High School, 66–68, 76, 79–80, 117–19
Student Nonviolent Coordinating Committee (SNCC), 62

students, 61–65, 75–76; Our lady of Lourdes School, 28, 39–40, 43, 112–13. *See also* enrollment
St. Vincent de Paul Catholic Church, 65
sub-Saharan Africa, 19, 35
suburbs, 10, 84, 118
Summerhour, Adele, 112
Supreme Court, U.S., 42, 71–72
Sweet Auburn District, 7, 16–17, 36, 50. *See also* Old Fourth Ward
Syllabus on Racial Justice (Hallinan), 75

Talmadge, Herman, 68
Tanyard Bottom (neighborhood), 42
Taves, Ann, 90, 93
teachers, 39–40, 47; lay, 78, 115–17, 119, 122
teaching licenses, 68, 115, 120
teaching orders, women led, 1, 27, 115, 120, 124
teaching sisters, 1, 27, 73, 112, 120–21; decline in, 113–15, 117, 124–25, 131
territorialism/territorial boundaries, 10, 31, 84–87, 140, 143
Third Plenary Council of Baltimore of 1884, 113–14
Thomas, Adelaide, 131
Thomas, Marshall, 62, 142
Thomas, P. (Sister), 112
Thomas, Roscoe, 1
Thomistic revival, 29–30
threats, 25–26, 39–40, 65–66
TLM. *See* Tridentine Latin Mass
Toollen, Thomas Joseph (Bishop), 13
Total Gift of Self (SBS), 123, 127
Tra Le Sollecitudini (Pius X), 96
translation, 94, 96–97
Tridentine Latin Mass (TLM), 6, 23, 88–89, 93, 105, 107–8, 162
Trinity United Methodist Church, 3
"True Church," Catholic Church as, 16, 20, 163
tuition, 39, 83, 114, 125, 127–28, 130

Union Church, 48–49
United States (U.S.), 8, 13, 22, 93, 110, 161–64; Catholic school crisis in, 113–25; Liturgical Movement in, 6, 96–97, 101, 105–7
universality of Catholicism, 2, 12–13, 19, 75, 92, 162, 168
University of Georgia, 70
urban decay, 126, 167
Urban Exodus (Gamm), 9–10

Vandiver, Ernest, 68
Vatican, 19, 52, 92, 150–51
Vatican II (Second Vatican Council), 11–12, 15–16, 107, 113, 165–66; Civil Rights Movement and, 5–7, 28, 89, 163, 165–66; liturgical reform and, 17, 88–89, 94, 119–25; SBS and, 28, 119–25. *See also* post-Vatican II; pre-Vatican II
vernacular languages, masses/prayer in, 96, 97–98, 101–4, 109, 166
violence, 9, 30, 40, 139–40, 145–46; of Atlanta Race Riot, 42–43
vote/voters, Black, 38–39, 41, 46–47

Watkins, Carl, 92
Watson, Don, 139–40
Watson, Thomas Edward, 24–25
Wayne State University, 70
Welch, Ernest (Father), 57–58
West Hunter Baptist Church, 2
West Side (neighborhood), 42–43, 83
Whatley, Anita, 52, 54–55
"What We Have Seen and Heard" (letter), 145–46
Wheat Street Baptist Church, 3, 7, 44–46, 50
white: coreligionists, 10, 18, 21 27, 58, 165, 167; paternalism, 9, 30, 57; priests, 9, 11, 145; Protestants, 4, 8, 23–26, 58, 63–64; students, 75–76; women, 42–43, 55–56, 131

White, Valencia, 167–68
white Catholics, 4, 10, 19, 22, 52, 58–59, 67, 156–57; Black Catholics and, 85–86, 165; Civil Rights Movement and, 64–65; desegregation and, 70–71, 80; on Drexel Catholic High School, 77–78; Our Lady of Lourdes Church funded by, 9, 33, 56–57, 126; pre-Vatican II, 30–31; SBS interfacing with, 5, 37, 129–30; white flight by, 82–87
white ethnic Catholics, 7, 25–26, 140, 161–62; Protestants and, 4, 22–23
white flight, 81–87, 119
white parishes, 13–14, 32, 55, 83, 87, 116, 119, 159; majority, 111, 144, 155, 165
white supremacy, 11, 23, 25, 44, 58, 89, 145
"whitewashed," Black Catholics as, 4, 11
Whitt, D. Reginald, 152
Williams, Adam Daniel, 46–47
Williams, Barbara, 75
Williams-Jones, Pearl, 148–49
withdrawals, SBS, 17–18, 111–12, 122, 124–34
Wittberg, Patricia, 120
women, 96; Black, 39–41; Catholic, 32, 36–37, 55–56, 114; teaching orders led by, 1, 27, 115, 120, 124; white, 42–43, 55–56, 131. *See also* teaching sisters
Woods, James (Minister), 48
working class, 39, 82–83
World War I, 24
World War II, 7, 97, 98, 120

Xavier University of Louisiana, 15, 27, 65–66, 154–55

yellow journalism, 42–43
Young, Andrew, 146

Zaire Use, 151

ABOUT THE AUTHOR

LEAH MICKENS is the August Wilson Project Archivist at the University of Pittsburgh. She has a PhD in religious studies from Boston University, master's degrees in library and information science and digital media, and additional academic training in international studies and history. Her research interests focus on the evolution of the Roman Catholic Church in the United States, Black religious culture and traditions, the growth of atheism as a social/popular movement, and the political and social history of People of Color in the Western Hemisphere. She is the inaugural recipient of the Cyprian Davis, O.S.B. Prize, awarded by the University of Notre Dame's Cushwa Center for the Study of American Catholicism.